D0605175

The Maurice Moore-Betty Cookbook

Other books by Maurice Moore-Betty:

Cooking for Occasions

*The Maurice Moore-Betty Cooking School
Book of Fine Cookery*

The Great Cooks Cookbook (Dessert Section)

Mary Poppins in the Kitchen
with P.L. Travers

The Maurice Moore-Betty Cookbook

by Maurice Moore-Betty

Illustrations by Preston Fetty

The Bobbs-Merrill Company, Inc.
Indianapolis/New York

The author gratefully acknowledges permission to reproduce the recipes for *Pain Complet* and *Galette Persane* from the following book:
The Breads of France by Bernard Clayton, Jr.,
© copyright 1978 by Bernard Clayton, Jr. Reprinted by permission of the publisher, The Bobbs-Merrill Company, Inc.

Published by The Bobbs-Merrill Company, Inc.
Indianapolis   New York

Designed by J. Tschantre Graphic Services, Ltd.
Manufactured in the United States of America

Library of Congress Cataloging in Publication Data

Moore-Betty, Maurice.
    The Maurice Moore-Betty cookbook.

    1. Cookery.   I. Title.
TX715.M8269   641.5   79-2032
ISBN 0-672-52611-5

ACKNOWLEDGMENTS

Barbara Reiss, my editor, has been a tower of strength and support. Her guidance, patience, and encouragement, like the widow's cruse, never ran dry. To use the hackneyed phrase "Without her this book would not have been possible"—you can say that again!!

I am sincerely grateful to Mrs. Steven Halsey and Mrs. Harriet Burnett, who typed from my almost illegible handwriting, and to Bernard Clayton, Jr. for permission to use his recipes for my favorite breads, and to my very good friend, James Beard, for his superb recipe for a champagne sorbet.

M.M-B.

For Ilse who saved my life many years ago!

Contents

Introduction

"When did you first take an interest in food?" a man from a newspaper once asked me. "In the nursery," I answered. Then, emboldened by the sound of my own voice, I added, "in the cradle, actually." (This was within shouting distance of the truth. My second earliest memory—the taste comes straight back to my lips—is of eating soft-boiled eggs, crumbled whole-wheat bread, and home-made butter.)

Since those days, life and the quality of life have changed at such a rate that when I saw my mother's household file, recently come into my possession, her instructions for making bread brought back to me that totally vanished world. The instructions were spartan to a degree, uncluttered, and austere. Like a home-truth.

"Take two handfuls of whole-wheat flour and one of white, a pinch of salt, and a pinch of bicarbonate of soda. Moisten with day-old buttermilk and bake in a medium oven till done when tested."

My students of today, I fear, would be taken aback by the speculative simplicity of these directions. When my mother's recipes were written, cooking was a high art—built up to, worked up, *earned*; no two cooks made a dish the same way. It seems to me that nowadays the minute, deliberate, torrential pseudo-detail demanded of the cookbook reader amounts to a recipe for "Extinction of the Art of Cooking."

My father was a physician with a large and widespread practice in Ireland, and my mother was engaged in local affairs and running two houses, with their specialties and differences. We had a farm, a living thing that I loved, with a small Georgian house on it where we spent part of every summer, and a larger house in town. For years I saw my parents only after breakfast and before going to bed. Then one day, a pang of surprise, my younger sister and I were allowed to take our meals with them in the dining room. The world of the nursery was now behind us, along with the license to indulge in bad manners.

On days when there were no classes at school, Nurse Wilson, more parent than nurse, would take me home with her to a small hill farm. Sometimes, pleading a susceptibility to colds and infections, I would contrive to spend weeks on end there with my nurse's two sisters, brother, and mother, who seemed to be no less than one hundred years old. (Many years later she was to have the last lonely cackle on life by dying at exactly that age.) Like old, fanciful female peasants the world over, she bundled herself up in acres of black garments, and there were never less than three aprons tied round her middle—winter and summer.

Their farmhouse had four rooms on the ground floor grouped around the kitchen. The open hearth was the full length of one wall, and if the child I was stood in it and looked up, he could see the April clouds scudding across the sky. There were several other rooms under the eaves, kept cool in summer and cozy in winter by a foot-and-a-half-thick thatch on the roof. The kitchen was the vibrating heart of the house—indeed of the whole farm—where everyone gathered, ate their meals, rested after the day's work, and received callers.

Neighbors' visits were known by the Gaelic name *ceildh*. Crops and the weather (floods, gales, and droughts) were discussed, local news exchanged—the only other source of news being a weekly paper. Tea was offered, strong and sweet, having been brewed for three or four minutes over hot peat coals, and a slice of rich cake made with farm butter, eggs, and loads of dried fruits.

The open fire was never allowed to go out, and each night the last to bed "raked the fire" by heaping hot ashes on fresh clods of peat. In the morning there would be a mound of glowing coals on which to build a new fire, called *greechins* in sixteenth-century English. My nurse's family used other sixteenth-century words: *ganzi* for sweater, waistcoat, or pullover; *gallices* for suspenders; and *gazen boarden* for floor boards that did not quite meet.

These companions of my early years were hard-working, honest people, whose day began with sunrise and ended when the sun went down. However backbreaking their work, there was little grumbling, and what grumbling there was was sweetened by a sense of humor. Having no pretensions, they were not reluctant to offer a visitor—no matter how high and mighty—a part of the daily fare, in marked contrast to many of the insecure of today who will ask, when we are preparing a seemingly simple dish in my cooking school, "Is it good enough for company?"

The Wilsons cooked with a natural grace and instinct, as these people had done for generations. Chickens, ducks, and geese were cooked in a heavy cast-iron Dutch oven standing on three short legs with a snug-fitting lid. The oven was placed on a bed of hot glowing coals, then more coals were heaped on the lid. The bird was smeared with goose fat, if it was a goose or duck, and if it was a plump chicken, with homemade butter or lard. Seasoning was nothing more exotic than salt and pepper and, for a wonder, it was "good enough for company." It made its own juices and it was done when it was done, according to the cook who tested it in her own way. In all the years that have passed since then, I have not succeeded in duplicating that flavor. And even if I could replace the insipid bird of today with that superb "dung-hill cock," I could never recapture the peace, simplicity, and balm of Nurse Wilson's world, where my heart was opened to the greatness of simple food.

Let's not dwell in the past, but make the best of the day and age we live in.

Since my formative years, changes in food preparation have been formidable. Electric appliances have simplified many methods that previously were time-consuming in the extreme. The making of a purée, for instance, by rubbing through a hair sieve, took hours on end, but can now be accomplished literally in a matter of seconds. All one needs is one of the many food processors available on the market today.

Rapid transport and refrigeration have widened the horizon. In most areas it is possible to buy products from the four corners of the earth—in and out of season. Fruits and vegetables out-of-season are double-edged swords: They both alleviate food boredom and produce it. I personally prefer to use those in season. I eat asparagus in May and June, strawberries in June and July until I am tired of both, and then put them aside and wait for the following year. I tend to follow the seasons, and thereby look forward to each one and what it brings to my table.

A word of advice to the reader, and one I always give to my students: Learn to use your knives. Slicing, julienning, and carving are all facets of the culinary art, and the sooner they are mastered, the sooner you will feel independent of electricity—free and equipped to cook wherever you are, provided you have your knives. And another pearl of wisdom I drop in the laps of students at the start of each class: The recipe is a guide, not a gospel. In a nutshell, follow the recipe where chemistry is concerned, but don't complain if the seasoning is not to your liking—that is a personal matter and up to you. The third and last pearl: Take infinite care and use your imagination when presenting a dish. The shortest route to the stomach is through the eye, and if there is a slight discrepancy in a dish that is eye-shattering in its beauty, you can get away with murder—which brings me to menu-planning, the novice's biggest stumbling block.

There are three basic needs: color, texture, and flavor. No two dishes in a well-planned three-course menu should repeat the same color, texture, or flavor. The most common fault of all is the use of cream sauces in two, or maybe three, of the dishes. I personally prefer a menu that progresses from lightness through richness to lightness again: for example, a light piquant first course such as consommé, followed by a well-sauced meat or fish, ending with a light dessert that might well be as simple as fresh fruit. The wines I select, if I'm having more than one, would follow the same pattern of light to heavy, with this exception: A sweet dessert wine would accompany the dessert.

Don't attempt to impress your guests. Serve dishes that you are most at home with, that will turn out as close to perfection as can be. Don't overload plates. Large helpings are unsightly, unnecessary, and guaranteed to blunt the edge of the keenest appetite, and it is most unlikely that any of your guests are suffering from malnutrition. It is good to remember Brillat-Savarin's words, "When you invite a man to dinner, never forget that during the short time he is under your roof his happiness is in your hands."

Throughout this volume you will see these symbols at the end of recipes:

> A—Can be prepared ahead
> B—Suitable for freezing
> C—Suitable for large quantities
> D—Easily prepared

My advice is to treat these as guides. Don't deliberately freeze a dish because the symbol indicates it can be frozen. Double the recipe if you feel like it and freeze half for a rainy day.

Large quantities are another matter. Large is so vague. For the person who lives alone, a large party may mean six or eight people; while for the busy hostess, it could be any number up to a few hundred. Use your common sense and judgment.

The number of servings expected from each recipe is indicated at the top of each recipe. I am constantly being asked by my students how many servings there are in a recipe. It is virtually impossible to give an answer. Those partaking of the repast might well be four or six strapping youths sitting down to dinner after a hard game of football, or three or four temperate eaters carefully watching their weight. Once again, use your judgment and common sense. And a final word of advice: Make the servings small.

Maurice Moore-Betty

The Kitchen

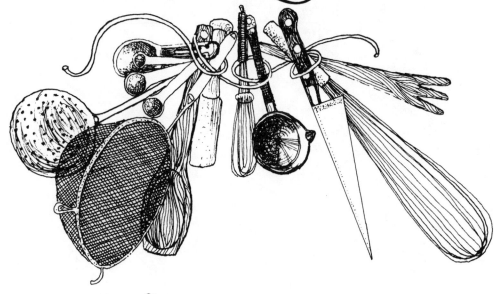

The Kitchen

Since fire was first accidentally stumbled on dark, distant ages ago, the cooking center—or kitchen—has been the pivot on which the family revolved. Recently, within the last hundred years, it has been described as the heart of the house—it most definitely has been the hearth.

As dwellings grew grander, the kitchen was installed farther and farther from the other domestic apartments, but its importance never varied, no matter how grand and commodious. Its supervision was the responsibility of the mistress or the lady of the house. No matter how great the wealth of the householder or the number of hands that were employed, the only truly successful cuisine that emerged from the kitchen was one supervised by a skilled mistress who gave it the personal stamp by which the house or family was identified. A careless, untrained chatelaine was the hallmark of a badly run household.

The farmhouse kitchen is perhaps the best example of the role a kitchen played in the past. It was the pulse of the family, the farm, and the house. The life-giving food was prepared in it, the workers and the family met in its comforting, appetite-stirring warmth for their three meals a day, and in the evening it was where they sat to rest and discuss the events and work of the day. It was the very heart of that small community.

After the opulence and grandeur of the Victorian and Edwardian eras, there are few of us who can afford cooks or chefs, even if they could be found. We have come full circle, and the rule rather than the exception is that we must "do" for ourselves, with as much comfort and as little fuss as possible, making use of the many labor-saving devices available.

A separate dining room for use on the rare occasion when one can find help is a white elephant. The wheel has turned and we are back to the "eat-in-kitchen"—and I don't have the "dinette" in mind. Cooking and eating in the same room is logical, and it can be as grand as you like. If you are planning to remodel, drop a mental dividing wall between your working space and where the dining area will be and create two separate units.

Wherever your taste lies, whether it be contemporary, eighteenth-century English, Spanish, French, or Mexican pull out all the stops and forget that your dining room will eventually be cheek by jowl with a sink, range, and refrigerator. The working area need not be large: ten by ten feet is ample; everything is within reach with plenty of working surfaces and a small mobile butcher-block table in the middle. Don't spare the pennies, for you'll find this is where you will spend the greater part of your day, and enjoy every minute of it.

Expensive and complicated equipment has not and never will improve the quality of the food but, within reason, it does lighten the burden of kitchen chores. For instance, sixty years ago a fine purée was made by rubbing the mixture, spinach or whatever, through a fine sieve—hours of backbreaking, boring work. Today, with one of the many food processors on the market, it's all over literally in a matter of seconds. If you can afford one, buy it, but if your budget won't allow it, be content with a hand-operated food mill. The Mouli, made in France, is excellent and inexpensive.

Don't over-equip your kitchen. I am one of the worst offenders—forgiven to be sure—as I'm constantly on the lookout for newer and better labor-saving devices, but don't follow in my footsteps. You can benefit from my mistakes and take my advice.

Let's begin with the basics: a graduated set of stainless-steel mixing bowls—they don't chip and will last a lifetime; stainless carbon steel knives made by a recognized cutter—a ten-inch butcher's knife, a paring knife, a slicing knife, and a bread knife. (To use your slicing knife for bread is a sacrilege; nothing dulls a knife faster than slicing bread.)

Pots and pans should be heavy to retain and evenly distribute heat: enamel-coated cast iron, stainless steel, or a new product, aluminum treated so that it is not affected by acids. Many of these have skillets to match and the pots may be used as casseroles in the oven. Have one cast-iron omelet pan and use it for omelets only. Select stainless-steel roasting pans and make sure the largest one will fit in your oven. Two baking sheets and two jelly-roll pans, also stainless steel, can be bought at the same time.

One set of measuring cups, a set of measuring spoons, and a pitcher or two—again stainless steel for long life and easy cleaning—are other essentials. Also necessary are two vegetable scrapers or peelers—one for you and one for the times when you need additional help. One large and one small wire strainer and two spatulas should complete the basic *batterie de la cuisine*.

One last word of advice. Remember that your kitchen must be functional first: easy to keep clean, easy to move about in, with everything you need close at hand. Your kitchen should work for you and not just for the architect, who more than likely has never dabbled in the culinary art.

Cocktail Food

Cocktail Food

The cocktail party is attributed to Alec Waugh in the Roaring Twenties, a year or two before my time. In its original form, if I remember rightly, it was a sort of muscle flexer for the festivities that followed: dinner, a night club, breakfast on the way home, then bed with the sun well above the horizon.

The form has changed. Instead of going home to dine or on to a restaurant, the cocktail party of today, in many cases, provides food and drink in sufficient quantity to make dining a superfluous part of the evening.

The cocktail party is a form of entertainment I rarely indulge in, either as a guest or host, but when I play the part of the latter, I provide food substantial enough to satisfy the hungry and act as blotting paper for the amount of alcohol consumed. It is a poor form of entertainment, but part of our way of life in the last quarter of a century. Yet it has the advantage of launching new products, new literature, new art, or maybe new friendships. It is the modern counterpart of the formal reception of the Edwardian Era, and it is here to stay.

The cocktail party is one function that I cannot and will not attempt to handle singlehandedly. There must, no matter how many one is catering to, be at least one pair of hands to cope with hot food—whether it be sautéing fillet Teriyaki or simply heating profiteroles in the oven—and one or two willing helpers to pass food, empty ashtrays, and keep the elderly and infirm who remain seated plied with refreshments. The other guests are usually more than eager to help themselves.

I've found that a round table strategically placed with a pâté and baked toast and a cold item or two helps to keep the guests circulating. And, if your house or apartment allows it, do not be backward about using your kitchen as well. A tidbit picked up from the kitchen counter, just hot from the range, is not a makeshift convenience.

And finally, set up the drinks table or bar where there can be no "bunching." Guests are inclined to home in on it and stay—unlike the bee who returns to the hive, deposits its nectar, and departs.

CHEESE CROUTONS

Approximately 36 pieces

2 cups Parmesan cheese, grated
1 cup mayonnaise (see page 277)

1 medium onion, grated
12 slices white bread

Mix the first three ingredients together thoroughly.

Toast the white bread slices. With a small round cookie cutter, cut out three rounds from each slice of bread.

Spread rounds thickly with the cheese mixture and run them under broiler until bubbling.

ACD

BELGIAN ENDIVE

Belgian endive
Gorgonzola or other blue cheese

Heavy cream
Parsley sprigs, finely chopped

When Belgian endive is in season in the winter, a pleasant combination is an endive leaf filled with Gorgonzola, or other blue cheese, mixed with cream to make a smooth paste.

Spoon the cheese mixture into the leaf or pipe it from a forcing bag fitted with a large star tube.

Sprinkle with finely chopped parsley.

A

WATER CHESTNUTS AND BACON

Approximately 20 pieces

1 pound sliced bacon
Water chestnuts, twice the number of bacon slices

Heat broiler to 450° to 475°F.

Cut bacon slices in half and if the water chestnuts are large, halve them as well. Wrap each chestnut piece in a bacon slice and arrange on a jelly-roll pan (to catch the fat), folded side down.

Broil until brown, then drain on paper towels. Serve on toothpicks.

For those who like it hot, a sprinkling of cayenne pepper satisfies their palate.

A

VEGETABLE BEIGNETS

Approximately 4 dozen pieces

Nancy Yurbi, who prepares the most beautiful and imaginative foods for her clients, makes a habit of serving fresh vegetables piping hot in a batter. She can, on rare occasions, keep up with the demand. Her catering service is such that no one would know that the food has not been prepared by the host or hostess, a rare achievement in this day of third-rate catering establishments.

Batter:

1 cup flour
4 whole eggs
1 cup water
1 teaspoon salt

Pinch of nutmeg
⅓ cup grated Parmesan cheese
2 egg whites

Sift the flour into a bowl and make a well in the center. Beat the four eggs lightly, and stir them with the water into the flour until you have a smooth paste. Add salt, nutmeg, and cheese; mix thoroughly.

Beat the egg whites until they form soft peaks and fold them into the batter.

Vegetables:

Choose vegetables to suit your taste. (For instance, some people detest cauliflower.) Here is my suggestion for vegetables, cut into bite-sized pieces:

Vegetable oil for frying
1 small cauliflower, broken into bite-sized pieces
4 carrots, peeled and cut into 1-inch pieces (may be blanched in boiling salted water)

4 small zucchini, cut into 1-inch pieces
4 small white turnips, peeled, quartered, and cut into 8 parts each
6 to 8 canned artichoke hearts, quartered
1 bunch parsley sprigs

Heat the vegetable oil in a deep pot or fryer to 360°F. on the thermometer or test with a cube of white bread: If the oil foams and turns the bread golden brown in fifty seconds or so, the temperature is right.

Dip the vegetable pieces into the batter to coat them and drop them into the hot oil. Turn with a slotted spoon or skimmer until golden brown.

Serve piping hot on a platter, garnished with sprigs of fresh parsley.

INDIVIDUAL PIZZAS

Approximately 12 pieces

Dough:

8 ounces flour
1 teaspoon salt
¾ ounces fresh yeast
1 teaspoon sugar

¼ cup warm milk
1½ ounces melted butter
1 egg

Sift the flour with salt into a warm bowl; cream the yeast and sugar together with a little warm milk. When spongy, make a well in the flour and pour in the rest of the warm milk, melted butter, and well-beaten egg. Beat until smooth.

Cover with a clean towel and allow the dough to double in bulk—about forty minutes.

Filling:

2 tablespoons olive oil
2 large onions, thinly sliced
2 small cloves garlic, chopped
1 medium can tomatoes, drained
1 tablespoon marjoram or ½ teaspoon
  dried oregano

Salt and pepper to taste
6 ounces cheese: Fontina, Port Salut, or
  Bel Paese
Anchovy fillets
Black olives

To prepare the filling, heat oil in a heavy skillet and cook the onion and garlic until soft and transparent.

Drain and chop the tomatoes; add them to the skillet. Cook slowly for about ten minutes until the mixture is thick.

Stir in the herbs and season with salt and pepper.

Heat oven to 475°F.

When the dough has risen, beat it for a minute or two, then shape it into three- to three-and-one-half-inch rounds on a greased baking sheet. Cover the dough with the onion mixture to within an inch of the edge.

Slice the cheese thinly and arrange the slices slightly overlapping on top. Decorate with anchovy fillets and black olives.

Bake for fifteen to twenty minutes in top third of oven. Serve piping hot.   *AB*

HOT CHEESE PROFITEROLES

Approximately 5 dozen

Profiteroles:

4 ounces butter
1 cup water
1 teaspoon salt

1 cup flour
4 eggs

Heat oven to 425°F.

Put the butter, water, and salt in a heavy pan and bring to a boil. When the butter is completely melted, add the flour all at once. Remove from the heat. Stir vigorously until the paste comes away from the sides of the pan. Over very low heat, stir for four to five minutes to dry out the paste.

Put the paste into a large bowl, and with a wooden spoon beat in the eggs one at a time. When one has been absorbed, add another.

Put the paste in a forcing bag with a plain tube. Grease a cookie sheet lightly and pipe small mounds three-fourths to one inch in diameter, until mixture is used up.

Glaze:

1 egg
1 tablespoon water

To glaze, beat one egg with one tablespoon of water and brush each profiterole.

Bake fifteen minutes. Lower the heat to 350°F. Bake twenty minutes more. Turn off the heat and leave the oven door open to cool the profiteroles.

Cheese Sauce:

3 tablespoons butter
3 tablespoons flour
1 cup milk

1 teaspoon salt
1 teaspoon pepper
4 tablespoons Parmesan cheese, grated

Melt the butter and stir in the flour. Cook gently for three minutes, taking care the flour does not brown.

In a separate pan, bring milk almost to the boiling point. Off the heat, add milk to the *roux* and whisk until smooth. Cook four to five minutes longer.

When smooth, add salt, pepper, and cheese. Allow the cheese to melt.

To fill the profiteroles, put the cheese mixture into a forcing bag with a small tube. Pierce a hole in the bottom of each profiterole and force in the cheese mixture until full. Reheat in a 300°F. oven for twenty-five minutes before serving. *A*

33

CARRIAGE HOUSE TERRINE

2 pounds fat belly of pork
1 pound pork liver
1 pound lean veal
½ pound flare or fat back (sometimes called "salt pork")
1 clove garlic

1 tablespoon coarse salt
12 black peppercorns
12 juniper berries
½ teaspoon mace
1 cup white wine
4 tablespoons brandy

Heat oven to 325°F.

Grind together, or chop very fine by hand, the fat belly, pork liver, and lean veal. Cut half the fat back into strips and dice it coarsely. Mix all together in a porcelain bowl.

Peel and crush the garlic clove with one tablespoon of coarse salt. Crush the peppercorns and juniper berries. Add the garlic, peppercorns, juniper berries, and mace to the pork mixture. Pour in the wine and brandy. Mix well and allow to stand for two hours.

To test for correct seasoning, cook two or three tablespoons of the mixture in a skillet for five to six minutes. Taste for seasoning. Correct the seasoning, if necessary, by adding more salt and freshly ground black pepper to the remaining uncooked mixture.

Turn the mixture into a one-quart terrine or loaf pan; smooth the top. Cut the remaining fat back into thin strips. Form the strips into a lattice pattern on top of the mixture. Place the terrine in a larger roasting pan. Add enough boiling water to come halfway up the terrine. (Add more water, if necessary, as it cooks.)

Cook for one and one-half hours. Cool. If it is to be kept longer than four or five days, pour melted butter or lard on top to seal it.   *A*

BAKED TOAST

1 loaf white bread
1 pound butter, softened

Heat oven to 350°F.

Remove the crusts from each slice of bread and cut the bread into four triangles. Spread each side generously with softened butter. Arrange on a baking sheet and bake in the middle of the oven until golden brown, about twenty minutes. Watch carefully to see they do not burn. Frozen, the toast keeps well.   *ABC*

BEEF TENDERLOIN TERIYAKI

Approximately 30 pieces

1 fillet, trimmed of all fat and membrane
Marinade: Teriyaki Sauce (see page 288)
1 pound butter

Cut the beef into one-and-one-half-inch cubes. Marinate in the Teriyaki mixture in a glass or enamel dish for half an hour.

Heat enough butter to generously coat the bottom of a heavy skillet. Over high heat quickly sauté beef cubes, turning them to brown all four sides. Serve piping hot.

A

SCOTCH EGGS

24 pieces

Scotch Eggs are to be found on the counter of almost any English pub. With a pickled onion, fresh bread, a piece of good Cheddar or Stilton cheese, they make a perfect inexpensive luncheon, washed down, of course, with a pint of the house's best ale. Try them on a summer day on the terrace or in the shade of your favorite tree.

1 pound sausage meat
6 hard-boiled eggs, shelled
2 eggs, beaten

2 cups well-seasoned fresh white bread
    crumbs
Oil for deep frying

Divide the sausage meat into six portions.

Dry the eggs and wrap sausage meat evenly around each one. Dip into the beaten egg and roll in bread crumbs.

Heat the oil until a piece of bread turns a light brown in less than a minute, about 365°F. on a frying thermometer.

Drop in the eggs two or three at a time; turn or roll them over now and again. Fry for four to five minutes. Drain on paper towels. When cool, cut each egg into four parts.   *A*

SHRIMP SCANDIA

6 servings

1½ pounds small shrimp (25 to 30 to the pound)
Sauce Scandia (see page 281)

Court Bouillon (poaching liquid):

1 small onion, chopped
1 rib celery, chopped
1 tablespoon salt

4 peppercorns
1 quart water

Combine all the ingredients for the court bouillon in a two-quart pot. Bring to a boil, lower the heat, and simmer, covered, for twenty minutes or so. Strain the liquid into a clean pot, discard the solids, and bring to a boil once more.

Add the shrimp, shelled, cleaned, and deveined, and bring to a boil again. Remove from the heat. Drain after two or three minutes. Cool.

Prepare Sauce Scandia.

Toss the cold shrimp in enough sauce to coat well. Serve the shrimp on toothpicks.   *A*

ABERDEEN SANDWICHES

8 to 10 servings

When I feel like throwing financial caution to the winds, I serve Aberdeen Sandwiches with cocktails. They are expensive and should be reserved for special occasions.

14 ounces pressed caviar
4 ounces unsalted butter, softened

Lemon juice and pepper to taste
1 pound thinly sliced smoked salmon

Mix the caviar and butter, and season to taste with the lemon juice and pepper. Spread this mixture thinly on a slice of smoked salmon. Lay a second slice of salmon on top to make a sandwich. Cut each sandwich into four pieces. Excellent served with drinks.   *A*

Appetizers

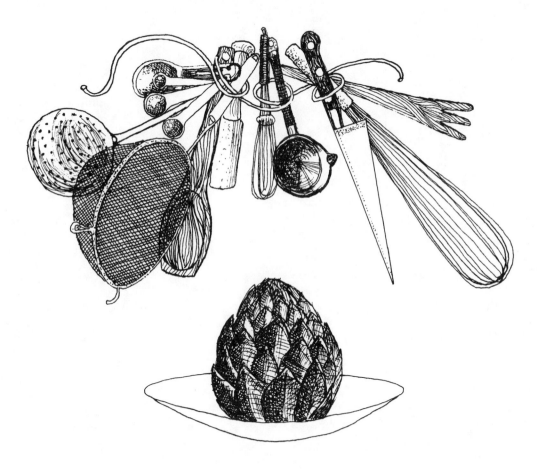

Appetizers

The appetizer, as it is called in America, is the European hors d'oeuvre. It is difficult to confine, as the term covers a wide range of ingredients, and many an appetizer comes under the heading of salad, fish, chicken, or vegetable. But, one rule should be adhered to: Make the serving small, whatever it be, and remember it is merely a preliminary or curtain raiser for what follows. It is a convenient course to serve. Without help, it can be on the table before you seat your guests. In many cases you will find that by doubling or tripling the recipe, you have a one-course luncheon dish.

AVOCADO AND TOMATO ICE

8 servings

8 ounces sugar
1 cup water
2 cups Italian plum tomatoes
  (approximately 1 pound), drained

Juice of 2 lemons
4 avocados, halved and brushed with
  lemon juice

Dissolve eight ounces of sugar in one cup of water. Boil together for exactly two minutes. Chill. Stir in two cups of Italian plum tomatoes, sieved. Stir in the juice of two lemons (or to taste).

Freeze the tomato mixture in refrigerator ice-cube trays or in a glass dish. As it freezes, mix with a fork from time to time to break down the crystals. Spoon into avocado halves and serve immediately. *A*

TOMATOES ANTIBOISE

6 servings

6 tomatoes
4 ounces peas, cooked and cooled
8 ounces lima beans, cooked and cooled
10 ounces good ham, julienned
½ cup mayonnaise (see page 277)

¼ cup Parmesan cheese, grated
Salt and pepper to taste
Chopped parsley
Shredded lettuce

Cut a slice off the stem end of each tomato and carefully scoop out the pulp and seeds. Turn the tomatoes upside down to drain.

Mix peas, lima beans, ham, mayonnaise, Parmesan cheese, salt, and pepper together. Spoon the mixture into the tomatoes and sprinkle with chopped parsley. Serve on a bed of shredded lettuce. *A*

TOMATES FARCIES AUX CREVETTES

8 servings

8 firm tomatoes, the size of tennis balls
1½ pounds small, cooked shrimp
2 cups mayonnaise (see page 277)
Heavy cream

Celery salt
Freshly ground black pepper
½ cup parsley sprigs, finely chopped

If you wish to remove tomato skins, drop tomatoes into boiling water, count to ten and lift them out with a slotted spoon. When cool enough to handle, the skin will slip off without difficulty.

Take a slice off the end opposite the stem. With a spoon or a melon baller scrape out the pulp, being careful not to puncture the fruit if it has been peeled. Stand tomatoes upside down to drain on a baking sheet covered with paper towels.

Slice the cooked shrimp in half lengthwise, setting aside one whole shrimp per tomato for garnish. Thin the mayonnaise with a little heavy cream and season to taste with celery salt and pepper. Mix shrimp with the seasoned mayonnaise. Mound into the tomatoes. Sprinkle with parsley and garnish with one whole shrimp.   *A*

KOHLRABI VINAIGRETTE

6 to 8 servings

2 heads kohlrabi
Vinaigrette Sauce (see page 290)
Parsley, finely chopped

Peel the hearts of the kohlrabi and cut into fine julienne strips. This may be done in the food processor with great ease. Keep them in a bowl of iced water until needed.

Drain and dry them, then mix with the dressing. Sprinkle with finely chopped parsley before serving.   *A*

CELERIAC REMOULADE

6 to 8 servings

2 small heads celeriac (celery root)
Rémoulade Sauce (see next page)
Parsley, finely chopped

Wash, peel, and shred celeriac. If you have a food processor, shredding takes little or no time, otherwise it must be done by hand. Keep shredded celeriac in a bowl of acidulated water (water to which a few drops of lemon juice or vinegar have been added) until needed.

(Continued)

Rémoulade Sauce:

2 cups mayonnaise (see page 277)
2 tablespoons finely chopped cucumber
    pickle
2 tablespoons drained, chopped capers
2 teaspoons imported Dijon mustard

1 teaspoon finely chopped parsley
1 teaspoon chopped tarragon
1 teaspoon chopped chervil
1 teaspoon anchovy paste (optional)
Lemon juice (optional)

Combine all the above ingredients, except lemon juice, and mix well. Add the lemon juice if you think the sauce is not sharp enough.

Drain the celeriac, pat dry, and mix it with enough Rémoulade Sauce to moisten. Sprinkle with a little chopped parsley before serving.
                                                                                                    A

ASPARAGUS

Asparagus must be fresh. Limp spears and shrunken stalk ends are telltale signs of age. If they are not to be used right away, cut a slice off the end of each spear and stand it in a pan of water as you would do with fresh-cut flowers. Allow six to eight spears per serving.

Cut a piece off the end to make all the spears the same length. Remove the outside skin with a vegetable peeler. Wash well under cold, running water to remove any sand that may cling to the tip. Tie in bundles of six to eight.

Bring a pan of water to a boil. Add one tablespoon of salt for each quart of water. Cooking time depends on the size and age of the spears, but three to four minutes is ample for fresh young asparagus.

Serve hot with Hollandaise Sauce (see page 277) or with melted butter seasoned with lemon juice, which is my favorite. Serve cold with Sauce Vinaigrette (see page 290).

ARTICHOKES WITH SAUCE MALTAISE

1 artichoke per serving
Vegetable oil

Salt
Sauce Maltaise (see page 278)

With a heavy, sharp knife cut the top off each artichoke, down to the tip of the third layer of leaves. This makes a sizable opening, enabling you to remove the choke. With scissors, cut off the thorny leaf tips. Cut off the stem end so that the artichoke will sit upright on its plate.

In a pan large enough to hold the artichokes, bring water to a boil. Add one tablespoon salt per quart of water and one tablespoon vegetable oil. Plunge the artichokes into boiling water and cover with a layer of cheesecloth. Cheesecloth will allow sufficient steam to partly cook the leaf ends but not enough to discolor the vegetables completely. Artichokes are never bright green when cooked. Boil gently for thirty to thirty-five minutes, depending on their size and age.

Lift the artichokes out and drain upside down. When they are cool enough to be handled, spread the leaves to allow you to get your thumb, first, and second fingers around the inner leaves that cover the choke. Twist and lift the leaves out. Set them aside. The choke, a tough, fibrous cap covering the "heart," is now visible. Scrape it out with a sharp-edged teaspoon.

Replace the leaves that covered the choke and reshape the artichoke with your hands. Serve at room temperature with Sauce Maltaise.

ARTICHOKES WITH MUSTARD SAUCE

4 servings

The globe artichoke is architecturally beautiful and gastronomically pleasing, but the California artichoke is the most beautiful of all—big, bold, and with a wealth of delicate "meat." Artichokes are the perfect first course, served either hot or cold.

4 artichokes
1½ tablespoons salt
1 tablespoon olive oil

Trim the stem and small outer leaves from each artichoke. Cut about one-quarter inch off the top of each artichoke and snip off the tips of the outer leaves with scissors.

Pour seven quarts of water into a large, non-aluminum pan; add oil and salt. Bring to a boil. Add the artichokes, cover with a layer of cheesecloth, and boil for thirty-five minutes, or until the outside leaves pull away easily. Lift the artichokes out and drain them upside down.

Mustard Sauce:

2 tablespoons Dijon mustard
3 tablespoons boiling water
½ cup olive oil

Salt, pepper, and lemon juice to taste
1 tablespoon finely chopped parsley

Place the mustard in a mixing bowl and stir in the boiling water. Add the olive oil drop by drop, whisking until it is completely absorbed. Add seasonings and lemon juice and stir in the parsley.

BRAISED JERUSALEM ARTICHOKES

4 to 6 servings

I describe the Jerusalem artichoke—which is not an artichoke—in the soup chapter (see page 58). This is my favorite way to serve the tuber. It is an excellent first course, since the flavor is wasted if served with any other food.

2 pounds Jerusalem artichokes
A little vinegar or lemon juice
2 cups dry red wine
4 tablespoons butter

1 teaspoon salt
Freshly ground pepper
2 tablespoons finely chopped parsley

Heat the oven to 350° F.

Peel the artichokes—a good, sharp paring knife is essential. Place them in a bowl of water with a little vinegar or lemon juice until ready for use. Drain.

Place artichokes, red wine, butter, salt, and pepper in a heavy pan with a tight-fitting lid.

Bring to a boil on top of the range, then cover and cook in the oven for thirty minutes, or until tender. Test for doneness with a fork or toothpick. They should be firm, rather like a properly done boiled potato.

Remove the artichokes from the liquid with a slotted spoon. Reduce the liquid in the pan to three-quarters of a cup over high heat. Pour over the artichokes. Serve them at room temperature, sprinkled liberally with chopped parsley.

COURGETTES A LA GRECQUE

6 to 8 servings

6 small zucchini
⅓ cup olive or salad oil
1 medium yellow onion, skinned and
  sliced very thin
1 small clove garlic, crushed
⅓ cup tomato purée

½ teaspoon dried thyme
¼ teaspoon black pepper, or 4 to 5 twists
  of the pepper mill
½ teaspoon salt
Lemon juice to taste
1 tablespoon parsley, finely chopped

Wash the zucchini. Do not peel. Cut off the ends and slice into rounds about one-quarter inch thick.

Heat the oil in a heavy skillet or saucepan. Add the sliced onion; cook until wilted and golden yellow. Do not allow onions to burn.

Add the zucchini and all the other ingredients, except the lemon juice and parsley. Cook slowly, stirring from time to time. Cooking time varies but it usually takes four to six minutes (the zucchini should be "al dente"). Stir in the lemon juice.

Serve at room temperature, generously sprinkled with finely chopped parsley.

MUSHROOMS A LA GRECQUE

4 to 6 servings

Mushrooms cooked "à la Grecque" are far too good to be served in any other way except alone as a first course.

4 shallots
2 tablespoons oil
2 tablespoons butter
1½ pounds fresh, medium mushrooms
½ tablespoon salt
2 tablespoons tomato paste

1 ripe tomato, peeled, seeded, and
    chopped
Lemon juice to taste
½ cup chopped parsley
Lettuce leaves

Chop the shallots and sauté them in the oil and butter. Do not allow them to brown.

Wipe the mushrooms clean; cut off the stems flush with the caps, and quarter them. Add to the shallots. Cook, turning them for approximately five minutes. Add salt and cook longer until the mushroom juices run.

Stir in the tomato paste. Add the tomato and sauté for three to four minutes more.

Pour the mixture into a bowl to cool; correct the seasoning; add the lemon juice and parsley. Serve on lettuce leaves at room temperature.

BAKED MUSHROOMS

2 medium or 1 large mushroom
    per serving
Melted butter

Lemon juice
Salt and pepper

Heat oven to 350°F.

Butter an oven-proof dish, one with a lid if you have it. If not, cover with wax paper and seal with foil.

(Continued)

Wipe mushrooms clean with a damp towel and remove the stems. Arrange mushrooms in the dish, cup side up.

Melt the butter and add lemon juice to taste. I like it very lemony. Add two teaspoons of melted butter to the mushrooms. Sprinkle lightly with salt and pepper.

Bake covered for ten to fifteen minutes until just tender but not soft and floppy. Serve with a little of the pan juice spooned over each mushroom. *A*

MELONS AND GINGER

Melon   Powdered ginger
Juice of fresh lime   Cantaloupe, 1 half per serving
Superfine sugar

Select melons of your choice, the best that are in season. Use two varieties, if possible, for a contrast in color and flavor.

Scoop out the melon with a melon baller and sprinkle with fresh lime juice.

Mix superfine sugar and powdered ginger in a proportion of three parts sugar to one part ginger. Dust melon balls lightly with this mixture and pile them into scooped-out cantaloupe halves.

Serve the remaining mixture in a sugar castor, if you have one, or in a bowl. *A*

PILAF

6 to 8 servings

Pilaf is usually served with a meat of sorts, but I like it as an introduction to a light meal in much the same way that pasta is used in Italian menus. It is highly nutritious and eliminates the necessity for a starch further on in the menu. Make the servings small.

4 tablespoons butter   Pinch of thyme
1 small onion, diced (about ½ cup) ½ teaspoon salt
1 cup Bulgur wheat   4 ounces prosciutto or smoked
1 stick celery, diced (about ½ cup)   ham, diced
2 cups strong chicken stock   3 to 4 mushrooms, quartered
Pinch of turmeric   ½ cup parsley sprigs, finely chopped

Heat oven to 350°F.

Melt the butter in a heavy casserole or one-quart pan with close-fitting lid. Sauté the onion and Bulgur wheat until onion is transparent. Do not allow the onion to burn. Add the celery, chicken stock, turmeric, thyme, and salt.

Bring to a boil on top of the range. Transfer the pilaf to the oven and cook, covered, for thirty minutes. Add the ham and mushrooms, and cook ten minutes longer. Stir in the chopped parsley and serve hot.

SHRIMP, AVOCADO, AND CARRIAGE HOUSE SAUCE

6 servings

1 pound small shrimp, approximately
2 quarts boiling water
2 tablespoons salt
3 avocados

Lemon juice
Carriage House Sauce (see page 282)
Watercress

Allow approximately three to four fresh, small shrimp for each serving as a first course. Clean, shell, and devein the shrimp.

Bring to a boil two quarts of water and two tablespoons of salt. Add the shrimp and bring to a boil again. Turn off the heat, and after two or three minutes, drain the shrimp.

Allow half an avocado per serving. Brush the inside of the avocado with lemon juice.

Mound shrimp in the center of the avocado and coat with Carriage House Sauce. Garnish with fresh watercress and serve with thinly sliced brown bread and butter.

SMOKED EEL

This is not everyone's dish of fish.

Smoked eel
Parsley sprigs
Lemon wedges

Horseradish Sauce (see page 289)
Brown bread, sliced thin and buttered

Smoked eel is usually sold complete with head and tail. First cut eel into three-inch pieces, then skin it and take out the bone. It is easier to bone small pieces than the whole fish. Discard the head and tail. Each three-inch piece, halved, will provide one serving.

Arrange on a serving dish. Garnish with parsley sprigs and wedges of lemon. Serve with Horseradish Sauce and thinly sliced brown bread and butter.   *A*

DEVILED CRAB PROFITEROLES

About 2 dozen

2 teaspoons Worcestershire sauce
2 teaspoons fresh lemon juice
Dash of Tabasco sauce
1 teaspoon salt
½ teaspoon dry mustard
¼ teaspoon white pepper

1½ cups thick Béchamel Sauce (see page 275)
1 pound frozen crabmeat (known as fresh frozen or Alaskan crab legs), coarsely chopped

Heat oven to 350°F.

Mix Worcestershire, lemon juice, Tabasco, salt, mustard, and pepper and stir into the Béchamel Sauce. Stir enough Béchamel Sauce into the crabmeat to bind it. It should not be too heavy, but you may like to use all of the Béchamel Sauce. It makes the crabmeat go farther.

Profiteroles:

1 cup water
4 ounces butter
Pinch of salt

1 cup all-purpose flour
4 large eggs

In a heavy pan heat water. Add the butter and salt. When the butter has melted, bring the water to a boil. Off the heat, pour in all the flour at once. With a long-handled spoon for leverage, stir the mixture until it comes away from the bottom and sides of the pan. Cool. Beat in the eggs one at a time; when one has been absorbed, add another. If you own a food processor, it is a simple operation.

Heat oven to 425°F.

Using a forcing bag and a one-quarter-inch plain tube, pipe mounds of pastry, two to three inches apart, onto a lightly greased cookie sheet, or drop the paste from a spoon. The amount should be a little more than a tablespoon. Drop the cookie sheet on counter to "settle" the profiteroles.

Glaze:

1 egg
1 tablespoon water

Mix the egg and water and brush the profiteroles with the glaze. Bake in middle of the oven for fifteen minutes. Reduce the heat to 350° F. and bake twenty-five to thirty minutes longer. Cool on a wire rack.

To fill with the deviled crab, cut a hinged cap in each profiterole with a sharp knife and scrape out any loose partly cooked pastry. Spoon in the crab mixture, then replace cap and refrigerate until needed. Profiteroles freeze well unfilled.

A

Soups

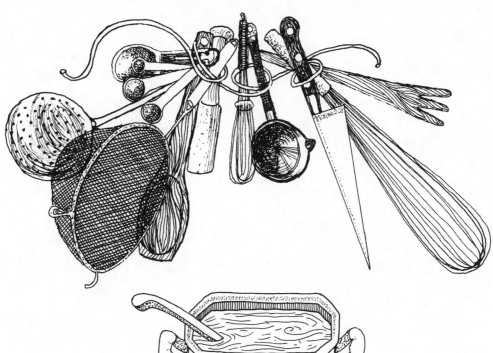

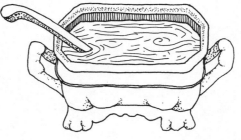

Soups

Soups, soups, glorious soups—warming, comforting, satisfying. Soups are surely the most versatile production to come from the kitchen. They are to be found on the table of the rich and mighty and in the kitchen of the poorest peasant, from truffled double consommé to coarse bread in seasoned hot water.

In the past, soups have been outrageously neglected by the uninformed cook who thought them too plebian for the double damask draped table, overlooking the fact that a cup of consommé does more to stimulate the appetite than a dry martini on the rocks.

The base, or stock—whether it be beef, chicken, veal, or lamb—is inexpensive to make, and no freezer should be without a quart or two. With the addition of vegetables, eggs, or meats, a course or a whole meal is there for the making. Lamb stock is the base for one of the most satisfying soups I know, and the ingredients—barley and vegetables and scraps of lean lamb—are to be found in most kitchens. With a good crusty bread, there is nothing better for a midday meal. And, as a starter, a cup of strong beef consommé spiked with a spoonful or two of dry Madeira, encourages the gastric juices to flow. Use your imagination and a food processor and you will be surprised by what you come up with, combinations that are not to be found in the cookbook library.

WHITE STOCK

2½ quarts

I include this recipe to encourage you to make your own white stock, which is used as a base for consommé and soups, and freeze it. Liquids frozen in one-quart milk containers are convenient and space-saving. When frozen solid, cut away the carton and seal the "brick" of stock in plastic wrap. Stack in the freezer. The bottom quarter of the milk carton makes a one-cup container.

4 pounds veal knuckles (veal shanks), cut
　　into 3 or 4 pieces
2 pounds shin of beef, cut into 3 or 4
　　pieces
Poultry bones, if available (Be nice to the
　　butcher and he will provide.)
6 quarts cold water
2 onions studded with 2 cloves

2 carrots, coarsely chopped
2 leeks, washed
1 celery stalk, chopped
1 tablespoon salt
12 peppercorns
Bouquet garni: 3 to 4 parsley stalks, 1 bay
　　leaf, and 1 small sprig of thyme, all
　　tied together

Put the veal, beef, and the chicken bones into a large saucepan, add the water, and bring slowly to a boil. Skim off the scum as it rises, occasionally adding a little cold water, as this will help bring the scum to the top.

After all the scum has been removed, add the prepared vegetables, the tablespoon of salt, the peppercorns, and the bouquet garni. Simmer for five hours over very low heat.

Strain the stock into a large bowl and chill. Remove every particle of fat.　　　　　　*BC*

BROWN STOCK

2 quarts

This is a base for soups and sauces.

6 pounds shin and marrow bones
4 quarts cold water
8 black peppercorns
6 whole cloves
1 bay leaf
1 teaspoon thyme

3 sprigs parsley
1 large carrot, diced
3 ribs celery, diced
1 cup drained, canned or fresh tomatoes
1 medium onion, diced
1 small white turnip, diced

Cut the bones into pieces and brown them in a 350° F. oven. Place the browned shin and marrow bones in a large stockpot with cold water. Bring slowly to a boil; reduce the heat and simmer, uncovered, for about thirty minutes.

Remove scum and add the remaining ingredients. Bring to a boil and then simmer partly covered for at least six hours.

Strain the stock. Cool uncovered, then refrigerate uncovered. Remove the fat when the stock is cold.

BC

CREME DU BARRY

8 to 10 servings

1 large or 2 small cauliflowers
5 ribs celery, chopped
6 cups chicken stock (homemade or from
  bouillon cubes)
3 to 4 tablespoons chopped onion

3 cups milk or light cream
Grated nutmeg
Salt and pepper to taste
½ cup parsley sprigs, finely chopped

Prepare cauliflower by breaking into small heads and removing most of the woodlike stalks. Put aside a few of the best-looking and smallest pieces for garnish.

Cook cauliflower and celery in a heavy pan, with enough stock to cover them, until tender, for ten to fifteen minutes.

Purée in a food processor or blender with the chopped onion until smooth. Return the cauliflower purée to a clean enamel-lined or stainless-steel pan. Stir in the milk or cream and remainder of the chicken stock.

Heat gently, but do not boil. Season to taste with grated nutmeg, salt, and pepper.

To serve, put a pinch of chopped parsley and two or three very small, uncooked heads of cauliflower in each heated bowl. Ladle in the hot soup. It also freezes well.   *A*

THE DIETER'S VEGETABLE SOUP

6 servings

3 medium carrots
2 ribs celery
1 small onion
1 tablespoon butter
1 quart chicken stock, or 2 cans (13 ounces
  each) clear chicken broth

¼ teaspoon celery salt
½ tablespoon salt
Freshly ground black pepper
1 tablespoon sugar
¼ cup dry vermouth
1 tablespoon chopped parsley

(Continued)

Scrape and dice the carrots. Wash and dice the celery. Chop the onion very fine. Melt the butter in a heavy two-quart pan.

Cook three-quarters of the chopped vegetables very slowly in the covered pan. Set aside the rest of the vegetables for a garnish.

Add about two cups of the chicken stock to the vegetables and blend in the blender until smooth.

Return the mixture to the pan and add the remaining chicken stock. Add the seasonings, sugar, and dry vermouth. Stir in the uncooked garnish. Bring to a boil and simmer for five minutes to marry the flavors.

Put a pinch of finely chopped parsley in the bowl before spooning in the soup.

(Approximately seventy-nine calories per serving.) *A*

CREAM OF CARROT SOUP—SANS CREME

6 servings

This is one of my many cream soups without cream. The most ardent "waist-watcher" can have it without the slightest twinge of regret.

6 medium carrots, scraped and chopped
1 small onion, peeled and chopped
1 bay leaf
2 tablespoons butter
3 cups chicken stock

2 teaspoons sugar (optional)
Salt and pepper
1 tablespoon grated lemon rind
1 tablespoon chopped parsley

Combine the carrots, onion, bay leaf, and butter in a heavy pan. Cover. Cook over a very low flame until the carrots are tender. Keep the lid on to create condensation. The moisture will help to prevent burning. The cooking time is approximately eight minutes. Cool slightly and remove the bay leaf. Add one cup of chicken stock.

Pour the mixture into an electric blender; turn first to low and then to high. Blend on high for one minute.

Return the mixture to the pan in which you cooked the carrots. Add the other two cups of chicken stock and the sugar. Season to taste with salt and pepper.

After the soup is poured, add grated lemon rind and parsley to each serving. *A*

CREAM OF CELERY SOUP—SANS CREME

6 servings

1 head celery
1 knob celeriac or two small potatoes
1 medium onion
1 quart chicken stock

Freshly ground pepper and celery salt
  to taste
¼ cup parsley sprigs, finely chopped

Wash the celery ribs, removing the "strings" with a vegetable peeler, and cut up the ribs coarsely. Wash, peel, and slice the celeriac or potatoes. Dice the onion.

In a two-quart pan with a tight-fitting lid, simmer the vegetables in half the stock until tender, for about fifteen minutes. Strain them into a clean pan and purée the solids with some of the liquid.

Stir the purée into the first pan and add the remaining stock. Season to taste with pepper and celery salt. Go lightly on the pepper.

Garnish with finely chopped parsley. Serve the soup hot or cold. *A*

VINDALOO SOUP

6 to 8 servings

Vindaloo in Hindustani means the blending of spices. By now you will have realized that many of my "cream soups" are lacking in cream. I have used a "self thickening" method—making a purée of the solids to create a thickening agent—for many years and find it to be both healthful and convenient.

5 ribs celery
6 carrots
6 cups stock, beef or chicken
Rind of ½ lemon, chopped fine

2 tablespoons tomato purée (optional)
2 teaspoons imported curry powder
½ cup dry vermouth
Salt and pepper

Wash the celery and carrots. Peel the carrots. Chop coarsely four of the carrots and three of the celery ribs. Set aside two of each to be used later.

Place the chopped carrots and celery in a two-quart heavy pan with a lid. Add the stock and simmer gently for half an hour. Strain and reserve the stock.

Purée the cooked vegetables and chopped lemon rind in a blender or rub them through a fine sieve. Add a little stock to the blender, as it will help in the blending process.

(Continued)

Put the purée of vegetables, the tomato purée, and the stock in the same pan. Dice the remaining two carrots and two ribs of celery very fine and add to the pan. Stir in the curry powder and dry vermouth.

Heat gently for five to six minutes. Season to taste with salt and pepper. A sprinkling of finely chopped parsley may be added as a garnish, if desired. *AB*

SUMMER SQUASH SOUP

6 to 8 servings

Summer Squash Soup is velvety and versatile. Although there is no cream or starch thickening in the recipe, it is not advisable to serve it on a menu that includes a cream sauce.

2 medium yellow squash
2 small zucchini
1½ cups celery leaves
3 tablespoons butter

6 cups chicken stock
Celery salt
Salt and pepper to taste
¼ cup parsley sprigs, finely chopped

Wash, but do not peel, the squash and zucchini. Chop them, but do not remove the seeds. Cook them in a covered pan with celery leaves in butter over a very low heat until tender, approximately six or seven minutes.

Purée the mixture in a blender, adding a little stock to assist in blending. Mix purée with the remaining stock. Correct the seasoning by adding celery salt, salt, and pepper.

Garnish the soup with finely chopped parsley. Serve hot or cold. *A*

SORREL SOUP

6 to 8 servings

During the summer months wild sorrel can be found growing in shaded spots all over the country, and many gardeners cultivate it. The wild leaf is spearhead-shaped, easily recognizable either by appearance or by taste when crushed a little on the tongue. The soup is rich but I forgive it, because the season is short and it can't become part of one's daily diet.

3 cups sorrel leaves, tightly packed
2 teaspoons butter
6 cups chicken stock (of your own
   making, or a good, clear, canned broth)
4 egg yolks

¾ cup heavy cream
2 tablespoons frozen green peas or
   lima beans, puréed in a blender or by
   forcing through a wire strainer (optional)
Salt and freshly ground pepper

Remove the midrib from the sorrel with a sharp knife and discard. Then wash the leaves in cold running water and drain. Chop finely and sauté in the melted butter until wilted. There will be only about three tablespoons left.

Bring the chicken broth to a boil and add the hot chicken stock to the sorrel. Simmer gently for a minute or so. Remove from heat.

Beat the egg yolks in a small bowl. Stir the cream into them and add very slowly to the sorrel and stock mixture, which should be hot but no longer boiling.

Heat gently until the soup thickens, being careful not to let it boil. Then add the purée of green peas or lima beans, if desired.

Season to taste with salt and pepper. Reheat slowly and gently so as not to curdle the egg yolk.   *A*

WATERCRESS SOUP

6 to 8 servings

1 small onion, chopped	3 tablespoons flour
4 tablespoons butter	6 cups chicken stock
4 cups watercress leaves and young stalks	Heavy cream (optional)
Salt	

Cook the onion in butter in a covered pan for seven to eight minutes. Do not allow to brown. Stir in the watercress (set aside a few leaves for garnish) and salt, and cook five to six minutes longer. Sprinkle with flour, then cook four to five minutes more.

Heat the chicken stock. Remove from heat and gently beat it into the watercress mixture. Rub through a fine sieve or purée in a blender. Correct the seasoning. Stir in a little heavy cream. Garnish with fresh watercress leaves.   *A*

POTAGE ST. GERMAIN

6 servings

When garden peas are in season, don't let the opportunity go by without making this soup at least once. And, if you like it, make it again for freezing.

1 small head Boston lettuce, shredded	4 cups strong chicken stock
1 medium onion, chopped	3 cups fresh green peas (about 3 pounds)
1 small handful celery leaves	Bay leaf (optional)
Parsley sprigs	2 tablespoons flour
4 tablespoons butter	Salt and pepper

(Continued)

In a heavy pan large enough to hold three quarts, sauté the shredded lettuce, chopped onion, celery leaves, and parsley in two tablespoons of butter until tender, about two to three minutes. Add two and one-half cups chicken stock, two cups peas, and a piece of the bay leaf. If the pea pods are young and tender, add a dozen or so. Cook, covered, until soft.

Put through a food mill or push through a strainer with a wooden spoon.

Simmer the remaining cup of peas in rest of the stock until tender, about five minutes. Set aside.

To bind, melt two tablespoons of butter and stir in the flour. Cook gently for two to three minutes. Add one cup of the strained soup all at once, and whisk until smooth. Pour the flour and soup mixture back into the soup pot and whisk until blended.

Stir in reserved whole peas and their stock. Reheat. Correct seasoning with salt and pepper.

AB

POTAGE POIRES DE TERRE

6 to 8 servings

The Jerusalem artichoke is an interesting vegetable and although indigenous to the North American continent, it has until quite recently been ignored. Its Latin name is Helianthus tuberosis. *It is not an artichoke and has nothing to do with Jerusalem; it is a member of the sunflower family. The early French Canadian settlers called it* poire de terre, *but when it eventually reached Italy, more aware of its relationship to the sunflower, the Italians dubbed it* girasole, *which later was corrupted to Jerusalem. It is versatile and the dieter's darling—low in calories, fat, and sodium, and high in iron. On a French menu it is* topinambaur.

1 pound large Jerusalem artichokes, peeled and sliced
1 medium onion, chopped
1 clove garlic, crushed with 1 teaspoon coarse salt
½ rib celery, chopped

2 slices lean bacon, chopped
4 tablespoons unsalted butter
5 cups good, strong chicken stock (substitute canned consommé, if necessary)
½ cup finely chopped parsley

Peel the artichokes and put them in a bowl of acidulated water (water with lemon juice, vinegar, or ascorbic acid added to prevent discoloration).

Cook the onion, garlic, celery, and chopped bacon in the butter until the vegetables are soft. Add the artichokes and one cup of chicken stock. Cook, covered, until the artichokes are tender. Purée in a blender or food processor until smooth.

Heat the remaining stock and stir in the purée. Correct the seasoning, if necessary, with salt and pepper. Stir in two or three tablespoons of chopped parsley and serve in heated soup plates or bowls.

AB

GREEK EGG AND LEMON SOUP

4 to 6 servings

Anyone who knows anything about Greece will know of Egg and Lemon Soup, Avgolemono. It is light and takes its place on hot-weather menus without embarrassment. Served cold, it titillates the palate.

2 ounces uncooked rice (6 ounces cooked)
1 quart chicken stock, plus 1 extra cup
2 eggs

Juice of 1 lemon
Salt and pepper
½ cup parsley sprigs, coarsely chopped

Cook the rice in a little chicken stock until tender but not soft, approximately ten minutes. Set aside.

Heat the remainder of the stock in a heavy pan. Whisk the eggs and lemon juice, and dribble them into the boiling stock through a wire sieve. Correct the seasoning by adding salt and pepper.

Put one tablespoon of rice in the bottom of each warmed bowl or plate and pour in the soup. Sprinkle with a little freshly chopped parsley. This soup may also be served cold.

A

INDIAN RIVER SOUP

6 servings

Indian River Soup, named for the citrus region of Florida, is a delightfully refreshing soup, hot or cold. Usually I make it in quantity to be drunk cold on hot summer days.

1 can (1 pound) plum tomatoes with basil
   included
1 carrot, shredded
½ medium onion, chopped
1 bay leaf
Rind of 1 lemon, grated
6 peppercorns
3 cups clear chicken consommé

2 tablespoons sugar
½ cup dry vermouth
Salt and freshly ground pepper
   (preferably white)
Rind of 1 orange
Juice of 1 orange
½ cup parsley, finely chopped

In a heavy two-quart pan bring the tomatoes, carrot, onion, bay leaf, lemon rind, and peppercorns to a boil, then simmer very gently for eight minutes.

Strain carefully into a clean pan. Discard the solids. Stir in the chicken consommé.

Place the soup over moderate heat and add the sugar and vermouth. Continue heating almost to boiling point, then remove from heat. Season with salt and freshly ground pepper. Proceed cautiously with the pepper.

(Continued)

Meanwhile, peel the orange very carefully, avoiding the white pith; cut the peel into very thin strips, one-half inch long. Put the peel aside to be used as garnish. Squeeze the orange and strain, adding the juice to the soup.

Reheat the soup gently. Ladle the soup into bowls or soup plates and sprinkle with finely chopped parsley and the orange rind. This soup may be served hot or cold.   *AB*

ICED CUCUMBER SOUP

6 servings

2 cucumbers
½ cup finely chopped onion
3 cups chicken stock
1 cup sour cream

½ teaspoon fresh dill, finely chopped or
  ¼ teaspoon dried dill
Salt and pepper to taste
¼ cup parsley, finely chopped

Peel one cucumber. Cut it lengthwise, remove the seeds, and dice it. Place diced cucumber in a saucepan, adding the onion and two cups of chicken stock. Simmer covered for fifteen minutes or until tender.

Pour the mixture into the blender and purée, or press it through a fine sieve into a mixing bowl. Add the remaining cup of chicken stock.

Peel and remove seeds from the second cucumber. Grate it coarsely. Stir the sour cream, grated cucumber, and chopped dill into the purée.

Season with salt and pepper; chill. Sprinkle with finely chopped parsley before serving.
          A

ICED BORSCHT

8 to 10 servings

This is one of the many variations of borscht. It is my favorite. On occasions when I'm not in the mood for a cold soup, I've heated it gently and served it with a spoonful of sour cream.

5 large beets
1 onion
1½ quarts cold water
1 cup tomato purée

Salt and pepper to taste
Sugar to taste
1 tablespoon lemon juice

Peel and grate the beets. Peel the onion and chop it coarsely. In a heavy pan, combine the beets, onion, and cold water. Bring to a boil and simmer gently for forty minutes.

Add the tomato purée, salt, pepper, sugar, and lemon juice to taste. Simmer gently for another thirty-five minutes.

Purée in a blender or food processor until smooth. Correct the seasoning.

The character of this soup is its sweet-and-sour taste. Add more sugar and lemon juice, if needed. Serve chilled.   *AB*

COLD FISH CONSOMME

8 to 10 small servings

This is one of the most delicious cold soups to serve on a hot summer day. Do not be alarmed by the length of the instructions. So much of it can be done in advance. Serve in glass bowls, if you have them.

Stock:

2 pounds bones and head of white fish
2 ribs celery, coarsely chopped
1 large onion, unpeeled and chopped
2 small carrots, washed and chopped
2 small bay leaves

1 tablespoon salt
2 quarts cold water
2 cups dry white wine
6 peppercorns

Put all the ingredients, except the peppercorns, in a large enameled or steel-lined pan. Bring to a boil, reduce the heat, and cook uncovered. Skim frequently until no more scum rises. Add the peppercorns. Simmer gently for two hours. Strain and cool.

To clarify:

1 egg shell
1 egg white
2 small carrots, peeled and chopped

1 rib celery, chopped finely
1 quart stock

Crush the shell and add it to the egg white and chopped vegetables. If the stock is not cold, add an ice cube or two.

Stir the egg and vegetable mixture into the fish stock and bring to a simmer over very gentle heat. Take particular care that it does not boil or you will have to start all over again.

Simmer very gently for thirty minutes. The solids will rise to the surface with the egg white and vegetables and form a definite crust. You may poke a hole in the crust to see that the simmer is gentle.

Take the stock off the heat and allow it to cool and rest for half an hour. Lift off the crust and strain the liquid through two thicknesses of wet cheesecloth.

(Continued)

Consommé:

3 to 4 ounces small uncooked shrimp
4 ounces bay scallops
1 small cucumber
Salt and pepper

White wine or sherry (optional)
A sprig or two of fresh dill
Lemon wedges

Clean, shell, and devein the shrimp. Bring them to a boil in what is left of the stock. Let the shrimp sit for three to four minutes, then lift them out and, when cool enough to handle, slice them paper-thin.

Cook scallops in the same stock. Boil for one minute, drain, and cool.

Slice the cucumber into paper-thin slices.

Season the consommé with salt and pepper. Flavor with additional white wine or sherry, if you prefer. Add the scallops.

As the consommé sets, add the sliced shrimp and cucumber so that the slices float. Push some of them down in the consommé so that they are submerged. Garnish with a sprig of dill and serve very cold with a wedge of lemon.
A

DOUBLE CONSOMME

6 servings

Consommé is the best remedy for a jaded appetite. A small serving is all that is needed to start the gastric juices flowing.

1 egg white, lightly beaten
1 egg shell, crushed
4 ounces lean ground beef
Tomato skins, chopped
1 carrot, chopped

1 celery stalk, chopped
1 quart strong, cold beef stock, free of all
   fat
¼ cup Madeira
Salt and pepper

In a bowl mix the egg white, egg shell, beef, and vegetables with your hand. Stir in the cold stock.

Bring the mixture carefully and gently to the simmer. Allow to simmer for ten to fifteen minutes. Be very careful that the mixture does not boil or you will have to start all over again.

Allow to rest for twenty minutes or so. Strain carefully through two thicknesses of wet cheesecloth.

Add the Madeira and reheat. Season to taste with salt and pepper.
AB

CONSOMME

6 to 8 servings

2 quarts beef stock
½ pound shin of beef
1 onion
1 stalk celery
1 carrot
2 egg whites and shells of 2 eggs, crushed
1 sprig of thyme or ½ teaspoon dried
   thyme

1 sprig marjoram or
   ½ teaspoon dried marjoram
1 bay leaf
2 cloves
12 peppercorns
4 ounces dry sherry
Salt

Remove all the fat from the cold stock. Grind the meat finely. Prepare the onion, celery, and carrot, and cut them into good-sized pieces. Mix the egg whites and crushed egg shells together.

Combine whites and shells with the ground meat and add a tablespoon of cold water. Place the vegetables and egg and meat mixture with the stock, herbs, and spices in a large pan. Stir the ingredients over heat until they almost reach a boil.

Let simmer very gently for ten minutes, then add the sherry. Bring almost to a boil again and remove from the heat. Let stand for five minutes.

Strain carefully through four or five thicknesses of cheesecloth. Return to the pan, reheat, and season to taste. *AB*

MUSHROOM CONSOMME

4 to 6 servings

The dried, imported mushroom has a true mushroom flavor, and the resulting consommé is a perfect starter to an elaborate meal.

2 packages imported dried mushrooms
1 quart strong clarified beef or chicken
   stock

Pepper and celery salt to taste
¼ cup dry Madeira
2 firm fresh mushrooms for garnish

Soak the dried mushrooms in the beef or chicken stock for one hour. Bring them to a gentle boil and simmer for thirty minutes.

Strain the liquid into a clean saucepan. Discard the mushrooms. Season the consommé to taste with pepper and celery salt, and add one-quarter cup of dry Madeira.

Serve hot or cold with one or two very thin slices of fresh mushroom in each soup bowl. *AB*

COLD TOMATO CONSOMME

6 servings

Here is a summer soup to please the most fastidious. Instead of Bloody Marys, add a shot of vodka to the consommé and serve before luncheon on a summer day.

2 cups canned Italian plum tomatoes with
   basil included
1 quart chicken stock
1 tablespoon sugar

¼ cup dry vermouth
Salt and pepper to taste
½ cup parsley sprigs, chopped
Rind of 1 lemon

In a stainless-steel or enameled pan, simmer the tomatoes and chicken stock for five minutes. Rub the mixture through a fine sieve. Add the sugar and vermouth. Season with salt and pepper to taste.

Serve the soup hot or cold, garnished with chopped parsley and shredded lemon rind.

AB

PUMPKIN SOUP

8 to 10 servings

Pumpkin pie is not my favorite dessert. To maintain tradition and give the pumpkin its place of honor on the Thanksgiving table, I turn the pumpkin into soup—and very good it is at Thanksgiving or on any other day.

2 pounds fresh pumpkin, with peel and
   seeds removed
2 cups water
3 cups milk
2 tablespoons brown sugar
1 tablespoon butter

Salt and pepper
Ginger
Cinnamon
½ cup ham (the best quality), finely
   julienned
Parsley, finely chopped

Cut the pumpkin into chunks and simmer in water until tender, for about five minutes. Drain. Purée the pumpkin in a blender or rub it through a fine sieve.

Heat the milk in a heavy pan. Stir in the pumpkin purée, brown sugar, and butter. Season to taste with salt and pepper. Add very little ground ginger and cinnamon. Heat, but do not allow to boil.

Divide the julienne of ham between the heated soup bowls. Ladle in the soup and garnish with a little chopped parsley.

A

OYSTER SOUP

6 to 8 servings

Oyster Soup is very much at home on the Thanksgiving or Christmas Day menu. On both occasions the entrée is usually a bird of one kind or another that will not spoil by waiting while the soup course is being heated.

4 tablespoons butter
2 tablespoons finely chopped shallot or
    scallions (white end only)
4 pints oysters with their liquid

4 cups half-and-half or light cream
Grated nutmeg
Salt and white pepper
1 cup parsley sprigs, finely chopped

Melt the butter in a small, heavy pan and add the finely chopped shallot or scallions. Cook very gently until they are transparent, being careful not to burn them.

Place the pan in a larger pan of hot water over medium heat. Add the oysters and their liquid. Stir carefully until the oysters curl at the edges.

Heat the half-and-half or light cream at just below the boiling point, then stir it into the oysters. Season to taste with grated nutmeg, salt, and white pepper. Heat gently, but do not allow the soup to boil.

Before serving, stir in the chopped parsley. Serve with croutons. *A*

SCOTCH BROTH I

10 to 12 servings

This wonderful, hearty soup freezes beautifully and I'm deliberately giving you large proportions for just that reason. Serve it for luncheon with French bread and fruit to follow, Sunday night supper, or just to comfort you on a cold winter night.

2 pounds neck of lamb, trimmed of all fat
    and cut into chops
10 cups water
½ cup dried peas
2 small white turnips, peeled and diced
3 carrots, peeled and diced
1 large onion, peeled and sliced

1 leek, the white part and half the green
    sliced
3 ounces barley
1 small green cabbage, shredded
Salt and pepper
½ cup parsley sprigs, chopped

Put the lamb in a heavy pot with the water and bring to a boil. Skim off all the scum as it rises to the surface.

(Continued)

Add the dried peas, turnips, carrots, onion, leek, and barley, and one tablespoon of salt. Cover the pan and simmer for twenty minutes.

Add the cabbage. Simmer ten minutes longer. You may, if you wish, remove and discard the bones, first removing any meat that clings to them. Put the meat back in the pot. Correct the seasoning. Stir in parsley before serving.

AB

SCOTCH BROTH II

6 to 8 servings

Lamb Stock:

Lamb bones
1 onion, chopped but not peeled
1 small carrot, chopped but not peeled
1 small bay leaf

1 rib celery, chopped
A few parsley stalks
4 peppercorns
Salt

Cover lamb bones with water to a depth of two inches. Simmer for five minutes or so, and skim off the scum as it rises. Add all the other ingredients and simmer, covered, for one hour. Add salt to taste.

1 pound lamb trimmings,
    trimmed of all fat
4 heaping tablespoons barley
2 medium onions, diced
2 medium carrots, diced

2 ribs celery
2 leeks thoroughly washed, white and
    half the green sliced thinly
Salt and pepper
½ cup finely chopped parsley

Simmer cut-up lamb in stock for ten minutes, skimming off scum as it rises. Add the barley and all the vegetables, except parsley. Cook slowly, covered, for about two hours. Season with salt and freshly ground pepper.

Serve hot in bowls generously sprinkled with finely chopped parsley. This soup is a meal in itself when served with crunchy French or Italian bread.

AB

Fish

Fish

Fish cookery is an art in itself. Cooks who instinctively know how to cook—and how long to cook—this finned and scaled delicacy have no need for formulas and timetables. But for the others, the inexperienced and the student, the Canadian government's Department of Fisheries has given us a foolproof method, and if it is followed without doubt or fear, there is no possible chance of being left with a salmon steak that resembles pink papier-mâché.

The rules governing the gentle art of fish cookery are simple in the extreme. First, measure the fish in inches, vertically, at its thickest part. Allow ten minutes of cooking time for each inch. For instance, to poach a fish three inches thick will take thirty minutes, that is, thirty minutes after the court bouillon comes to a gentle simmer. To bake the same fish will take thirty minutes at a temperature of 450°F. And from there we come to the fillet and baking *en papillote* (in envelopes). The average fillet of fish is one-quarter of an inch thick. The tapered tail is tucked under. One-quarter of ten is two-and-a-half. Therefore, the fillet will broil, bake, or grill in two and one-half minutes at a high temperature, say 450°F.

It is difficult to turn over fillets of flounder and other soft-fleshed fish. They are cooked on one side only. Dover or Channel sole, on the other hand, has a firm flesh and may be turned with ease. It is classed as "game" and improved by being aged for a day or two. Unless it is fresh and flown in daily, we must be content with frozen Dover sole in the United States. My advice, therefore, is not to open your purse to pay for frozen Dover sole; wait until you are in Europe to have perfect fish, grilled on the bone and sprinkled with a little lemon juice.

Black sole, fished off the west coast of Ireland and in Donegal Bay, was considered a delicacy by my grandparents. It was a rare delicacy, not because of a shortage of fish, but a shortage of fishermen who fished only when ready cash was badly needed for such mental and bodily comforts as Guinness Stout or John Jameson's aged Irish whiskey. The black sole would be brought to the kitchen door by a young man, jaunty, red-cheeked, and smiling, from the bay, eighteen miles away. By the time it got to the range, it was in perfect condition for whatever method it was to be cooked by. But, I remember it best grilled, brushed with homemade butter, and served with a boiled potato—a potato that can only be found in Ireland, white and soufflé-like and with a flavor that needed nothing more than a little salt to improve it.

I prefer fish cooked with the head on and, in spite of protests from my students, this is how I serve a whole fish. Those who are offended by the cooked head would dearly love a fish that could be bred headless.

Grilled fish is infinitely better with the bone left in. The backbone is a good conductor of heat, which ensures even cooking. It is more time-consuming to eat, but well worth the trouble.

Deep frying is not one of the most popular cooking methods, but, properly done, it is both simple and nutritious. The temperature must be right—375°F. is roughly correct—and I find the electrically heat-controlled fryer a great convenience. There is no smell of frying and no spatter; it is a good investment.

When buying fish, look for clear, bright eyes and glistening scales. Open up the gills and put your nose right in. If there is the slightest odor of fish, it is not fresh. Frozen fish loses much of its nutritional value as it thaws out; liquid containing salts, minerals, and vitamins is lost during the thawing process.

Fish is no longer inexpensive, but penny for ounce, it is good value for your money and highly nutritious—high in protein and very satisfying. Treat fish with the respect it demands, and you have a most welcome addition to your menu.

SAUMON EN PAPILLOTE

6 servings

Envelope-cooking is simple and unmessy and has been in use for generations all across the world—wrapping meats or fish in banana leaves, for example. The flavor is retained and an adequate amount of sauce produced. It is, in fact, a one-dish meal. The amount of salmon I've used in this recipe is ample for a main dish; halve it and you have a splendid opening to a luncheon or dinner.

2 medium tomatoes
4 large mushroom caps
3 tablespoons sweet butter
1 tablespoon finely chopped shallots
1 heaping tablespoon flour
⅓ cup dry white wine
1 cup heavy cream
¼ cup finely chopped parsley

6 salmon steaks, 8 ounces each
1 teaspoon salt
¼ teaspoon pepper
3 sheets parchment paper (15 by 18 inches each)
1 egg
1 tablespoon water

Heat oven to 400°F.

Plunge the tomatoes into boiling water for ten seconds. Lift them out and when cool enough to handle, remove their skins. Cut them in half, remove the seeds, and dice.

Wipe the mushroom caps clean with a damp cloth and slice them. Heat the butter in a saucepan; add the tomatoes and mushrooms; sauté until soft. Add the shallots and cook another two minutes.

Sprinkle the flour over the vegetables and cook for an additional two minutes. Add the wine and continue cooking for three or four minutes. Pour in the cream and cook, stirring, until the sauce thickens. Remove from the heat and add the parsley.

Season the salmon steaks with salt and pepper. Cut each sheet of parchment paper in half and brush each piece with melted butter.

Fold each piece in half, then open it and place two tablespoons of sauce near the fold. Place a salmon steak on top and cover the steak with three tablespoons of sauce. Fold the paper over and pinch the edges to form a half-moon shape. Brush the entire package with melted butter.

Beat one egg with one tablespoon of water and brush the edges of the paper with the egg mixture to seal. Repeat the procedure for the remaining steaks.

Place the packaged salmon steaks on a greased pan on the top rack in the oven and bake for fifteen minutes. Serve in the paper bags. Cut your own bag first so that your guests, should they be confused, can follow suit.

TRUITE EN PAPILLOTE

This is one of the exceptions when the Canadian method does not apply. Compensation is made for foil and wax paper. Both act as insulators and cooking time will be longer.

1 trout per person, cleaned, but with head
    left on
Salt and pepper
1 sixteen-inch square of wax paper and
    foil for each fish

8 tablespoons butter
Lemon juice
½ cup parsley sprigs, finely chopped
Lemon wedges

Heat oven to 450°F.

Dry the trout, and season inside and out with salt and pepper. For each fish, lay a piece of wax paper over one of foil and place the fish across them diagonally. Dot with three or four dabs of butter and sprinkle with a little lemon juice. Fold to seal, making a neat package. Arrange on a baking sheet and bake for twelve minutes.

To serve, open the package at one end and slide out the trout with its juices onto a hot plate. Sprinkle with a little chopped parsley and garnish with lemon wedges. A steamed potato counteracts the richness.

A

POACHED STRIPED BASS

8 to 10 servings

1 striped bass, weighing 7 to 8 pounds
Watercress
Lemon wedges

Court bouillon:

2 sticks celery
12 peppercorns
1 bay leaf
2 carrots, thinly sliced
1 onion, sliced

Pinch of thyme
3 quarts water
2 tablespoons salt
1 quart dry white wine

To make the court bouillon, tie the celery, peppercorns, bay leaf, carrots, onion, and thyme in a cheesecloth bag. Place the bag and the other ingredients in a fish kettle. Bring to a boil and simmer for half an hour. Discard the bag of aromatics; they have served their purpose.

Scrape the fish with the back of a knife to remove the scales, if the fishmonger has not done this for you.

Place the bass on the grid and put it in the fish kettle with the gently simmering court bouillon. Simmer for about thirty minutes or ten minutes per inch at the thickest part of the fish. Do not allow to boil. Allow to cool sufficiently before handling.

Remove the skin and dark flesh close to the backbone. Carefully slide the fish onto a long fish platter. Garnish with watercress and lemon wedges. Serve with melted butter, Green Sauce (Sauce Verte), Sauce Tartare, or Mousseline (see chapter on sauces).

POACHED SALMON STEAKS

Court bouillon (see instructions in recipe
    for Poached Striped Bass, page 72)
1 salmon steak per person, about 1 inch
    thick

Melted butter
Finely chopped parsley
Lemon wedges

Prepare the court bouillon.

Tie loose ends of steaks together with string to hold them in place and give the steaks an oval shape. Place steaks into court bouillon and poach for ten minutes for every inch of thickness, measured at the thickest part. (The definition of poaching, according to Mme. Prunier, is to keep the court bouillon just gently trembling so that cooking proceeds by gradual penetration of heat into the fish.)

Lift out the steaks with a spatula, cut the strings, and peel off the skin. Scrape off the dark grayish meat; it is unsightly, but otherwise as edible as the pink meat. Brush the salmon steaks with melted butter and sprinkle with parsley before serving with lemon wedges.

BAKED RED SNAPPER

6 to 8 servings

2 three-pound red snappers
Salt and pepper
Flour seasoned with 1 tablespoon salt,
    3 to 4 twists of the pepper mill
8 tablespoons butter

1 cup orange juice
1 cup dry vermouth
4 oranges
Watercress

(Continued)

Heat oven to 450°F.

Have ready a non-aluminum baking pan about two inches deep, large enough to hold the fish. Prepare the snappers for cooking by scraping the scales, seasoning the inside with salt and pepper, and dusting the outside with seasoned flour.

Melt butter in the baking pan. Add one cup of orange juice and one cup of dry vermouth. Bring to a boil and simmer for two to three minutes.

Lay the fish in the pan and baste with the juices. Cook for thirty to thirty-five minutes in the oven basting thoroughly and frequently. Test for doneness: The flesh should spring back when pressed with a finger.

Remove the snappers to a serving platter. Reduce the pan juices and pour them over the fish.

Garnish with orange slices or wedges and watercress.   *A*

CREAMED, SMOKED HADDOCK

6 to 8 servings

Smoked fish is widely used in Europe, especially Northern Europe. Smoking was one of the early methods of curing meats and fish. Smoked fish is an acquired taste—and once acquired, seldom abandoned. Creamed, Smoked Haddock—make sure it is haddock and not cod dyed to impersonate it— is one of my most useful stand-bys. For a late supper after the theater, it is unbeatable.

2 pounds smoked haddock to make approximately 4 cups of cooked and flaked fish	3 tablespoons flour
	Scraping of nutmeg
	Freshly ground pepper
Milk, sufficient to cover fish	½ pound small, fresh mushrooms
3 tablespoons butter	

Heat oven to 400°F.

Soak the haddock, in enough milk to cover it, for one hour; then bring the haddock and milk slowly to a boil in a heavy pan. Allow it to cool. When the haddock is cool enough to handle, drain and reserve the milk. You will need two cups of the milk later on. Remove the haddock's skin and all the bones.

Make a *roux* by melting three tablespoons of butter in a heavy pan and stirring in three tablespoons of flour. Cook gently for two to three minutes, being careful not to burn it.

Heat two cups of the milk in which the haddock was cooked and, off the heat, pour it into the *roux* all at once. Add the nutmeg, whisk until smooth, return to gentle heat, and cook for five to six minutes, stirring all the time. Correct the seasoning with the addition of freshly ground pepper. You will find that extra salt will not be necessary.

Wipe the mushrooms clean, cutting off the stems flush with the caps. If the mushrooms are large, halve or quarter them; the pieces should be no larger than a "quarter." Add them to the sauce and cook for two to three minutes more. Stir the sauce into the flaked fish and pile it into an oven-proof dish. Bake until bubbling, about ten to fifteen minutes.

To prepare ahead of time, refrigerate the sauce and fish separately if you are cooking them a night ahead. Wait until the morning to stir the flaked haddock into the sauce and heat thoroughly.

CODFISH STEAKS

6 servings

Not many years ago cod was on the bottom rung of the gastronomic fish ladder, much the same as herring was in Europe—food for the masses. And, I believe, the reason was its low cost. That no longer applies since cod has risen in price. Why should anything take a back seat because it is inexpensive? Cod—and codling (scrod)—is delicious when carefully prepared. It is rich and nutritious and makes a splendid one-dish meal.

½ cup vegetable oil
1½ cups white bread, trimmed of crusts
    and cubed (about 3 slices)
2 teaspoons salt
½ teaspoon freshly ground white pepper
6 one-inch-thick codfish steaks,
    approximately 3 pounds

½ cup flour
8 tablespoons sweet butter
1 to 4 tablespoons lemon juice
2 large lemons, peeled and cut into
    ½-inch cubes
4 tablespoons capers, drained
½ cup parsley sprigs, finely chopped

Heat three tablespoons of oil in a skillet until hot and add the bread cubes. Toss them so that they brown evenly on all sides. Lift out and drain on paper towels.

Sprinkle the salt and pepper on both sides of the fish steaks and dip them in the flour to coat. Shake off the excess. Heat three tablespoons of butter in each of two heavy skillets; add the remaining oil. When the oil mixture is foaming, add the fish. The steaks must not touch each other. Cook over medium heat for about five minutes. Turn the fish and cook for another five minutes.

Arrange the fish steaks on a warm serving platter, sprinkle with lemon juice, croutons, lemon cubes, and capers.

Melt the remaining two tablespoons of butter in a clean skillet until it turns light brown. Pour the hot butter on top of the fish, sprinkle with parsley, and serve immediately with steamed potatoes.

GOUJONNETTE OF SOLE

6 to 8 servings

Goujonnette of Sole is excellent as a first course.

6 fillets of sole
2 eggs, beaten
2 cups fresh white bread crumbs
Vegetable oil for frying

Lemon wedges
Fried parsley (see page 172)
Sauce Tartare (see page 286)

Cut the fillets across the width in strips approximately one-quarter inch wide.

Dip the strips in beaten egg and then in bread crumbs. Lay them on paper towels until all have been breaded.

Heat the oil and test the heat with a small cube of bread. If the bread takes on a healthy tan, the temperature is about right for deep frying (approximately 370°F.). Do not overcrowd the fryer—the cooking time will be little more than a minute.

Lift the fish out with a slotted spoon as the pieces are done and drain on several layers of paper towel. Keep them warm in the oven until all the fillets have been cooked.

Garnish with lemon wedges and fried parsley. Pass the Sauce Tartare separately.

TURBAN OF SOLE, SAUCE JOINVILLE

8 to 10 servings

The Turban of Sole is one dish I serve when in an expansive mood. It is both beautiful to look at and to eat. The ingredients are costly, so save it for special occasions. Don't be put off by the length of the instructions. Read them through several times to fix them firmly in your mind. When the time comes to put the recipe together, it will be no stranger. And now the good news: It can be prepared ahead of time, completely ready for the oven.

If you need a starch to go with it, try plain boiled rice. But, personally, I prefer it on its own with a salad to follow.

4 large gray soles, filleted to make 8 fillets
2 egg whites
2 teaspoons salt
¼ teaspoon nutmeg
Rind of 1 lemon

White pepper
Dash of cayenne pepper
2 cups heavy cream
Sauce Joinville (see recipe next page)

Heat oven to 350°F.

Take two fillets, and set aside the other six. Cut the two fillets in half lengthwise and pull out the connecting "string." Cut up the fillets coarsely and mix with the egg whites. Add the salt, nutmeg, lemon rind, white pepper, and cayenne. Pulverize half the mixture in a blender or food processor with one cup of cream. Repeat, using the remaining half of the mixture and the other cup of cream. Combine the mixtures and correct the seasonings. Refrigerate the mousse until needed.

Cut the remaining six fillets in half lengthwise and pull out the connecting "string." Arrange the fillets in a six-cup buttered ring mold, with the broad ends hanging over the outside edge and the narrow ones over the inside. Fill with the chilled mousse. Fold flaps of sole over the mousse, thin ends first and broader ones on top. Cover with wax paper or foil and refrigerate until needed.

To cook, place the mold in a roasting pan with enough hot, not boiling, water, to come half-way up the mold. Cover with foil or wax paper and bake for twenty-five to thirty minutes. Turn out the mold onto a warm dish and drain off the liquid that will eventually ooze out.

Sauce Joinville:

½ pound raw shrimp
½ cup dry white wine
¼ pound tight button mushrooms
4 tablespoons unsalted butter
1 tablespoon flour
Salt and freshly ground pepper

½ cup heavy cream
2 tablespoons dry sherry
2 egg yolks
2 tablespoons lemon juice, or to taste
Finely chopped parsley

Rinse the shrimp under cold running water and place them in a heavy skillet with all the water that clings to them. Add the wine. Place over a high heat, cover, and cook until the shrimp turn pink, about three minutes.

Drain the liquid into a measuring cup and reserve it. Cool the shrimp immediately under cold water to stop the cooking. Then shell, devein, and chop them very fine. Set aside.

If necessary, wipe the mushrooms with a clean, damp cloth. Cut off the stems flush with the caps. Quarter the mushrooms.

Melt two tablespoons of the butter in a skillet. Add the mushrooms and sauté until lightly browned. Lift them from the skillet with a slotted spoon and combine with the shrimp. Combine any liquid in the pan with the reserved shrimp liquid.

Make a *roux* with the remaining butter in the same skillet: When the butter is melted, stir in the flour and cook until smooth, stirring constantly until the mixture foams, about three minutes.

If the reserved shrimp liquid doesn't measure one cup, add enough fish broth or wine to make up the difference. Stir the liquid into the *roux* and cook, whipping constantly, until the sauce thickens slightly. Season to taste with salt and pepper.

(Continued)

Combine the cream, sherry, egg yolks, and lemon juice together. Add to the sauce while stirring. Stir in the shrimp and mushrooms and bring to a boil. Do not cook further. Reheat when needed.

Just before serving, stir in the chopped parsley. Spoon a little of the sauce over the crown of the ring and pour the remaining into a warmed sauceboat. *A*

SEA HARVEST

6 to 8 servings

"Any man who has to ask the annual upkeep of a yacht cannot afford one," so said J.P. Morgan. The same applies to many of the ingredients we use in cooking today. Nevertheless, the Sea Harvest is good value and makes a splendid dish for a buffet and—served with well-seasoned rice—it goes a long way.

1 four-ounce piece fresh squid (optional)
½ pound raw shrimp
½ pound bay scallops
1 tablespoon sweet butter
1 tablespoon finely chopped shallots
½ cup fish stock or clam juice
½ pound mushrooms, quartered
½ cup dry vermouth

1 teaspoon salt
½ teaspoon white pepper
½ pound lobster meat
½ cup heavy cream
2 tablespoons tomato paste
Beurre manié: 2 tablespoons sweet butter,
    2 tablespoons flour
½ cup parsley sprigs, finely chopped

Wash the squid thoroughly, remove skin from inside and out, and cut into one-inch pieces. Clean, shell, and devein the shrimp. Cut them in half lengthwise if they are large. Wash the scallops under cold running water and drain.

Melt the butter in a heavy two-quart saucepan and sauté the shallots over low heat for two minutes. Add the squid and cook, stirring, until it turns white. Add the shrimp and cook for another five minutes. Add the scallops and cook for a further three minutes. Stir in the fish stock or clam juice, mushrooms, vermouth, salt, and pepper.

Pick over the lobster meat to remove the cartilage, if any. Wash, drain, and cut into one-inch pieces. Add the lobster meat to the saucepan and stir in the cream and tomato paste.

Combine the two tablespoons of butter and flour (beurre manié) to make a paste and stir into the mixture. Simmer until the sauce has thickened, but do not allow it to boil. Garnish with finely chopped parsley.

MOULES MARINIERE

4 servings

Coquïllages are as fresh as their source. True, but obviously a reliable fishmonger knows where the mussels come from and will give assurance as to their untainted condition. When you personally buy the mussels, make quite sure they are tightly closed. The French say a half-open mussel is "yawning." Allow approximately one quart per person. If you plan to serve more than four or five people, add an extra quart to allow for mussels that have to be discarded—those that float or are open or broken. Since mussels are comparatively inexpensive, the extra quart will amount to no major drain on the purse.

4 quarts clean mussels
2 cups dry white wine
1 small onion, peeled and coarsely
  chopped
1 small carrot, peeled and chopped
1 rib celery
1 small clove garlic

8 or 10 parsley stalks
Sprig of fresh thyme or a pinch of dried
  thyme
1 bay leaf
8 peppercorns
½ cup parsley sprigs, finely chopped

Scrape the mussels with the back of a small knife, removing the beard and any small barnacles. Leave them for as long as possible in a large pan under cold running water. Grit will float off. The mussels are now ready for use.

Bring the wine to a rolling boil in a large pan with all the ingredients, except the mussels and the parsley. Add the mussels and cover the pan. Shake and toss the pan until the mussels open.

Lift the mussels out with a slotted spoon or skimmer and pile them in a deep, heated dish or soup tureen. Sprinkle with chopped parsley. Strain the pan liquid and serve along with a fresh, crusty French loaf for mopping up the juices.

CHARITHES ME FETA

6 servings

Corfu, where I spend part of each year, is an island remarkable for its food. Fish, lamb, pork, rich yellow cream—thick enough to support a large hard-boiled egg—local cheese, fresh fruits and vegetables make it a cook's paradise.

Shrimp baked with Feta cheese is one of the Corfiots' specialties that emigrates successfully. It is a splendid first course, may be prepared in advance, and has the advantage of making shrimp go farther.

(Continued)

2 medium onions, thinly sliced
¾ cup olive oil
1½ pounds tomatoes, peeled and chopped
2 cloves garlic, mashed to a paste with
   coarse salt
Salt and pepper to taste

½ cup parsley sprigs, finely chopped
2 pounds raw shrimp, cleaned, shelled,
   and deveined
½ pound Feta cheese
Lemon wedges

Heat oven to 450°F.

In a skillet, sauté the onions in one-half cup of oil until tender. Add tomatoes, garlic, salt, and pepper. Cook over low heat, stirring now and again for fifteen to twenty minutes. Stir in the chopped parsley.

Spoon the mixture into six cocottes (flat, porcelain dishes) or scallop shells and arrange five or six shrimp on each. Brush the shrimp with the remaining one-quarter cup of oil; dust with salt and pepper, and sprinkle with crumbled Feta cheese.

Bake in the oven for fifteen minutes. Serve very hot with wedges of lemon.   *A*

Poultry and Game

Poultry and Game

"When in doubt, serve chicken." Good advice, but not the only reason for serving this universally available bird. Its versatility is astonishing, from a half chicken simply broiled to the complicated time-consuming boned or half-boned and reshaped bird to everything in between. Surely, there is nothing on two legs or four, except perhaps the porker, that provides you with such variety. There is little waste, the beak perhaps, the feet most certainly not.

Nowadays, when a great many people shun the red and heavier meats, chicken fills the void and, as my opening line suggests, it is without doubt the safest of all entrées to serve to guests whose tastes are unknown.

The recipes that follow range from the simple broiled or roasted chicken to the rich and grand chicken pie.

The flavor of the modern bird cannot be compared with the "dung-hill cock" that roamed the farmyard picking up tasty morsels with the addition of a few handfuls of grain now and again. In winter months this diet was augmented by a hot "mash" to help ward off the cold. The modern bird is confined to a pen, and its diet is very far from à la carte. Nevertheless, the lack of flavor is compensated by careful seasoning and cooking. Imagination and common sense play an important role in the cooking of poultry.

Whenever possible buy fresh birds, weighing not less than three pounds each. To me, it seems the smaller fryer or broiler has as much bone as its heavier counterpart and, therefore, is not as good value for your money. Save the wing tips and giblets. Freeze them, and when there are enough, make chicken stock. Freeze the livers separately (the liver is rarely added to the stock pot), for certain sauces, risottos, and stuffings. The stock, as I have mentioned in the soup chapter, freezes beautifully and is a splendid stand-by for a soup base or sauce. If by chance you have a chicken for which you have no immediate use, rub it lightly all over with vegetable oil, chill it, wrap securely in plastic wrap, and freeze—oil eliminates the risk of freezer burn and drying out.

Whether the chicken is to be roasted, poached, or the humble hen boiled, learn and use the trussing method. The result is a neat, compact appearance and a bird easier to carve.

ROAST CHICKEN

4 to 6 servings

Many years ago Eleanor Noderer, a very good and generous friend of mine, and, I must add, a superb cook, gave the recipe for the best roast chicken in the world. That is what I called it when she first served it to me and that is what it has been called ever since. It is now generally known as Maurice's chicken—simple to prepare and cook in the extreme, and unfailing in its popularity. Served at room temperature with a good salad, cheese, and fruit, it makes the perfect Sunday luncheon.

1 three-pound roasting chicken	Juice of 1 lemon
Coarse salt	Freshly ground pepper
1 clove garlic	

Heat oven to 400°F.

Wipe the inside of the chicken with a damp cloth or paper towel. Sprinkle inside and out very generously with coarse salt. Peel the garlic clove, chop fine, and, using a small knife as a palette knife, crush it to a paste with one teaspoon of coarse salt. Rub the inside of the chicken with half the garlic paste.

Truss or tie up the chicken for the oven and smear the rest of the paste on the outside of the bird. Place it on a rack in a roasting pan. Pour half the lemon juice inside the chicken and pat the remainder all over it. Dust with a little more coarse salt and freshly ground black pepper.

Cook for one hour in the middle of the oven, without basting. Do not open the door.

I usually serve the chicken with watercress salad, but for those who need something a little more substantial, Carrots Vichy go very well with it.   C

BARBECUED CHICKEN

Allow half of 1 two-and-one-half-pound
   chicken per serving
Barbecue Sauce (see page 286)

Ask the butcher to split the chicken in half and remove the backbone. Wash and dry the chicken. Brush both sides of each chicken half with the Barbecue Sauce.

Broil for ten minutes over moderate heat, about six inches away from the heat source. Brush the chicken twice with the sauce during the first ten minutes.

Turn the chicken and broil for ten minutes more, brushing twice during this period.   D

VIRGINIA BAKED CHICKEN

8 servings

Chicken smothered in sour cream, cloaked in seasoned bread crumbs, and baked is a perfect picnic food. No plates, no knives or forks—just the hand is all that's needed when eating this extraordinarily moist and sharply flavored chicken. Children love it.

This is a recipe from Nancy van Sweringen, a friend of mine of long standing and a great cook. For many years she created those marvelous products sold by Soupson in New York City. Her boundless energy gave her time to work with me while I was food consultant for the American Express Company and the owner of a small catering company. Nancy's approach to life is that crises and disasters must be overcome. She now lives in Florida in retirement, which means she only works ten hours a day, instead of eighteen.

2 broiler chickens, weighing
   approximately 2½ pounds, cut into 8
   serving pieces each
2 cups sour cream, approximately

2 cups bread crumbs, seasoned with
   1 tablespoon salt and 1 teaspoon
   dried thyme
4 ounces butter, melted

Heat oven to 375°F.

Skin the chicken pieces and coat them generously with sour cream. Don't be afraid of using too much. Roll the chicken in seasoned bread crumbs.

Arrange the pieces on a baking sheet. Dribble the melted butter over each piece of chicken and bake for forty-five minutes. Serve hot or at room temperature.   *AC*

POULET NORMANDE

8 to 12 servings

6 whole chicken breasts, boned and
   halved
Flour
6 tablespoons butter
Salt and pepper
⅓ cup Calvados (Applejack may be
   substituted)

½ cup white wine
½ cup heavy cream
Sautéed Apple Rings
   (see recipe next page)
Cherry tomatoes
Watercress

Remove skin from the chicken breasts and dredge them lightly with flour.

Melt enough butter to generously coat the bottom of a heavy skillet. Cook the chicken three to four minutes on each side over medium heat, being careful not to brown the breasts. Add more butter as it is needed. Season with salt and pepper.

(Continued)

Heat the Calvados and pour it over the chicken. Set alight. Add the white wine, and cook four to five minutes longer. Remove chicken to serving platter and keep hot.

Gradually pour the cream into the pan juices, and cook over low heat, stirring to reduce and thicken the sauce. Correct the seasoning. Spoon the sauce over the chicken breasts.

Sautéed Apple Rings:

6 apples, peeled, cored, and sliced about ¼ inch thick	4 tablespoons butter Sugar

Sauté the sliced apples quickly in butter over moderately high heat; sprinkle lightly with sugar, and cook until the edges are slightly crisp.

Wash and dry the tomatoes. In a separate pan melt the remaining butter and toss the tomatoes for one to two minutes. Add one teaspoon of sugar.

Garnish the platter with slices of apple, tomatoes, and watercress.

CHICKEN IN WHITE WINE SAUCE

6 to 8 servings

6 whole chicken breasts, skinned and boned	½ cup white wine
3 ribs celery	½ cup chicken stock, made from breast bones and celery trimmings
½ pound small, fresh mushrooms	Beurre manié: two tablespoons flour and two tablespoons butter, softened
4 tablespoons unsalted butter	½ cup parsley sprigs, finely chopped
Salt and freshly ground pepper	

Heat oven to 350°F.

Cut the chicken breasts into two-inch-square cubes. Wash the celery stalks and scrape them to remove coarse fibers. Cut into one-inch pieces on the bias. Wipe the mushrooms with a damp paper towel or cloth. Cut the larger ones in halves or quarters to match the smallest mushrooms.

Heat two tablespoons of the butter in a heavy skillet or casserole. Season the chicken pieces with salt and pepper. When the butter foams, quickly sauté a few pieces of chicken at a time for a minute or so, on each side, and remove them to a casserole. Add more butter as needed and continue cooking the chicken.

When all the chicken has been sautéed, pour the white wine into the skillet and turn up the heat. Scrape the skillet thoroughly to loosen the solids and boil for three to four minutes. Add the chicken stock. Pour the liquid over the chicken in the casserole. Add the celery. Cook, covered, in the oven for twenty-five minutes. Add the mushrooms and continue to cook for ten minutes longer.

Blend two tablespoons of flour with two tablespoons of softened butter (beurre manié). Add bit by bit to the casserole liquid until you have the thickness you want. Sprinkle generously with chopped parsley. Serve with plain boiled rice. *AC*

ESCALOPE DE VOLAILLE

8 servings

When one has a hankering for Escalope de Veau and does not feel up to opening the purse that wide, chicken breasts come in a very close second. I have known the deception to be complete. Each half breast has a fillet. It is easily recognizable. It is finger-shaped and held to the half breast by a thin covering of membrane. Grasp it with a piece of paper towel and it will pull out. Dry and freeze the fillets until you have enough for Goujonnette of Chicken (see page 88).

4 whole chicken breasts, skinned, boned, halved lengthwise, and with finger-shaped fillets removed
1 whole egg, beaten with 1 tablespoon water
1½ cups fine, white bread crumbs, seasoned with salt, pepper, and ½ teaspoon crushed dried sage

Oil and butter for sautéing
½ cup dry Marsala
Flour for dredging
1 cup strong chicken stock
½ cup Sauce Espagnole (Brown Sauce, see page 275)

Flatten each chicken breast half between sheets of wax paper with the flat side of a cleaver. I have often used a rolling pin or a bottle full of water. Make them as thin as possible.

Dip the chicken escalopes in egg and then in seasoned bread crumbs. Refrigerate on a cookie sheet for an hour or so.

Heat one tablespoon of oil and one tablespoon of butter in a heavy skillet. Remove the chicken from the refrigerator and sauté quickly over moderately high heat, turning once. Add more oil and butter as needed. Rearrange the chicken on a cookie sheet. Do not refrigerate again if escalopes are to be used the same day.

Deglaze the pan with Marsala, scraping the pan bottom to loosen the particles. Dust pan juices lightly with flour from a dredger (a small container with holes in the lid). Stir in the chicken stock and cook over high heat, adding dredged flour two or three times. Stir in Sauce Espagnole. Cook until slightly thickened.

Heat oven to 350°F.

Reheat escalopes in the oven for fifteen to twenty minutes. Serve with purée of lima beans and pass the sauce. *ABC*

GOUJONNETTE OF CHICKEN

The goujonnette in this case is the finger-length fillet of chicken found on each side of the breast and described in the recipe for Escalope de Volaille (see page 87). It is treated in exactly the same way as Goujonnette of Sole and served with the same Sauce Tartare. This is a splendid first course to a grand meal or a single course for luncheon or dinner.

Chicken fillets, allow 3 per person as a
    first course and 5 or 6 as a main dish
3 eggs, beaten with 2 tablespoons water
1½ cups fine dry bread crumbs seasoned
    with one generous pinch dried sage,
    1 tablespoon salt, freshly ground pepper

Light vegetable oil and butter in equal
    proportions for sautéing
Sauce Tartare (see page 286)

Dip the fillets in beaten egg, roll in bread crumbs, and lay them on a baking sheet. Refrigerate for at least one hour.

Heat the oil and butter in a heavy skillet until almost smoking. Cook the prepared fillets for two minutes, no more, turning once or twice to brown them evenly. Lift them out with a slotted spoon and drain on paper towels.

Place the fillets on a baking sheet and reheat in a 350° F. oven for six to seven minutes. Serve with Sauce Tartare.

The goujonnettes may be frozen after being dipped in egg and bread crumbs.   *AC*

POULET SUPREME MEURICE

6 servings

This I can claim as my own. I had in mind the Hotel Meurice in Paris when I named it, the spelling of my own first name being too pretentious. It is delicious cold, sliced and served with a good salad.

½ pound fresh mushrooms
½ cup fresh white bread crumbs
1 tablespoon finely chopped fresh
    tarragon or ½ teaspoon dried
1 cup parsley sprigs, finely chopped
½ cup finely chopped ham
    (about ¼ pound)
1 tablespoon salt
5 to 6 twists of the pepper mill

¾ cup dry Marsala
6 tablespoons melted butter
6 whole chicken breasts, boned and with
    fillets removed (see page 87)
Salt and pepper
Flour for dusting
½ cup chicken stock
Watercress

Heat oven to 450°F.

Wipe the mushrooms with a damp cloth and chop them finely. In a mixing bowl combine the mushrooms, bread crumbs, tarragon, parsley (all except one tablespoon), ham, salt, and pepper. Add about one-quarter cup of Marsala and three tablespoons of melted butter, sufficient to moisten the filling.

Lay each chicken breast out flat, skin-side down. Brush with melted butter and season with salt and pepper. Place about one tablespoon of filling on each breast. Fold each side to the center and roll to resemble a closed fist. Place folded-side down on a well-buttered roasting pan. Brush with melted butter, and dust lightly with flour, salt, and pepper.

Bake for twenty minutes, basting now and again with pan juices. Dust again with flour and bake ten minutes more, basting once. Add a little stock or water if the bottom of the pan looks too dry.

Remove the chicken breasts to a serving platter and keep them hot. Deglaze the pan with chicken stock and the remaining Marsala and reduce the liquid until it thickens. Correct the seasoning.

To serve, arrange chicken on a heated platter. Spoon the hot sauce over the breasts. Sprinkle with finely chopped parsley. A large bunch of watercress in the center completes the arrangement. Green beans, fresh garden peas, or fresh lima beans are good with this dish and do not detract from the unusual flavor.   *A*

CHICKEN BREASTS EN PAPILLOTE

8 servings

1 sheet parchment paper, approximately
   16 by 15 inches for each chicken breast
Melted butter or oil
4 half chicken breasts, boned and each
   sliced in half horizontally

¼ pound ham, finely chopped
8 tablespoons Mint Butter (see page 274)
Salt and pepper
2 eggs, lightly beaten

Heat oven to 350°F.

Fold the parchment in half and open up again. Brush with the melted butter. Lay each chicken breast on one half of the paper and smooth the chopped ham over one half of the breast. Dot with Mint Butter and fold over the other half of the breast. Season lightly with salt and pepper.

Fold the parchment over the breast and brush the edge of the paper with beaten egg. Start rolling paper tightly from one corner to make a well-sealed paper bag. Brush the rolled fold again with beaten egg and the whole bag with melted butter or oil.

Bake on a baking sheet for thirty minutes. Slide the breast out of the bag onto a plate and serve with a purée of lima beans.

CHICKEN CROQUETTES

4 to 6 servings

3 chicken thighs
Chicken stock, if available, or water
   seasoned with 4 peppercorns and
   1 tablespoon salt
1 cup Béchamel Sauce (see page 275)

1 egg, beaten
1 cup bread crumbs seasoned with salt,
   pepper, and a pinch of thyme
Vegetable oil for deep frying

Place the chicken thighs in a pan and cover with the stock or seasoned water. Bring to a boil and simmer, covered, for ten minutes. After the meat is cool enough to handle, remove it from the thigh bone and discard the skin and bone. Dice the chicken rather coarsely; mix with the Béchamel Sauce and chill.

When cold, roll the mixture into a sausage shape and cut into two-inch croquettes. Dip in beaten egg and roll in the seasoned bread crumbs. Chill again.

Heat about two inches of oil in a saucepan or skillet. When the temperature reaches 380°F., drop the chilled croquettes into the oil—watch the oil for spitting. Fry three to four croquettes at a time to a rich brown color, turning them now and again.

Drain on paper towels and serve piping hot with crisp, buttered haricot verts.   *A*

NANCY'S CASSEROLE OF CHICKEN

6 servings

I am incapable of putting recipes together for a book or, for that matter a class, without including another of Nancy's creations.

3 whole chicken breasts, boned
4 chicken thighs
6 carrots
3 ribs celery
½ pound small mushrooms
1 cup flour seasoned with 1 tablespoon
   salt and ½ teaspoon pepper

1 tablespoon butter
1 tablespoon oil
2 cups chicken stock
½ cup dry vermouth
½ cup parsley sprigs,
   finely chopped

Heat oven to 350°F.

Skin the chicken breasts and cut them into one-inch pieces. Remove the skin from the thigh joints and cut the meat from the bone. As nearly as possible, cut evenly sized pieces.

Wash and scrape the carrots. Slice the larger carrots in half lengthwise, and cut them into pieces on the bias. Cut the celery in the same way. Wipe the mushrooms clean with a damp cloth. Cut off their stems and cube, if large; if small, leave them whole.

Put the chicken pieces in a bag with the seasoned flour. Shake until thoroughly coated. Heat one tablespoon of butter and one tablespoon of oil in a heavy skillet. Brown the chicken.

Transfer the chicken to a casserole. Add the chicken stock and bake for thirty minutes. Then add the carrots, celery, and vermouth and cook ten minutes more. Stir in the mushrooms and cook five minutes longer.

Turn out onto a hot, deep, serving platter and sprinkle with finely chopped parsley.

ABC

CHICKEN "243"

6 to 8 servings

When I lived at 243 East 53rd Street in Manhattan, I was stuck for a title for this recipe. It is one of my favorites—not because it's my own, but for its usefulness. It freezes beautifully; the sour cream can be stirred in after the chicken has been thawed and reheated. Undercook if you intend to freeze it: Cook it for twenty-five instead of thirty-five minutes.

½ ounce imported dried mushrooms
2 to 3 tablespoons unsalted butter
2 two-and-one-half to three-pound
  chickens, cut into 16 serving pieces
  (Use the back, wing tips, gizzards, etc.,
  for stock. Freeze the livers for other
  dishes.)
4 tablespoons brandy
1 tablespoon finely chopped onion
2 cloves garlic, chopped and crushed with
  salt

1 tablespoon meat glaze (Bovril is an
  excellent substitute and may be
  purchased in most markets.)
1 tablespoon tomato paste
3 tablespoons flour
1 cup chicken stock
½ cup dry white wine
Salt and pepper
1 cup sour cream
½ cup parsley sprigs, finely chopped

Heat oven to 350°F.

Cover the mushrooms with boiling water and allow them to soak for an hour.

Melt enough butter in a heavy skillet to cover the bottom of the pan. Brown the pieces of chicken, a few at a time. Add more butter as it is needed. Transfer the chicken to an oven-proof casserole with a tight-fitting lid.

(Continued)

Allow the skillet to cool slightly and stir in the brandy. Scrape the bottom of the skillet to loosen the solids.

Drain the mushrooms, reserving the liquid. Chop the mushrooms and add them with the onion and garlic to the skillet. Stir in the meat glaze, tomato paste, and flour; mix thoroughly. Gradually add the mushroom liquid, chicken stock, and white wine. Cook slowly until thickened, while stirring. Season with salt and pepper.

Pour the sauce over the chicken, cover, and bake in the oven for about thirty-five minutes, or until tender.

Remove the chicken pieces from the casserole and arrange them on a heated serving dish. Stir sour cream into the sauce remaining on the bottom of the casserole. Correct the seasoning and pour over the chicken. Garnish with finely chopped parsley. Plain boiled rice is the ideal accompaniment.

ABC

CHICKEN MARENGO

6 to 8 servings

Here is an economical version of the classic veal dish—equally good and not nearly so costly.

3 tablespoons oil
1 three-and-one-half-pound chicken cut
   into 8 serving pieces
1 medium onion, chopped
½ cup tomato purée
2 tablespoons potato flour
2 cups chicken or veal stock
1 cup dry white wine
1 clove garlic, crushed with 1 teaspoon salt

2 bay leaves
1 teaspoon dried thyme
Salt and pepper to taste
12 small white onions
¼ pound mushrooms
3 tomatoes
Black pitted olives, approximately 1 dozen
Finely chopped parsley

Heat oven to 350°F.

Heat the oil in a heavy casserole with a cover. Add the chicken and brown evenly all over. Peel and chop the medium onion; add to the chicken and cook for three minutes.

Stir in the tomato purée and potato flour and mix thoroughly. Gradually pour in part of the stock and the white wine. Add the garlic, bay leaves, thyme, salt, and pepper. Cover the casserole, and bake in the oven for fifteen minutes.

Peel the small onions. To do this easily, put them in boiling water for two minutes first. Cook the onions until tender in enough reserved stock to cover, then add the onions and stock to the casserole.

(Continued)

Wipe the mushrooms clean with a damp cloth and slice them. Peel the tomatoes and cut them into quarters. Add the mushrooms and tomatoes to the casserole and cook, covered, for another thirty minutes, or until the chicken is tender. The length of time will depend upon the quality and age of the chicken.

Just before serving, add the olives, and sprinkle with chopped parsley. Serve with rice, plain or tossed with chopped parsley, or steamed potatoes. *ABC*

POLLO TONNATO

6 to 8 servings

Helen McCully, food editor of House Beautiful *for many years and a good and generous friend, devised this variation of tonnato. I have decided I like it much more than the original, Vitello Tonnato.*

1 boiling fowl or 2 roasting chickens,
  totaling six and one-half to seven
  pounds
1 veal knuckle
1 can (7½ ounces) tuna fish in oil, drained
1 can flat anchovies, drained
2 cups dry white wine
½ sour pickle
2 medium carrots, chopped
1 large onion, sliced
4 stalks celery, chopped

2 cloves garlic, finely chopped
1 small bunch parsley
16 peppercorns
2 cups long-grain rice
2 cups parsley sprigs, chopped
2 tablespoons capers, drained and
  chopped
Mayonnaise (see page 277)
Lemon juice
1 hard-boiled egg

Put the fowl or chicken and the veal knuckle in a large pot together with all the ingredients up to and including the peppercorns. Cover with cold water and bring to a boil. Simmer gently until the fowl is done, which can be determined by testing the drumstick. It should move freely. Cool the bird in the cooking liquid; then lift it out and set aside, but do not refrigerate.

Place the pot with the cooking liquid and veal knuckle back on the range and boil slowly until there are only about two to two and one-half cups of liquid left. Strain the liquid through three thicknesses of damp cheesecloth; reserve for making the finished sauce.

Cook the rice "al dente" (to the tooth), so that each grain is separate and firm. While the rice is cooking, skin the chicken and slice the meat from the legs and breast. Mix the rice with about three-fourths of the chopped parsley, reserving the rest for garnishing the finished dish. Mound the rice on a suitable platter. Arrange the sliced chicken on top and sprinkle with chopped capers.

(Continued)

The reduced cooking liquid should by now be on the point of setting. Mix the jellied liquid with sufficient mayonnaise to make a sauce thick enough to adhere to the chicken when spooned over it. Season with lemon juice to taste. Spoon the sauce over the sliced chicken to cover completely; pass the rest in a sauceboat.

Shell the hard-boiled egg and press the yolk through a strainer or sieve, using a wooden spoon. Decorate the mounded chicken with one border of chopped parsley and another of egg yolk.

The dish may be assembled two hours or more before it is needed and refrigerated, but do not garnish with egg and parsley until the last minute. *AC*

CHICKEN PIE

6 to 8 servings

This is no ordinary chicken pie, but one I keep for special occasions. It takes both time and cash to make, but is well worth the time and expenditure. Use foie gras if you can get it—failing that the best pâté de foie gras. Plan your menu carefully—this chicken pie is rich and should have star billing with light dishes on either side of it.

All-Purpose Pastry for one-crust pie
  (see page 300)
1 pair sweetbreads
1 three-pound chicken, trussed (reserve
  the giblets)
Salt and freshly ground pepper
¼ teaspoon each of nutmeg, ground
  clove, and cinnamon
6 tablespoons butter
1 carrot, sliced

2 small white onions, sliced
½ cup diced, cooked ham, about 4 ounces
¼ pound mushrooms, washed and sliced
Juice of ½ lemon
3 tablespoons cognac
3 tablespoons port
3 cups heavy cream
1 tablespoon pâté de foie gras
Glaze: 1 egg yolk mixed with 1 tablespoon
  cream

Heat oven to 450°F.

Prepare the pie pastry according to the recipe. Refrigerate until needed.

Soak the sweetbreads for one hour. Drain them and add enough salted water to cover. Bring to a boil; simmer for five minutes and drain. Rinse the sweetbreads under cold running water. Cool under weight. Trim or pare away the skin and tubes of the sweetbreads. Slice the sweetbreads and cut into bite-sized pieces.

Sprinkle the chicken inside and out with salt and pepper. Place the nutmeg, clove, and cinnamon inside the chicken. Heat half the butter in a large, oven-proof skillet, and turn the chicken to coat it on all sides in butter. Let the chicken rest on one side.

(Continued)

Add the giblets, carrot, and onions, and roast for ten minutes; baste, using a large spoon. Turn the chicken on its other side and roast and baste for a further ten minutes. Place the chicken on its back and continue roasting and basting for about twenty-five minutes more, or until done. Leave the chicken in the skillet while completing the preparation.

Heat the remaining butter in another skillet and add the sweetbread pieces. Cook, turning occasionally, about two minutes. Add the ham, mushrooms, and lemon juice. Continue cooking, gently stirring once in a while, about five minutes.

Cut the chicken into serving pieces—there should be eight—and place them in a deep one-quart pie dish. Add cognac and port wine to juices in the skillet in which the chicken was cooked. Bring to a boil and stir to dissolve the brown particles at the bottom of the skillet. Add salt to taste and all but two tablespoons of the cream. Strain into a saucepan and add the sweetbread mixture. Simmer three or four minutes.

Blend the reserved two tablespoons of cream with the pâté de foie gras and add to the saucepan. Pour this sauce over the chicken and cover the dish with pastry. Brush the pastry with egg yolk mixed with cream. Bake fifteen minutes, or until crust is a rich golden brown.

CAPON, SAUCE SUPREME

6 servings

1 capon, about six and one-half pounds,
    dressed and trussed
2 stalks celery with leaves
12 peppercorns
1 leek, trimmed
A few parsley stalks
1 bay leaf
3 sprigs thyme, or 1½ teaspoons dried
    thyme

1 teaspoon salt
1 onion, peeled
1 carrot, scraped
5 tablespoons sweet butter
4 tablespoons flour
1 cup heavy cream
1 teaspoon lemon juice

Place the capon in a large saucepan or kettle and add the celery and peppercorns. Cut the leek down the center almost to the base of the root. Wash the leek carefully under tepid running water. Add the leek to the kettle along with the parsley, bay leaf, thyme, salt, onion, and carrot. Add water to cover the capon.

Bring to a boil, then simmer, partially covered, for about two hours. Prick the joint between the thigh and drumstick with a fork. When the juice runs clear, remove the capon and keep it warm. Skim the fat from the stock. Reduce the stock by about half over high heat; strain the stock. Set aside four cups and put the rest back in the kettle. Return the capon to the remaining stock in the kettle to keep it hot and moist.

(Continued)

Melt four tablespoons of the butter in a saucepan and stir in the flour. Cook, without browning, for three to four minutes. Add four cups of the reserved stock, stirring vigorously with a whisk until smooth. Lower the heat and simmer the sauce very gently until thickened, approximately thirty minutes.

Just before serving, stir the cream into the sauce, thinning, if necessary, with more stock. Add the lemon juice and the remaining tablespoon of butter; correct the seasoning.

Cut the capon into serving pieces; place on a warm serving dish. Spoon a little of the sauce over each piece and serve the remaining sauce separately. Plain boiled rice goes well with this.

BLANC DE DINDONNEAU ITALIEN

8 servings

Friends of mine were giving a dinner party for one hundred twenty-five and asked me to plan a menu that would be: a) not too costly, b) easy to prepare ahead of time, and c) stylish.

This was the entrée. The end result was spectacular. Most of the guests were convinced they had been served veal. I advised the hosts not to disillusion them.

16 pieces turkey breast,
   thinly sliced
1 cup flour seasoned with 2 teaspoons
   salt, 5 or 6 twists of the pepper mill,
   and a pinch of dried sage
Oil and butter in equal amounts for
   sautéing

¼ pound mushrooms, stems removed
   and thinly sliced
1 cup chicken stock
¼ cup dry Marsala
2 teaspoons cornstarch, blended with just
   enough water to make a thin paste
1 cup parsley sprigs, finely chopped

Dry the turkey-breast slices carefully and dredge in seasoned flour. Shake off the excess flour and brown for about one minute on each side in the oil-butter mixture. Set aside and keep the slices warm.

Sauté the mushrooms quickly in the same pan after the turkey has finished browning. Remove from the pan and spoon over the turkey.

Add chicken stock and Marsala to the pan along with the moistened cornstarch. Cook until the sauce has the desired thickness; it should have the consistency of heavy cream. Strain and season to taste with salt and pepper.

Pour the sauce over the mushrooms and turkey. Garnish with finely chopped parsley. This dish freezes well.

ABC

BOILED TURKEY AND CELERY SAUCE

8 to 10 servings

Boiled turkey is delicious. It was a common enough method of cooking the yuletide bird in Victorian times, but since then has fallen out of favor. It makes a welcome change from the eternal roasted and, more often than not, gargantuan turkey served at Thanksgiving.

Parsley and Lemon Stuffing (see page 321)
1 fourteen-pound turkey

Stock:

4 medium carrots, sliced
1 turnip, peeled and sliced
1 rib celery, sliced
3 onions, unpeeled and stuck with
   3 cloves each
15 black peppercorns, slightly crushed

1 heaping tablespoon salt, or to taste
2 bay leaves
4 sprigs thyme
Bunch of parsley stalks, left from the
   stuffing

Prepare the Parsley and Lemon Stuffing according to the recipe.

Stuff the turkey and wrap it in cheesecloth so that it can be lifted easily. Put it breast-down on a small rack or trivet in a large pan with a lid.

Add all the stock ingredients, and enough cold water to barely cover the bird. Bring to a boil and simmer gently for two hours, or until the turkey is cooked. The simplest way of judging this is to pull the bone-end of the drumstick; if the leg moves easily from the body, the bird is done. Keep the stock for soup.

Place the bird on a heated platter, and remove the cheesecloth.

Celery Sauce:

1 head of celery
6 tablespoons unsalted butter
1½ cups Béchamel Sauce (see page 275)

Salt and pepper
½ cup parsley sprigs, finely chopped

To make the sauce, wash, trim, and scrape the celery ribs. Cut them into strips about three inches long. Blanch them in boiling salted water for five to six minutes. The celery should be almost, but not quite, cooked.

Drain it well, place it in a pan with the butter, and cook, tossing the celery, for two to three minutes.

Add the Béchamel Sauce, stir to mix, and bring to the boiling point. Adjust the seasoning with salt and pepper; stir in the chopped parsley and pour into a heated vegetable dish.

Carve the turkey in the usual way and pass the sauce separately.

DEVILED DRUMSTICKS

6 to 8 servings

Turkey drumsticks, cooked

Devil Sauce:

2 teaspoons Dijon mustard, preferably
   coarse Moutarde de Meux
2 teaspoons anchovy paste
2 teaspoons red wine vinegar

1 teaspoon Worcestershire sauce
1 tablespoon mango chutney, finely
   chopped
Salt and pepper to taste

Mix all sauce ingredients together. The consistency should be a reasonably smooth paste. (A good homemade green tomato chutney—see page 288—could take the place of the mango chutney.)

Make several deep gashes in the drumsticks with a small, sharp knife. Open them up so that as much paste as possible can be forced in. Brush the outside of the drumsticks with the remaining paste.

Broil about four to five inches from the heat until they sizzle and are thoroughly heated.

GOOSE

6 servings

It is not a simple matter these days to find a good young goose. If, by chance, you are sold an old bird, abandon the effort of roasting it and fall back on a dish of well-scrambled eggs. Nowadays, one is forced to rely on the supplier. It is impossible to test the frozen bird for age.

The young goose, preferably one that has roamed the cornfields after the harvest, is a delicacy. There are many ways to prepare it. The following is one of my favorites.

1 eight- to eleven-pound goose
3 to 4 tablespoons flour, well seasoned
   with salt and pepper

1 pound chestnuts, approximately
2 pounds apples, approximately

Heat oven to 400°F.

Remove all visible fat from the bird. Rub the goose all over with seasoned flour.

Shell and blanch the chestnuts in boiling salted water for five minutes. Peel, core, and chop the apples. Combine the apples and chestnuts in a proportion of approximately two to one. Season with salt and pepper.

Stuff the goose with the apple-chestnut mixture and truss for roasting.

Place the bird on a rack in a roasting pan and roast in the center of the oven for thirty minutes. Remove from the oven and prick all over—breast, back, legs, and between the thighs—with a sharp fork, wherever there is fat. Pierce the skin only and not the flesh underneath.

Reduce the temperature to 350°F. and roast for an hour more. Prick again. An eight-pound bird will need one and one-half hours cooking time—an eleven-pound bird, two hours. If the breast becomes too brown, cover it with a piece of foil.

Serve with a purée of potatoes, braised celery, and the chestnut-apple stuffing.

ROAST DUCK

Serves 4 in a pinch

When duck is good, it is very good and when it is not, it is inedible. The farmyard duck is naturally fat, but the commercially raised bird is outrageously fat. Careful cooking and seasoning does wonders for it.

If it is to be eaten in a restaurant, order it in advance. The cooking time is roughly an hour and a half, and if the restaurateur is given fair warning, your meal should proceed without fuss and no waits. Many lesser restaurants cook the birds in large batches hours ahead of time and reheat them as ordered.

My favorite recipe is simple and has a splendid stuffing. Remember Trollope's words: "The duck is an awkward bird, too big for one and not enough for two."

1 four- to four-and-one-half-pound duck

Stuffing:

2 large onions, peeled and chopped
½ teaspoon sage
4 ounces fresh white bread crumbs, about
    8 to 9 slices
Grated rind of 1 lemon

Salt and pepper
1 stick melted butter
Powdered ginger
Flour for dusting

Mix all the above ingredients, with the exception of the flour and ginger, to make the stuffing.

Stock:

Duck giblets: neck, gizzard, and heart
1 cup water
1 cup dry white wine
1 onion, chopped

A few celery leaves
Small piece of carrot, chopped
Salt and pepper

Bring all of the above ingredients to a boil, reduce the heat, and remove the scum as it rises. Lower the heat and simmer, covered, while the duck is cooking.

(Continued)

Heat oven to 375°F.

Sprinkle the inside of the duck with salt. Fill loosely with stuffing to allow for expansion and truss for the oven. Rub the duck all over with coarse salt and dust it lightly with powdered ginger.

Place the bird on its side on a rack in a roasting pan, and bake for twenty minutes. Prick carefully all over to allow the fat to flow. Turn it to its other side and cook for a further thirty minutes. Reduce the temperature to 325°F. Turn the duck breast-side up and cook forty-five minutes more. Total cooking time is calculated at twenty minutes to the pound.

For the last ten minutes dust the bird with flour and baste with boiling fat to produce a crisp skin. Remove the duck to a heated dish and keep it hot. Untruss.

Pour off all the fat from the pan and add two cups of stock, scraping and loosening the bits on the bottom of the pan. Bring to a boil and cook until reduced to one and one-half cups, approximately. Correct the seasoning. Serve in a warmed sauceboat. New potatoes and fresh mushrooms go perfectly with this dish.

DUCK WITH GREEN PEAS

4 to 6 servings

6 tablespoons butter
1 three-and-one-half- to four-pound duck
3 tablespoons flour
Salt and pepper
1 cup stock made from giblets
1 small onion, finely chopped
2 packages (10 ounces each) small frozen peas

2 small heads of bib lettuce, chopped
2 sprigs thyme, 2 sprigs marjoram, and
  6 small sprigs mint, tied in cheesecloth
⅛ teaspoon ground mace
⅛ teaspoon nutmeg
½ cup heavy cream

Melt four tablespoons of the butter in an oven-proof casserole with a lid.

Rub the duck with one tablespoon of flour, and salt and pepper. Prick the duck's skin all over with a fork. Brown the duck on all sides in the butter in the casserole. Pour off all the fat.

Add the stock, onion, peas, lettuce, and bag of herbs to the duck in the casserole. Cook, covered, over gentle heat for forty minutes, shaking and stirring now and again. Stir in the mace and nutmeg.

Blend the remaining two tablespoons of flour with the remaining two tablespoons of butter. Stir this paste into the casserole liquid and add the cream.

Remove the duck to a warm platter. Discard the bag of herbs and pour the peas and liquid over the duck.

SALMI OF DUCK

4 to 6 servings

Henry IV of England, Chaucer, and his son all enjoyed Salmi of game, fish, or duck. In the language of the day, it would have been called Salomene or Salome. The recipe originated in France in the fourteenth century and made its way across the English Channel through cooks at court. It is a splendid supper dish and has survived in much the same way for more than five centuries.

1 four- to five-pound duck
1½ cups stock, made with duck carcass
   (see recipe below)
¼ pound mushrooms
4 tablespoons unsalted butter
Lemon juice

Salt and pepper
½ cup dry red wine
4 slices white bread, crusts removed and
   each slice cut in half diagonally
1 orange, quartered

Roast the duck until it is rare (forty minutes at 400°F.), and when the duck is cool enough to handle, cut off the breast meat in long, thin slices. Remove the bones from the drumsticks and thighs and scrape the meat from the wishbone and collar bone. Reserve all the meats.

Stock:

Duck bones
1 rib celery, chopped
1 small carrot, sliced

½ small onion
4 peppercorns
½ bay leaf

Break the duck bones into sizable pieces.

Put all of the above ingredients in a two-quart saucepan and pour in six cups of water. Bring to a boil and simmer for one hour, covered.

Boil gently, uncovered, for a further half hour until there are only one and one-half to two cups of liquid left. The stock by now should have a strong flavor of duck.

Strain and set aside one and one-half cups for the sauce.

Sauce:

4 tablespoons unsalted butter
3 shallots, finely chopped
3 tablespoons flour

4 parsley stalks, 1 bay leaf, a pinch of
   dried sage, the thinly sliced peel of
   1 orange, all tied in a cheesecloth bag

Melt four tablespoons of butter in a heavy one-and-one-half- to two-quart pan. Add the shallots and cook slowly until soft and a rich golden color.

(Continued)

Stir in the flour and cook for one minute.

Add one and one-half cups of stock and the bag of seasonings. Simmer for thirty minutes or so, until you have a rich sauce rather like heavy cream.

Slice the mushrooms and sauté them in one and one-half tablespoons of butter. Add the mushrooms, lemon juice, salt, pepper, and wine to the sauce. Simmer for five minutes.

Sauté the bread triangles in the rest of the butter.

Add the duck meat to the sauce and heat thoroughly but do not allow to boil. Serve in a shallow dish with bread triangles tucked around the sides and orange segments between each triangle.

PIGEONS

4 servings

4 pigeons, trussed
2 ounces salt bacon
¼ cup carrot, finely chopped
¼ cup celery, finely chopped
1 tablespoon shallot, chopped
Small piece bay leaf
Juice of 1 lemon

4 tablespoons unsalted butter, melted
Flour for dredging
Salt and pepper
¼ cup brandy
Watercress
Sauce (see recipe next page)

Heat oven to 400° F.

Singe the birds to rid them of down.

Dice the bacon and cook it over medium heat in a heavy skillet. Lift out the pieces of bacon with a slotted spoon and brown the birds in the fat. Remove the birds and reserve.

Place the vegetables, including the shallot, on the bottom of a roasting pan and cook them in the same fat for three to four minutes. Add the bay leaf. Arrange the birds on top. Pour a little of the lemon juice inside each bird and sprinkle the remaining on the outside. Dribble the melted butter over the breasts and dust them lightly with flour, salt, and pepper.

Roast the pigeons in the oven for ten minutes. Warm the brandy and pour it into the pan and flame. Return the pan to the oven when the flame has died down and roast for an additional twenty minutes.

Place the birds on a warm platter and keep them warm while the sauce is being prepared. Strain the pan juices through a fine sieve into a clean saucepan and set aside.

Sauce:

½ cup strained pan juices
¼ cup port wine
1 cup Sauce Espagnole (see page 275)

1 orange, peeled, sectioned, and chopped
½ cup seedless white grapes

To the reserved juices add the port wine and sauce, and cook until slightly thickened. Stir in the orange and grapes, and reheat. Serve in a heated sauceboat. Garnish with watercress. Serve with brown rice or wild rice.

BRAISED PHEASANT

4 servings

Unless I am absolutely certain the pheasant is a young bird, I braise it instead of roasting. If it is an old one, braising will give it a youthful, moist tenderness.

2 medium onions
8 tablespoons unsalted butter
1 pheasant
4 tablespoons sweet tomato chutney
1 cup dry red wine

2 cups very strong chicken stock
Salt and pepper
Beurre manié to thicken sauce
  (see page 274)

Heat oven to 300°F.
Peel and slice the onions. In a skillet, brown the onions in half the butter. Add more butter if needed, taking care the onions do not burn. Remove the onions to a casserole with a lid, one just large enough to hold the pheasant.

Brown the pheasant on all sides in the skillet, adding more butter if necessary. Place the pheasant on top of onions in the casserole. Add the chutney, wine, stock, two teaspoons of salt, and a few twists of the pepper mill.

Bring to a boil on top of the range, then cook the casserole in the oven, covered, for one hour. By this time, the meat should be about to fall off the bone. Remove the pheasant to a heated platter.

Over low heat add the beurre manié, bit by bit, to the sauce in the casserole until the sauce reaches the desired thickness; it should resemble heavy cream. Correct the seasoning.

Carve the pheasant and serve the sauce from a sauceboat. Haricots verts and a purée of potatoes go well with this dish.

CIVET DE LAPIN DE BORDEAUX

6 servings

The lovely, lovable rabbit is much neglected as a food on this side of the Atlantic. In Northern Europe it is a delicacy. In America sentiment and ignorance are largely responsible for the disinterest.

Before teaching my students to cook this dish, I put it to a vote. Twenty percent will have nothing to do with it, and sixty percent have never eaten it but are willing to give it a try. The others have already sampled it in Europe or French provincial restaurants here and are delighted by the suggestion. The doubtfuls, once they have sampled the dish, were grateful for yet another recipe that can be prepared ahead of time and added to their repertoire. It freezes well.

4 ounces fat bacon, cubed
4 tablespoons butter
1 two-and-one-half to three-pound frozen rabbit, cut into serving pieces
2 tablespoons brandy
4 cups good red wine
4 tablespoons flour
1 tablespoon dark brown sugar
1 clove garlic, crushed with 1 teaspoon salt

1 small whole onion, peeled
6 large shallots, peeled and coarsely chopped
½ teaspoon each of salt and pepper
Pinch of nutmeg
Pinch of allspice
Bouquet garni: a few parsley stalks, small bay leaf, and a sprig of thyme tied together in cheesecloth

Heat oven to 350°F.

Dice the bacon. In a skillet cook the bacon over medium heat until quite dry, but not burned, and free of fat. Remove the bacon with a slotted spoon and set it aside. Cool. Pour off half the fat and set it aside.

Melt half the butter in the same skillet, add the rabbit pieces a few at a time, adding more butter as needed, and cook over medium heat until well-browned all over.

Transfer the rabbit with the cooked diced bacon to a casserole with a lid. Pour about one-quarter of a cup of the pan fat over the rabbit and set the casserole over low heat. Discard the fat that remains in the skillet.

Pour brandy over the hot rabbit and set it alight. Shake until the flame dies down. Remove from the heat.

Put the skillet back on the range over low heat and pour in about one cup of the wine. Scrape the skillet with a wooden spoon to loosen the brown bits. Pour over the rabbit in the casserole along with the rest of the wine.

In a small bowl, blend the flour and brown sugar with a little of the liquid from the casserole to make a smooth, thin paste. Stir it back into the casserole. Add crushed garlic, onion, shallots, salt, pepper, nutmeg, allspice, and bouquet garni. Bring to a boil on top of the range, then cover and cook in the middle of the oven for one and one-half hours, approximately, or until tender. Ideally, steamed potatoes are best with young rabbits.   *A*

Beef

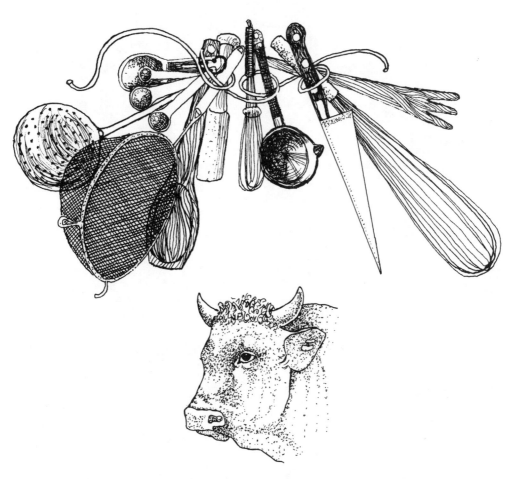

Beef

To many people beef is still the most important item on the menu. And there are those who simply cannot be weaned from the meat-and-potatoes diet. But economics, travel, and the ever-growing interest in cooking and eating are eroding die-hard habits. Fortunately, the taste for prime beef perfectly cooked cannot be beaten and I, personally, every so often crave the well-cooked standing rib roast or the sirloin with Yorkshire pudding, horseradish sauce—fresh I might add—and potatoes roasted alongside the beef. And after I have tired of cold beef, what is left goes into Cottage Pie.

For those who like a little spice in their lives, there is always a curry; you will find a recipe for Curry Sauce in the sauce chapter.

Whatever cut you buy, try to find aged beef and look for the marbling—the streaks of fat running through it. The fat on shell steaks, roasts, and sirloin should be appetizingly white.

MEAT LOAF DE LUXE

8 servings

Meat Loaf de Luxe has been named for a very good reason. It is without doubt the best hot pâté I have encountered. "Meat loaf" has an every-day ring to it. To please and pamper my students, I call it "Pâté Chaud," for that is what it is in France. It is, on the other hand, equally good cold.

2 pounds ground beef (top round or
    sirloin)
1 pound ground veal
1 pound ground pork
1 cup cottage cheese
1 cup fresh bread crumbs
1 cup chopped onion

½ cup bottled chili sauce
3 eggs, beaten
3 tablespoons chopped green pepper
Salt and pepper to taste
½ cup good red wine
1 cup tomato sauce

Heat oven to 400°F.

Combine the beef, veal, and pork, and mix thoroughly. Add the cottage cheese, bread crumbs, onion, chili sauce, eggs, and green pepper. Season with salt and pepper.

Shape into a loaf and place in a roasting pan. Pour the wine over the meat loaf, and spread on the tomato sauce.

Bake in the oven for thirty minutes, basting frequently. Reduce heat to 350°F., and bake until done, about one hour.

VARIATIONS ON GROUND-BEEF PATTIES

2 tablespoons capers, drained and
    chopped, or 1 cup parsley sprigs,
    finely chopped
4 tablespoons soft, unsalted butter

Lean round of beef, ground once
Worcestershire sauce
Salt and pepper

Mix capers or the chopped parsley with softened butter and roll into small balls about one-half inch in diameter.

For large patties, allow eight ounces of beef per serving. To make each patty, roll the ground meat around a butter ball to enclose it. Broil according to your taste. Sprinkle with a little Worcestershire sauce and dust with coarse salt and pepper before serving.

For small patties, allow one pound of beef for six small patties. Cut each butter ball in half and enclose it in ground meat. Broil as you would a larger patty.   *C*

COTTAGE PIE

8 to 10 servings

2½ pounds top round or lean chuck,
   ground
2 onions, chopped
2 tablespoons butter
Salt and freshly ground black pepper

Juices from roast beef, leftover gravy,
   or beef stock to moisten
2 pounds potatoes, boiled in their jackets
½ cup parsley, finely chopped

Heat oven to 425°F.

In a large frying pan or skillet, cook the ground beef for four to five minutes, stirring constantly. Turn it into a large bowl.

Peel and chop the onions. Add two tablespoons butter to the pan in which the beef was cooked. Cook the onions until they are golden and tender. Mix them with the beef. Season with salt and freshly ground black pepper. Add the pan juices or beef stock to moisten the beef mixture.

Spoon the mixture into an oven-proof dish, ten by seven by two inches. Using a potato ricer, cover the mixture evenly with peeled, riced potatoes. If you don't have a ricer, lightly spread mashed potatoes over the top with a fork.

Bake in the oven until the potatoes are brown and crisp, about fifteen to twenty minutes. Sprinkle with finely chopped parsley before serving.   *A*

MINUTE STEAK

Shell roast, allow one thin slice per
   person
Freshly ground black pepper

Clarified butter (see page 345)
Lemon juice
Salt

Ask your butcher to slice the shell roast for you. Trim off the fat, if any. Dust the steak with pepper.

Melt enough butter in a chafing dish or skillet. When the butter is almost smoking, add the steak. Cook for one minute. Turn and cook the steak for another minute. Transfer it to a heated platter. Continue until all the steaks have been cooked.

Deglaze the pan with lemon juice and pour over the steaks. Dust with salt at the last minute.

BEEF IN MADEIRA

4 to 6 servings

2 pounds fillet of beef
½ cup flour
2 to 3 twists of the pepper mill
3 tablespoons butter
1 tablespoon oil
¾ cup onion, finely chopped
1 tablespoon shallots, finely chopped

½ pound small mushrooms
2 cups beef stock
2 medium tomatoes, or 2 whole canned
 tomatoes
½ cup Madeira
Salt and pepper
½ cup parsley sprigs, finely chopped

Heat oven to 350°F.

Cut the beef into one-and-one-half-inch cubes. Mix together the flour and pepper. Dredge the cubes in the seasoned flour.

Melt the butter and oil in a large skillet and sauté the meat over high heat until brown. Transfer the meat to a two-quart oven-proof casserole with a cover.

Add the onions and shallots to the skillet and cook until soft and transparent. Wipe the mushrooms clean with a damp cloth.

Add the contents of the skillet to the beef, pour in the beef stock, and add the mushrooms. Peel and seed the tomatoes and press them through a sieve into the beef mixture.

Add the Madeira, season with salt and pepper to taste, cover, and bake in the oven for forty-five minutes. Test for doneness after thirty minutes. Just before serving, sprinkle the surface with finely chopped parsley.

A

BRAISED STEAK

6 to 8 servings

Braised steak is hearty winter fare. Once it has been assembled, your only concern is to see that it does not overcook.

3 pounds top round of beef in one piece
2 medium onions
2 tablespoons oil
6 ounces salt pork or unsmoked bacon
2 shallots, chopped
2 small tomatoes, skinned, seeded, and
 coarsely chopped
2 small carrots, scraped and sliced

1 large clove garlic, crushed
Bouquet garni: thyme, bay leaf, parsley
 sprigs, and 8 peppercorns, tied
 together in cheesecloth
1 teaspoon salt
Rind of 1 lemon, chopped
1 cup good red wine

Have the butcher tie the meat securely.

Heat oven to 325°F.

Slice the onions. Heat the oil in a skillet and cook the onions until golden. Add the diced pork or bacon and cook until it gives off its fat.

Brown the beef on all sides in the fat, then transfer the steak to an oven-proof casserole with a cover. Add the cooked onion and bacon. Also add the chopped shallots, tomatoes, sliced carrots, crushed garlic, and the bouquet garni. Sprinkle with a teaspoon of salt and the lemon rind. Pour the wine over the meat and bring to a boil on top of the range.

Cover the casserole first with wax paper, then the lid, and cook in the oven very slowly for approximately three and one-half hours. Check it from time to time to make sure it is not over-cooking, since meats vary.

Place the meat on a serving dish or in a clean casserole. Press the ingredients that remain in the original casserole through a fine sieve or a food mill. Correct the seasoning and pour over the meat. Serve with a purée of potatoes.   *A*

DAUBE OF BEEF

6 servings

1 pound lean sliced bacon
4 pounds shoulder of beef, trimmed of all
    fat and cut into 1½-inch cubes
Salt and pepper
4 large onions, quartered
20 cloves garlic, about 2 heads, peeled

2 strips orange peel, 1 bay leaf, 1 teaspoon
    dried thyme or a sprig of fresh thyme,
    all tied in a piece of cheesecloth
1 quart good dry red wine
1 cup parsley sprigs, finely chopped

Heat oven to 350°F.

Cook the bacon in a large casserole until all of its fat has been extracted. Remove the bacon and reserve it.

Cook the cubed beef, a little at a time so as not to overcrowd the casserole, until brown all over. Sprinkle the beef cubes with salt, about two teaspoons, and a few twists of the pepper mill.

Add the onions, garlic, the bacon crumbled, and the bag of seasonings. Pour in enough red wine to cover. Bring to a boil on top of the range.

Cover the casserole with its lid and cook in the oven for two and one-half hours. Test for doneness. Cool and, when cold, refrigerate.

The following day remove all the surface fat and reheat thoroughly. Before serving, sprinkle with chopped parsley. Plain steamed potatoes are the perfect accompaniment.

CASSEROLE OF BEEF

4 to 6 servings

This is my favorite beef casserole. It is uncomplicated, fool-proof, and comforting when the snow lies deep on the ground. And there is no "browning" or searing of the meat involved.

3 pounds of chuck, top round, or sirloin, trimmed of fat
2 large onions
2 cloves garlic

1 tablespoon coarse salt
Freshly ground pepper
½ cup parsley sprigs, finely chopped

Heat oven to 350°F.

Cut the beef into one-and-one-half-inch cubes and place in a heavy casserole with a tight-fitting lid. Peel the onions and chop them finely. Crush the garlic with the coarse salt. Add the onions, garlic, and a dusting of freshly ground pepper to the casserole.

Cover and cook in the oven for one and one-half hours. Skim off the fat and test for doneness. If necessary, continue to cook until tender. Correct the seasoning with additional salt and pepper, if needed. Sprinkle with parsley and serve with fresh, crusty French or Italian bread.

AB

CARBONNADES FLAMANDES

8 servings

Prepared mustard—Dijon is my preference—and dark beer give this excellent Belgian dish its unique character. It is perfect winter fare and freezes successfully. Double the recipe and freeze one half.

1 cup flour
1 tablespoon salt
3 to 4 twists of the pepper mill
½ pound lean bacon, cubed
4 tablespoons butter
5 to 6 large onions, thinly sliced
4 pounds boneless chuck, cut in 1½-inch cubes

Pinch of dried thyme or 3 to 4 leaves of fresh thyme
1 bay leaf
2 slices bread
Dijon mustard, enough to spread on one side of each slice of bread
2 bottles of dark beer (12 ounces each)

Heat oven to 320°F.

Mix the flour, salt, and pepper. Cook the bacon in a heavy skillet until most of the fat has been extracted. Transfer the bacon pieces to the casserole you will be using for the Carbonnade. Pour off all but three to four tablespoons of the fat.

Add the butter and heat until hot, but not smoking. Brown the onions, lift them out, and set aside. Dredge the meat cubes in the flour, shake off the excess, and brown them in the skillet.

Transfer the beef to the casserole. Cover with sautéed onions. Sprinkle with thyme and broken-up bay leaf. Spread slices of bread with mustard and lay them over the beef, mustard-side down. Pour the beer over the bread. Bring the casserole to a boil on top of the range, then transfer to the heated oven and bake for forty minutes.

Stir the bread into the beef and continue cooking for one and one-half hours, or until tender. After one hour test from time to time. Correct the seasoning. Serve with boiled potatoes. *AB*

POT ROAST

10 to 12 servings

Pot Roast, perhaps because of its name, is looked upon as plebian fare and nothing could be further from the truth. It is no longer inexpensive, but then what is? However, it is good value for your money and goes a long way. This variation is excellent but means thinking ahead. The lengthy marinating time produces a superb flavor and is guaranteed to transform the toughest cut into mouth-watering tenderness.

5 pounds round of beef in one piece
½ cup good red wine vinegar
2¼ cups onion, chopped
2¼ cups carrots,
   peeled and chopped
1½ cups celery, chopped
2 cups leeks,
   washed and chopped
2 cloves garlic, peeled, chopped, and
   crushed with a little salt

Bouquet garni: 1 small bunch parsley
   stalks, 1 teaspoon each of dried sage,
   rosemary, and marjoram, a dozen
   coriander seeds, tied in cheesecloth
1 quart of good red Bordeaux
2 teaspoons salt
Freshly ground black pepper
¾ cup salt pork, diced
¼ cup flour
2 cups beef stock

Place the beef in a large earthenware bowl.

Combine together the vinegar and one-half cup each of the onion and carrots, one cup of celery, all the leeks, the crushed garlic, and the bag of herbs. Bring to a boil in an enamel-lined or stainless-steel pan and simmer gently for five to six minutes.

Pour the vegetable mixture over the meat and add enough wine to cover. Sprinkle with two teaspoons of salt and a few twists of the pepper mill. Cover the bowl with plastic wrap and refrigerate for at least forty-eight hours.

When you are ready to cook the beef, lift it out of its marinade, and pat it dry. Strain the liquid and set aside three cups. Discard the remainder with the solids.

Heat oven to 350°F.

Cook the salt pork in a covered casserole until all the fat has been extracted. Lift out the pork pieces and reserve them. Brown the beef on all sides in the casserole and when brown, lift it out and keep it warm on a platter in a low oven.

Add all the remaining uncooked vegetables and pieces of salt pork to the casserole and cook, stirring until the onion is softened and golden. Sprinkle the vegetables with flour and stir until well-blended. Add the reserved marinade and the beef stock, stirring until thickened.

Return the meat to the casserole. Cook, covered, for approximately two and one-half hours, or until the meat is tender.

Remove the pot roast to a warm platter and bring the casserole liquid to a fast boil. Boil it down to a thickness resembling heavy cream. Steamed potatoes or a purée of potatoes go well with the pot roast.

STEAK AND KIDNEY PIE

6 servings

Steak and Kidney Pie is as British as John Bull. Before the day of the cultivated mushroom, oysters were incredibly inexpensive and used in place of the mushroom. Winston Churchill was once chided for this seemingly incongruous combination of beef and fish. His answer was Churchillian, "Why not? The Department of Agriculture and Fisheries is one." Either combination suits my taste.

2 pounds chuck steak
1 pound beef kidney
1 cup flour, seasoned with salt and pepper
6 tablespoons butter
1 large onion, chopped
½ pound mushrooms, sliced

Bouquet garni (see page 110)
1 cup beef stock
1 cup red wine
All-Purpose Pastry (see page 300)
1 egg beaten with 1 tablespoon of water

Heat oven to 300°F.

Trim the steak of all fat and cut it into one-inch cubes. Cube the kidney and cut away all fat. Dust lightly with seasoned flour, shaking off the excess.

Heat four tablespoons of butter in a skillet, add the onion, and cook slowly until it is golden and transparent. Transfer to an oven-proof casserole with a lid. Press the onion to extract the butter and pour the butter back into the pan.

Dredge the cubes of steak with seasoned flour and brown with the kidneys quickly, a few pieces at a time, in the hot butter. Add them to the onions in the casserole. Sauté the mushrooms in the remaining butter and add them and the bouquet garni to the steak and onion mixture.

Deglaze the pan with stock and wine, and cook over high heat to reduce and thicken the liquid a little. Add to the casserole, cover, and cook in the oven for one to one and one-half hours. Test after one hour. Place the steak, kidney, and onion mixture in a two-quart, deep pie dish.

Heat oven to 450°F.

Prepare the pastry dough according to the recipe. Roll out the dough from one-eighth to one-quarter-inch thick. Moisten the rim of the pie dish with egg yolk and water. Cover the dish with pastry and trim to the edge with a sharp knife.

Gather the remaining pastry into a ball and roll it out. Cut enough one-quarter-inch strips to go around the pie dish. Moisten the rim of pastry and press on the strips to seal the crust. Mark the crust with a fork, roller, or fingers.

Brush the entire surface with a mixture of one egg beaten with one tablespoon of water, and decorate in any way that takes your fancy.

Bake for fifteen minutes, then reduce heat to 350°F., and bake twenty minutes longer.

A

BEEF TENDERLOIN IN ASPIC

8 to 10 servings

1 four- to six-pound beef tenderloin, trimmed of all fat
½ pound bacon, sliced

Heat oven to 425°F.

Cover the tenderloin with slices of bacon. Place the tenderloin on a rack in a roasting pan and roast for thirty to thirty-five minutes, or until the meat thermometer registers 120°F. Remove and discard the bacon; cool the tenderloin.

Cut the cool fillet into slices one and one-half inches thick and chill.

Aspic:

3 cups strong chicken consommé
3 tablespoons dry white wine or dry
   vermouth
1 tablespoon lemon juice
2 egg whites

2 egg shells
2 tablespoons unflavored gelatin
1 cup port wine
1 whole truffle (optional—if you like
   gilding the lily)

(Continued)

In a stainless-steel or enamel-lined saucepan combine the consommé, wine or vermouth, and lemon juice. In a small bowl beat the egg whites lightly, crush the egg shells, and mix them with the whites.

Stir the egg mixture into the consommé mixture and heat almost to the boiling point but do not allow it to boil. There should now be a mat-like covering on the consommé and the liquid should be barely simmering. Simmer it for five minutes and turn off the heat.

Allow it to stand for fifteen minutes. Strain the consommé into a clean bowl, stir in the gelatin, and cool. Add the port wine.

Arrange the sliced tenderloin on a large platter. Spoon a little of the now-cooling aspic over each slice.

Slice the truffle and cut it into shapes to suit your fancy. Dip each truffle slice into the aspic and decorate the tenderloin with it.

Spoon enough aspic over the decorated tenderloin to allow the sauce to flow over and cover the bottom of the platter. Chill the tenderloin until needed.

BEEF WELLINGTON

6 to 8 servings

Beef Wellington is not my favorite dish. In the first place, it is expensive; second, the beef depends on the pâté for its flavor; last and far from least, the pastry, because it is in contact with the pâté, cannot be anything else but damp and soggy on the inside. But, in spite of these drawbacks, it never fails to draw oohs and ahs when it makes its appearance. It also has in its favor the advantage of being agreeable to preparation ahead of time.

I like to think of it being named for the shape, color, and high polish of the much-decorated Duke's boot.

Brioche Dough:

1 package dry yeast	½ teaspoon salt
2 tablespoons warm milk	2 eggs
1½ cups flour	8 tablespoons butter
1 teaspoon sugar	Flour for sprinkling

Sprinkle one package of dry yeast over two tablespoons of warm milk to soften.

In a bowl sift together one and one-half cups of flour, one teaspoon of sugar, and one-half teaspoon of salt, and make a well in the center. Break two eggs into the well, add the softened yeast, and begin to knead the paste to make a smooth mixture. With your hands beat in eight tablespoons of butter until the dough is thoroughly mixed.

Shape the soft dough into a ball and put it into a bowl sprinkled with flour. Cut a deep crosswise incision across the top.

Cover the bowl with a towel and let the dough rise in a warm place until it is doubled in size.

Punch the dough down, cover it again, and chill overnight.

1 fillet of beef, approximately 4 pounds, ready for the oven
Dry mustard
Larding pork or bacon strips
½ pound firm white mushrooms
¼ pound ham
4 chicken livers
2 tablespoons butter

½ clove garlic, crushed into a paste with 1 teaspoon salt
1 tablespoon tomato purée
1 tablespoon meat extract or Bovril
⅓ cup dry sherry
1 egg yolk for glazing
Sauce Madeira (see page 276)

Heat oven to 400°F.

Rub the fillet all over with dry mustard. Tie on the larding pork or bacon strips with string. Roast for twenty-five minutes. Cool. Remove the string and pork. Set aside the pan juices.

To make the pâté, chop the mushrooms, ham, and chicken livers. Sauté all of them in two tablespoons of butter for eight minutes. Add the garlic, tomato purée, meat extract, pan juices, and sherry. Cook five minutes longer.

When cool enough to handle, purée the mixture in a blender or food mill.

Increase the oven temperature to 425°F.

Roll out the brioche dough about one-half inch thick. Spread the center with some of the pâté. Place the fillet over the pâté in the exact center; spread the fillet with the remaining pâté. Fold the brioche dough over the fillet. Seal the edges. Put the fillet seam-side down on a rimless baking sheet. Brush with egg yolk, and decorate with cutouts made from leftover dough. Brush again with egg yolk. Bake thirty minutes more. Serve with Sauce Madeira. Green beans, braised celery or braised endive are suitable accompaniments.

NEW ENGLAND CORNED BEEF

Up to 14 servings

Corned beef surrounded by lightly cooked root vegetables and cabbage forms the backbone of one of the best winter meals in my repertoire. It can be prepared ahead of time, and a second point in its favor is that hash can be made from the leftovers.

12 to 14 pounds corned beef
4 medium potatoes
8 small carrots
6 small white turnips

1 small cabbage
Finely chopped parsley
Horseradish Sauce (see page 289)

(Continued)

Wash the corned beef under cold running water. In a pot large enough to hold it, cover the meat with boiling water. Bring the water to a boil again, then simmer gently. Allow about one hour per pound cooking time. Cool the corned beef in its liquid and refrigerate until needed. Reserve the liquid, chill, and remove the fat.

Peel the potatoes, cut in quarters, and shape each quarter to resemble a large olive. Scrape and halve the carrots if they are large. Peel and quarter the turnips. Quarter the cabbage and cut out most of the stalk, leaving only enough to hold the leaves together.

Cook the potatoes and carrots until they are almost tender in enough of the reserved beef liquid to cover them. Take care not to overcook them. Remove the vegetables with a slotted spoon to a second pot or shallow roasting pan. Add a ladle of beef liquid.

Cook the cabbage quarters and turnips together in the same beef liquid for approximately ten to fifteen minutes. Lift them out and add them to the potatoes and carrots.

Heat oven to 350°F.

Remove as much of the fat as possible from the corned beef. Slice the beef very thinly against the grain and lay the slices neatly in a shallow pan. Spoon some of the cooking liquid over the slices.

To serve, heat the sliced beef in its dish, covered with wax paper or foil, in the oven for fifteen to twenty minutes. Heat the vegetables in the cooking liquid on top of the range. Arrange the sliced meat and vegetables in a heated, deep platter with a little of the boiling liquid spooned over them. Sprinkle the vegetables with finely chopped parsley. Serve with Horseradish Sauce.

A

GLAZED CORNED BEEF

8 to 10 servings

The corned beef described in the preceding recipe makes a splendid display on a buffet at Christmas or at any other cold-weather festivity. The leftovers provide filling for sandwiches for days to come.

1 four-to-six pound corned beef,
   cooked and trimmed
Cloves

Glaze:

1 can (8 ounces) crushed pineapple
4 heaping tablespoons domestic prepared
   mustard

½ cup orange marmalade
8 whole cloves

To prepare the glaze, combine all the ingredients in a small, heavy pan and cook over medium heat until thickened.

Heat the oven to 375°F.

Place the corned beef on a greased jelly-roll pan. Trim off most of the fat. Stud the meat with a pattern of cloves, then brush it with the glaze. Bake for one hour, basting frequently and adding more glaze as necessary.

Remove the corned beef to a serving platter and allow it to reach room temperature before serving.
AC

CORNED BEEF HASH

6 servings

Oil and butter for browning
3 cups ground or finely chopped cooked
  corned beef
1 large raw potato, grated

1 medium onion, finely diced
Freshly ground black pepper
Celery salt

Heat enough oil and butter to grease a heavy skillet. Mix together all the other ingredients and spoon into the heated skillet.

Cook the mixture over medium heat until a crust forms on the bottom. Turn it and brown the other side. Cooking time is about thirty minutes.

During the last five minutes, press down the hash to make a large patty. Reheat thoroughly, turn out, and serve.
CD

Lamb

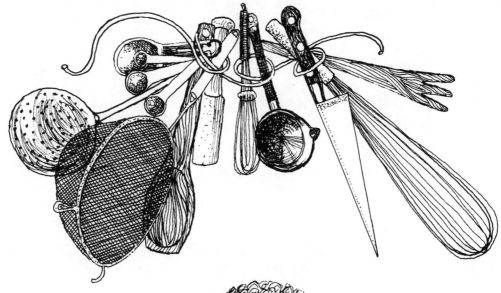

Lamb

Of the red meats, I prefer lamb. It lends itself to so many different cooking methods, flavors, and garnishes. As for flavors and garnishes, lamb is versatile; it marries contentedly with other ingredients. In Chinese cookery this is called "matchmaking," an apt title. But, whatever you decide to use as an accompaniment or seasoning, it must play a secondary role and do nothing to overwhelm the flavor of the lamb itself. The flavors may clash, such as apricots in a stuffing, but there must be a relationship.

The roast leg of lamb has been ill-treated by overcooking, particularly in America where no one in his right mind would dream of overcooking fine beef. The roast leg of lamb should be just as pink and succulent as the rib roast.

Choose cuts in which the fat is white, making sure there is not too much of it. In the case of a leg, pick out a small one. If what you are cooking needs boning, save the bones for lamb stock, the only true base for Scotch Broth.

BUTTERFLIED LEG OF LAMB

10 servings

"Butterflied" is an apt description of a leg of lamb boned and flattened. Sometimes I call it Puccini or Madame Butterfly. Unless you are a very skillful carver, the boned leg produces more servings. Carved against the grain with a very sharp knife, a small, boned leg should serve ten. And you have the bone and trimmings for stock.

1 leg of lamb, not more than 5 pounds,
   boned and flattened

Dressing:

2 tablespoons Dijon mustard
½ teaspoon salt
¼ teaspoon pepper
4 tablespoons brown sugar

2 tablespoons soy sauce
2 tablespoons olive oil
¼ clove garlic, crushed
⅓ cup lemon juice

Heat oven to 500°F.
   Combine all the ingredients for the dressing. Brush the lamb with the dressing. Lay it on a rack in a roasting pan. Add a little water to the pan to prevent burning.
   Cook for twenty-five minutes on the highest shelf, brushing and basting frequently. Turn the leg on its other side halfway through the cooking time.
   Allow the lamb to rest before carving. Slice it on the bias as you would London Broil. Serve with the pan juices and a hearty salad.   *A*

PLYMOUTH LEG OF LAMB

8 to 10 servings

This method produces an unusual flavor, but must be avoided by anyone allergic to the juniper berry.

½ cup juniper berries
1 cup gin
1 leg of lamb, weighing not more than
   5 pounds, boned

Coarse salt and freshly ground
   black pepper
4 to 6 ounces unsalted butter

Soak the juniper berries overnight in one-half cup of the gin, sealing the glass to prevent evaporation.
   In the morning, flatten out the leg of lamb and season the cut side very generously with coarse salt, freshly ground black pepper, and half the butter.

Spread the juniper berries over the seasoned lamb. Roll it up and sew the leg together with a large needle and string; then refrigerate until needed.

Heat oven to 450°F.

Remove the leg of lamb from the refrigerator and spread the rest of the butter over it. Season it again with salt and pepper.

Put the lamb on a rack in a roasting pan and cook for forty-five to fifty minutes, basting it with its juices from time to time. Remove from the oven and let it rest for ten to fifteen minutes on a heated platter. Remove the string.

Heat the other one-half cup of gin, pour it over the lamb, and set it alight. When the flames die down, carve the lamb into thin slices.

LEG OF LAMB WITH APRICOT AND RICE STUFFING

8 to 10 servings

This dish is based on an eighteenth-century English recipe, and a very good one it is. The flavor is delightfully unusual and, as more rice and apricots are made than go into the lamb, there is no need to serve anything else with it. A salad, perhaps, later. Now that you have the recipe for Apricot Rice, serve it with a baked fish such as red snapper sometime.

1 small 4- to 5-pound leg of lamb, boned
Salt and pepper
6 tablespoons melted butter

Heat oven to 375°F.

Bone the leg of lamb leaving the shank intact. Set aside the loin chops and bones for freezing. Make cuts in the thickest part of the leg and flatten to make an even, overall thickness. Season well with salt and pepper.

Apricot and Rice Stuffing:

8 ounces long-grain rice, uncooked	1 teaspoon powdered cinnamon
4 ounces apricots, soaked for an hour, then chopped	1 teaspoon powdered coriander
4 tablespoons golden raisins	1½ teaspoons powdered ginger
4 tablespoons slivered almonds	Salt and freshly ground black pepper

Cook the rice in one and one-half quarts boiling water with two tablespoons of salt for twelve to fifteen minutes until rice grains are still firm. Drain well and mix with the apricots, raisins, almonds, spices, salt, and pepper.

(Continued)

Spoon about one-third to one-half of the rice mixture onto the lamb, fold the meat over and reshape it to look like a leg.

Sew it up neatly with needle and string.

Place it on a rack in a roasting pan; brush generously with melted butter, and season it with salt and pepper.

Roast for approximately an hour and a half, or twenty minutes to the pound. Remove the lamb to a platter and keep it warm in a low oven.

Pour off the fat from the roasting pan and stir the pan juices into the rest of the rice. If it is too dry, add some of the melted butter. Arrange the rice around the lamb. Remove the string from the lamb before carving.

A

BOILED LEG OF LAMB, CAPER SAUCE

8 to 10 servings

Boiled Mutton and Caper Sauce for centuries has been a delicacy on English chop-house menus. And at Simpson's-in-the-Strand in London, it is still a favorite. Caper Sauce does wonders for it. The leg of lamb is a very good substitute for mutton.

1 four- to six-pound
  leg of lamb
Salt
3 medium carrots
3 small white turnips
4 to 5 medium potatoes
¼ cup milk

1 faggot: 3 to 4 parsley stalks; 1 rib celery, washed; 1 bay leaf; 1 teaspoon dried thyme or 6 to 8 leaves of fresh thyme; 6 peppercorns, crushed; all tied together and wrapped in cheesecloth
Freshly chopped parsley sprigs
Caper Sauce (see page 282)

Have the butcher break the shank bone and remove the irregular bone at the broad end.

Put the lamb in a pan and add enough cold water to cover. Add one teaspoon of salt for each quart of water.

Wash and scrape the carrots. Cut each one in half. If the carrots are large, quarter them. Peel the turnips, taking off the thick layer of bark-like peel, and quarter them.

Peel and quarter the potatoes. Leave the potatoes covered with cold water in a bowl. Add about one-quarter cup of milk. This prevents discoloration.

Put the vegetables, with the exception of the potatoes and the faggot, in the pot with the lamb. Bring to a boil and cook, simmering, for fifteen minutes per pound. Test the vegetables from time to time after the first half hour. If the vegetables are cooking too fast, remove them and return them to the pot later.

Cook the potatoes separately in boiling salted water. They take about twenty minutes.

Remove the lamb to a hot serving dish. Surround the lamb with all the vegetables, including the potatoes. Sprinkle with chopped parsley and serve with hot Caper Sauce. Save the cooking liquid. It is the perfect base for a Scotch Broth and can be frozen.

NOIX D'AGNEAU BRAISE

6 servings

Valerie Johnson of Palm Beach, Florida, is my sort of cook. She has the confidence so many people lack to serve perfectly marvelous food that many would consider "not good enough for company," a phrase some of my students use. I have taken a liberty and altered her recipe somewhat. My version is not quite as exotic as hers, but very good nevertheless.

1 cup flour
1 tablespoon salt
3 to 4 twists of the pepper mill
6 lamb knuckles
Vegetable oil for searing
3 cups stock, lamb, chicken, or beef
3 tablespoons tomato paste

2 cloves garlic, crushed to a paste with a
    teaspoon of coarse salt
1 small bay leaf, crumbled
½ teaspoon rosemary
Grated rind and juice of 1 orange
1½ tablespoons potato flour
½ cup parsley sprigs, finely chopped

Mix the flour, salt, and pepper. Dredge the knuckles in the seasoned flour, shaking off the excess.

Heat two or three tablespoons of oil in a large, heavy casserole with a lid and brown the lamb evenly all over. Heat the stock and pour it over the lamb. Add the tomato paste, garlic paste, bay leaf, and rosemary.

Bring to a boil, lower heat, cover the casserole and simmer gently for one to one and one-half hours, until the meat leaves the bone.

Take the knuckles out of the casserole and strip the meat from the bones. Chill the liquid left in the casserole, and when cold, remove the fat. Trim the lamb of any obvious bits of fat and, if the knuckles are large, cut them in half.

If the dish is not to be used in the near future, add the meat to the fatless liquid in the casserole and freeze.

(Continued)

To serve, add the juice and grated rind of the orange to the casserole. Blend the potato flour with a little of the casserole liquid and stir it into the casserole. Heat gently to thicken, stirring to make a smooth sauce. Correct the seasoning with salt and pepper, if needed. Serve very hot with rice or plain boiled potatoes and sprinkle with finely chopped parsley.   *AB*

BONED STUFFED SHOULDER OF LAMB

8 to 10 servings

½ pound sausage meat
1 onion, finely chopped and lightly
    sautéed
1 teaspoon parsley, chopped
1 cup fresh bread crumbs
1 egg
½ teaspoon salt and freshly
    ground pepper
1 lamb shoulder, boned
1 onion and 1 carrot, sliced

Bouquet garni or faggot: 3 to 4 sprigs
    parsley; 1 to 2 stalks celery; 1 leek, if
    available; ½ bay leaf; a pinch of thyme
    or 1 to 2 fresh sprigs; all tied in a piece
    of cheesecloth
2 or 3 tablespoons fat (butter or bacon
    drippings)
1 tablespoon flour
1 cup lamb stock or hot water

Heat oven to 425°F.

Mix together the sausage, cooked onion, parsley, bread crumbs, egg, salt, and pepper, and stuff the shoulder with this mixture. Roll up the shoulder and tie it with string.

Spread the sliced onion and carrot on the bottom of a roasting pan and add the bouquet garni or faggot. Rub the shoulder with a little salt and pepper, spread with the fat, and place on top of the vegetables in the roasting pan.

Bake, uncovered, in a moderately hot oven for about thirty minutes, turning often to brown on all sides.

Sprinkle flour on top of the vegetables, add the stock or water, and continue cooking at a moderate heat (375°F.) for about two hours, basting often. If the liquid cooks away, add more. Remove the bouquet garni.

Transfer the meat along with the vegetables to a serving dish. Strain the pan juices, remove the fat, reheat, and serve with the lamb. A braised vegetable such as endive or celery goes well with this dish.

A

CARRE D'AGNEAU

2 to 3 servings

The rack consists of not more than six chops. When trimmed of all fat with the chine bone cut to allow for easily cutting into the chops and the chop bones themselves of a uniform length, the rack is a delicacy. The brushing mixture coats the outside with a crust that brings out the flavor of the meat inside while the rack is roasting. It is a simple and quick cut to cook and is internationally popular.

Rack of lamb (half a rack of lamb serves two)

Brushing Mixture (makes approximately ½ cup):

2 tablespoons prepared Dijon mustard
½ teaspoon salt
¼ teaspoon pepper
4 tablespoons brown sugar
2 tablespoons soy sauce

2 tablespoons olive oil
¼ clove garlic, crushed
⅓ cup lemon juice
Watercress for garnish

Heat oven to 425°F.

Combine all the ingredients for the brushing mixture. Brush the lamb with the sauce before placing it in the oven. It is best to brush on the mixture half an hour in advance. Bake the lamb for fifteen minutes, remove from the oven, and brush again. Cook fifteen minutes more for pink meat, longer for well-done. Allow the lamb to rest for ten minutes.

Carve it into single chops and cover each bone end with a paper frill. Arrange on a heated platter, garnished with bunches of watercress.

ROAST SADDLE OF LAMB GARNI

6 servings

The saddle is the double rack. Try to imagine, and it is unlikely you would ever have to, putting a saddle on the back of a lamb. Well, that is where the saddle part of the lamb—the king of all cuts—is located. It is expensive to buy and not all that economical to serve. In fact, it is a luxury cut but, when one feels like self-pampering, well worth every penny. I class it as expensive simplicity. I was once asked to suggest a menu for one of the Rothschilds, and the saddle was my choice of entrée.

Saddle of lamb, approximately
  7 to 8 pounds
1 tablespoon coarse salt
1 small clove garlic
Freshly ground black pepper

2 tablespoons butter
2 tablespoons olive oil
1 cup lamb stock
2 tablespoons dry sherry
Salt and freshly ground pepper

(Continued)

Heat oven to 425°F.

Trim the side flaps, leaving enough to fold under the saddle. If your butcher has not already done so, remove the parchment-like skin. Rub the saddle with coarse salt and then garlic. Use the black pepper generously.

Put the butter and oil and then the lamb in the roasting pan. Cook for thirty-five minutes, basting frequently.

Turn the saddle on its back, open the flaps, and remove the fillets with a small, sharp knife. They run the length of the saddle, close and parallel to the bone. Close the flaps and replace the saddle right-side up. Lay the fillets on either side of the saddle. The fillets have been protected by the flaps and will now need direct heat. Close the oven door and cook for a further ten minutes. Remove the saddle and fillets from the pan and keep them warm.

Skim the fat from the pan juices. Scrape the bottom to loosen the solids. Add one cup of boiling stock. Cook until the liquids are reduced to approximately three-quarters of a cup. Add two tablespoons of sherry. Correct the seasoning and strain the gravy.

Carve the fillets so that everyone can get a sample and put them on a warm platter. Turn the saddle right-side up, and carve it in strips lengthwise, following the line of the backbone. Serve with green beans and pommes croquettes. *A*

CASEROLE OF LAMB

6 servings

3 pounds lean lamb shoulder, cut into serving pieces
3 tablespoons olive oil
1 tablespoon sugar
Salt and freshly ground pepper
3 tablespoons flour
2 to 3 cups lamb stock or canned beef bouillon
2 large, ripe tomatoes, peeled and chopped
2 cloves garlic, finely minced
¼ teaspoon thyme
1 bay leaf
12 small potatoes, peeled, and cubed if they are too large
6 carrots, scraped and cut into 1½-inch lengths on the bias
6 small turnips, peeled, and cubed if they are too large
12 small white onions
1 cup shelled peas or 1 package frozen green peas
1 cup green beans, cut in ½-inch lengths

Heat oven to 325°F.

Brown the meat on all sides in oil, a few pieces at a time. Transfer to a heavy casserole. Sprinkle the meat with sugar and place over moderately high heat for four to five minutes.

Season with salt and pepper, sprinkle with the flour, and cook for five minutes longer, stirring, occasionally.

Add enough lamb or beef stock to cover the meat. Add the tomatoes, garlic, thyme, and bay leaf, and bring to a boil.

Cover and bake in the oven one to one and one-half hours until the meat is almost tender. Test frequently. Do not overcook. Remove meat to a clean casserole.

Strain the sauce, skim the excess fat, and pour the sauce over the meat. Add the potatoes, carrots, turnips, and onions. Cover and bake for twenty-five minutes longer, or until the vegetables are almost tender.

Add the green peas and beans and bake for ten minutes. If frozen vegetables are used, add them only for the last five minutes.

This casserole freezes well. To freeze, cut cooking time by fifteen minutes and leave out frozen peas. Add them after thawing the casserole and before reheating. A salad would be an appropriate accompaniment.

AB

Pork

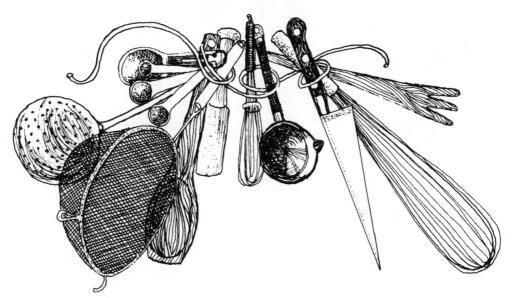

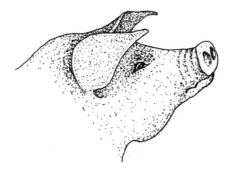

Pork

Long past are the days when pork was considered unsuitable as party fare. It was very much a family meat and in large households it was the entrée in the "servants' hall," while on the other side of the "green baize" door, poultry, game, or one of the red meats would be served. In my opinion, pork is a delicacy and the only reason for not serving it would be on religious grounds. The modern-day porker is a lean animal, with little waste of any kind. Its skin, its innards, and its whiskers (for bristle) are all put to good use. The by-products are legion.

The loin, the leg, and the chops are all delicious and greatly improved when accompanied by a compote of unsweetened fruits or stuffed with a mixture containing tangy fruit. Unless the leg or loin is unskinned, I prefer braising to all other cooking methods. Braising on a bed of aromatic vegetables keeps the meat moist and imparts a flavor all its own.

If one is fortunate enough to find a leg or loin with skin untouched, you then have a treat for the gods. Deeply scored with a small, sharp knife, the skin turns into brittle, crisp cracknel while roasting, and the moisture in the meat is retained.

The meat should be very white and, in spite of the fact that trichinosis is an uncommon disease today, for roasting the internal temperature should read 150°F. Cold, thinly sliced pork is almost better than hot. What is left over from the evening meal makes a splendid cold luncheon the following day.

ESCALOPES DU PORC

8 to 10 servings

1 loin of pork, boned, sliced thin, and
   flattened between sheets of wax paper
1 cup flour, seasoned with 1 tablespoon
   salt and 5 or 6 twists of the pepper mill
2 tablespoons olive oil

2 tablespoons unsalted butter
1 cup stock, chicken or veal
½ cup dry Marsala
½ tablespoon tomato paste
Chopped parsley

Dust escalopes liberally with the seasoned flour.

Heat the oil and butter in equal quantities, a little at a time as needed, in a heavy skillet. When foaming, sauté escalopes on each side for approximately one minute. Remove to a heated serving dish and keep them warm.

Add one cup of stock to the pan, turn up the heat, scrape the bottom and sides to loosen the brown bits, and cook over high heat until the liquid is slightly reduced. Add one-half cup of Marsala, stir in the tomato paste, and cook until slightly thickened. It should have the consistency of heavy cream. Correct the seasoning, if necessary.

Pour the sauce over the escalopes and sprinkle them with a little chopped parsley before serving. Serve with Potato Purée.

LOIN OF PORK, ALMOND SAUCE

8 servings

Lili Strepetoff, born Princess Thurn Taxis, now Countess Spinola, gave me the recipe for this unusual method of cooking pork. I understand it hails from Spain, one of the many, many countries Lili has connections with—she speaks at least eight languages fluently, which sometimes adds spice to conversation as words from all eight are likely to be heard in the course of a short conversation. Her talents are as many as her languages: painting, music, literature, couture, not to mention the "civilized art" of cooking.

½ cup clarified butter (see page 345)
Salt and pepper
1 loin of pork, weighing approximately
   4 pounds, boned and rolled, and tied
   back on the bone

4 cloves garlic, peeled and halved
2 cups almonds, blanched and peeled
Milk
½ cup parsley sprigs, finely chopped

Heat oven to 350°F.

Heat a little clarified butter in a heavy skillet. Rub salt and pepper into the loin. Brown the loin evenly in the skillet.

Transfer it to an oven-proof casserole with a tight-fitting lid. Add the garlic, almonds, and enough milk to cover the loin. Bring to a boil on top of the range, taking care that the milk does not boil over.

Place the casserole in the oven and cook covered for one hour and twenty minutes. Turn the meat once or twice during the cooking time. If the milk has evaporated, replenish with hot water. Test for doneness and avoid overcooking. The internal temperature on a meat thermometer should be 145° to 150°F.

If the loin is to be served hot, put it on a serving dish at the side of the range. Purée the remaining contents of the casserole and correct the seasoning with salt and pepper. If the almond sauce is too thick, thin it with a little light cream or milk. Spoon a little of the sauce over the pork; sprinkle with chopped parsley. Pass the remainder of the sauce separately. The loin of pork is equally good served with wedges of lemon. *A*

LOIN OF PORK

6 to 8 servings

2 carrots	Clarified butter (see page 345)
1 rib celery	1 four- to five-pound loin of pork, boned
1 small onion	and rolled, and tied back on the bone
3 to 4 parsley stalks	2 cups dry white wine
1 small bay leaf	Flour for dredging
Pinch of dried thyme	Salt and pepper
Rind of 1 lemon cut into strips	Lemon wedges
Peppercorns	

Heat oven to 350°F.

Scrape and slice the carrots and celery, and slice the onion. Make a bed of them with the parsley stalks on the bottom of an oven-proof casserole. Tie the bay leaf, thyme, lemon rind, and peppercorns in a piece of cheesecloth.

Heat some of the clarified butter in a heavy skillet. Rub salt into the loin and brown the meat thoroughly all over in the hot butter. Transfer the loin to the casserole.

(Continued)

Pour off the fat and deglaze the pan with a little white wine, scraping the bottom of the pan to loosen the brown bits. Pour the pan juices over the loin with the rest of the white wine. Dust the loin lightly with flour. Bring the pan juices to a boil on top of the range.

Transfer the casserole to the oven and cook, covered, for one hour. After half an hour, turn the loin and dust it with flour again. Repeat at the end of the hour and test with a meat thermometer. It should read not less than 150°F. Continue cooking until this temperature has been reached, taking care that the tip of the thermometer only goes to the middle of the roast and does not touch the bone. When you are satisfied it is done, transfer the loin to a warm serving dish. Untie it and remove the bone.

Pour the pan juices into a clean pan and skim off the fat. Press the solids through a sieve into the pan and correct the seasoning. Carve the roast in thin slices and serve with the pan juices, a purée of celery root and potatoes, and a compote of apricots. Garnish with lemon wedges.

A

FIDGET PIE

6 servings

All-Purpose Pastry (see page 300)

Filling:

1½ pounds pork with fat, ground
¼ teaspoon mace
1 teaspoon fresh thyme or ½ teaspoon
  dried thyme
½ cup parsley sprigs, chopped
2 teaspoons salt
1 teaspoon freshly ground black pepper

¼ cup fine white bread crumbs
  (approximately 1 slice of bread)
½ cup onion, chopped
1 tablespoon butter
1 hard, tart apple
1 egg yolk mixed with 1 tablespoon water

Heat oven to 425°F.

Prepare the pastry according to the recipe. Refrigerate until needed.

Mix together the ground pork, mace, thyme, parsley, salt, pepper, and bread crumbs. Cook a walnut-sized piece of the mixture in a hot pan to test for seasoning. Correct, if necessary. Sauté the onion in one tablespoon of butter in a saucepan until golden and transparent. Peel and core the apple. Grate it coarsely.

Pile half of the meat mixture in the pie plate. Spread half of the sautéed onion evenly over it, followed by all of the grated apple, and then the rest of the sautéed onion. Mound the remaining meat mixture on top to form a dome.

Roll out the pastry to one-quarter-inch thickness. Brush the lip of the pie plate with beaten egg yolk and one tablespoon water. Lay the pastry over the plate and trim the edges.

Roll the leftover pastry again and cut it into strips as wide as the pie plate lip and long enough to go around the rim of the dish when laid end to end. Brush the pastry edge with the yolk mixture and lay the strips carefully and evenly on the circumference. Press them into place with finger and thumb or with the tines of a fork. Decorate the top of the pie as you wish. Brush with egg yolk.

Bake at 425°F. for fifteen minutes.

Brush once again with egg yolk. Reduce the heat to 350°F. and bake for thirty minutes longer.

PORK CHOPS AND YELLOW PLUMS

Serves 6

1 large onion	1½ pounds firm, ripe, yellow or green plums
6 tablespoons unsalted butter	1 beef bouillon cube
6 pork chops	2 tablespoons red wine vinegar
1 cup dry white wine or dry vermouth	

Peel, slice, and chop the onion. Sauté gently in the butter for three to four minutes until it is almost soft.

Add the chops and, with great care, cook on both sides until they turn a light golden color. The butter must not turn brown and the onion must not burn.

Add about half the wine. Cover the pan and simmer gently for roughly twenty minutes, until the chops are tender. Set them aside and keep them warm.

Place the plums in a heavy pan with a tight-fitting lid, add two to three tablespoons of water, and cook them over very slow heat until they are tender but not falling apart. If the plums are too tart, add a very little sugar.

Pile the plums in the middle of a heated serving dish and arrange the chops around them.

Crumble the bouillon cube and add it with the rest of the wine and the vinegar to the juices in the pan. Stir while heating, then spoon over the chops.

FILLET DU PORC SAUVAGE

8 to 10 servings

Fillet du Porc Sauvage is as close in flavor to the wild boar as one can get. It is a dish for those who appreciate game. In cooking there is "mock" this and "mock" that—turtle, caviar, and so on—but, in my opinion, this is less "mock" than any of the others. If your butcher can give you the tenderloin, use it instead of the shoulder butt. It will cost more, take less time to cook, and will be delicious.

2 pork shoulder butts or "cushions,"
   approximately 2½ to 3 pounds each,
   tied as nearly as possible in a sausage
   shape with all visible fat removed
1 tablespoon oil

Marinade:

2 cups red wine
⅓ cup chopped onion
1 clove garlic, crushed
1 bay leaf
2 tablespoons salt

4 or 5 twists of the pepper mill
¼ cup finely chopped carrot
¼ cup finely chopped celery
¼ teaspoon dry sage

Wipe the pieces of pork and put them in a glass or enamel container just large enough to hold them.

Mix together all the marinade ingredients.

Pour the marinade over the pork and turn the meat twice to make sure it is liberally coated. For three to four hours, turn them every half hour. An alternative is to put the dish in the refrigerator overnight and turn the pork when you think of it or have time, the more often the better.

Heat oven to 350°F.

Wipe the pork pieces dry and remove any of the marinade solids. Heat one tablespoon of oil in a heavy skillet and brown them evenly on all sides.

Put them in an oven-proof dish with a well-fitting lid and strain the marinade over them. Cook for two hours. Remove the lid for the last half hour and turn the meat once. Test from time to time with a meat thermometer until temperature reaches approximately 170°F.

Serve with the sauce from the casserole. Alternatively, you may pour the marinade over the pork unstrained and cook as above. Before serving, strain the marinade into a small pan and force the solids through the strainer to make a thicker sauce.   *A*

JAMBON PERSILLE

10 to 12 servings

Jambon Persillé is famous in Burgundy at Easter. It is both beautiful to look at and to eat. Easter is springtime, and when I feel the world coming to life again after winter's long, dark sleep, dishes such as this emphasize this aliveness and activity once again. I always have Jambon on hand for the Easter weekend—it's made much earlier in the week—in case a dozen or so friends should drop in for a meal. It can return to the table several times and look as if each time was its debut. It is reassembled and regarnished on a new platter for each appearance.

1 four- to five-pound Virginia
    or Smithfield ham
1 knuckle of veal, chopped into
    pieces
2 calves' feet,
    boned and tied together
2 quarts dry white wine

Bouquet garni consisting of: 2 or 3 small
    branches of tarragon, a few sprigs of
    chervil, 1 small bay leaf, a pinch of
    dried thyme, 3 to 4 parsley stalks, and
    10 peppercorns tied in cheesecloth
2 tablespoons white wine vinegar
1 bunch parsley, coarsely chopped

In a ham kettle or large pan, cover the ham with cold water and bring slowly to a boil to get rid of the excess salt. You may have to repeat the operation if the ham is very salty.

When the "cleansing" is complete, cover the ham once again with cold water and bring slowly to a boil. Simmer very gently for about thirty-five to forty minutes.

Lift out the ham and when it is cool enough to handle, cut the meat off the bone in good-sized chunks. Put them in a clean pan with the knuckle of veal, calves' feet, and bouquet garni. Cover with the wine, bring to a boil, lower the heat, and simmer very gently for about an hour, skimming off the fat as it rises. The ham must be very thoroughly cooked, as it will be flaked later.

When you are satisfied that the ham is sufficiently cooked, pour off the liquid into a large mixing bowl through a strainer lined with three or four thicknesses of wet cheesecloth. Separate the ham from the veal and calves' feet. Stir two tablespoons of wine vinegar into the liquid and leave it to set slightly in the bowl or in a one-gallon mold.

Mash or flake the ham with a fork. It usually looks like coarse threads. Before the jelly sets, stir in the shredded ham and plenty of chopped parsley, about three-quarters of a cup at least. Pour over the ham in its bowl or mold. Stir to mix evenly. Refrigerate overnight to set.

To serve, turn out onto a large dish. Garnish with clumps of crisp, curly parsley. Serve with baked potatoes in their jackets. *A*

Veal

Veal

Veal is the meat of a calf that has known no food other than milk from its mother. No sooner does solid food become part of its diet than it ceases to be milk-fed veal. This accounts for its high cost which, in turn, makes it a luxury. As a luxury meat, veal should be treated with respect, and, because of its delicacy, as few ingredients as possible should be added to it while cooking. Salt, pepper, and lemon juice enhance the flavor and, in my opinion, are all that is needed.

Stewing veal, meat from an older calf that has indulged in grass or grain, is another matter. It is rosy pink, suitable for casserole-type dishes, and is in no way spoiled by the addition of herbs, spices, and aromatic vegetables. Do not, no matter how glib your butcher, allow him to palm it off as milk-fed veal.

SALTIMBOCCA

6 servings

12 thin slices veal	Butter
Dried sage	½ cup veal or chicken stock
Salt and pepper	½ cup Marsala
6 thin slices smoked or boiled ham	Parsley

Pound the veal slices and dust them with sage, salt, and pepper. Place a slice of ham on top of a slice of veal and cover with another piece of veal, pressing the slices together.

Melt butter in a skillet. Cook the veal until brown on both sides, three to four minutes. Add the stock and cook two or three minutes longer. Transfer the veal to a platter.

Scrape the solids from the pan bottom, add the Marsala and cook over high heat for three or four minutes, or until the liquid is reduced and thickened. Pour over the veal and garnish with parsley.

ESCALOPE DE VEAU MARSALA

6 servings

1½ pounds very thin veal cutlets, or 2 cutlets per serving	½ teaspoon salt
1 clove garlic, cut in half	Freshly ground black pepper
Flour	⅓ cup Marsala wine
¼ cup butter	1 teaspoon lemon juice
½ pound thinly sliced mushrooms	Finely chopped parsley

Pound the veal until very thin. Cut into two-inch pieces. Rub both sides of each piece with the cut garlic and sprinkle lightly with flour.

Heat butter in the skillet. Add the veal a few pieces at a time and brown them lightly on both sides. Keep them warm.

Return all the veal to the skillet and add the mushrooms. Sprinkle with salt, pepper, and the Marsala.

Cook, covered, over low heat for about ten minutes, or until the veal is tender. To serve, sprinkle with lemon juice and parsley.

ESCALOPE DE VEAU SUISSE

4 servings

8 escalopes of veal
Salt and freshly ground pepper
Flour for dredging
2 tablespoons butter

2 tablespoons olive oil
6 tablespoons Marsala wine
8 very thin slices prosciutto
8 thin slices Gruyère or Swiss cheese

Pound the meat lightly with a flat mallet, but without breaking the fibers. Sprinkle the veal slices on both sides with salt and pepper and dredge them all over with a little flour.

Heat the butter and oil in a heavy skillet large enough to hold the meat in one layer, and when it is very hot add the veal. Brown quickly on both sides and transfer the veal escalopes to a hot baking pan large enough to hold the pieces in one layer. Keep them warm.

Add the Marsala to the skillet and cook, stirring, over high heat until the wine becomes syrupy. Spoon this over the escalopes.

Top each piece of veal with one slice of prosciutto and one slice of cheese and run the escalopes quickly under the broiler until the cheese melts. Serve immediately.

VEAL ESCALOPES WITH MUSTARD SAUCE

3 to 4 servings

8 veal escalopes, about ¾ pound
⅓ cup flour
Salt and freshly ground pepper
4 tablespoons butter
2 tablespoons finely minced shallots

¼ cup dry white wine
½ cup heavy cream
1 tablespoon imported mustard, Dijon or
    Dusseldorf

Place the veal escalopes on a flat surface and pound them thin with a flat mallet.

Blend the flour with salt and pepper and dredge the escalopes on all sides.

Heat the butter in a large, heavy skillet until it is quite hot but not brown. Add the veal escalopes (they will shrink as they cook). Cook quickly until golden, about two minutes on one side. Turn and cook the other side.

Add the shallots to the skillet and cook them briefly, stirring. Add the wine and cook, stirring, until it has almost totally evaporated. Add the cream and, while stirring, let it come to a boil. Cook for about thirty seconds and turn off the heat. Stir in the mustard. Do not cook further.

Spoon the sauce over the escalopes. Serve with fine buttered noodles.

VEAL CORDON BLEU

2 small slices veal per serving
Salt and pepper
2 thin slices prosciutto per serving
1 thin slice Gruyère cheese per serving
Flour for dusting
1 egg, beaten

White bread crumbs
Butter
Dry vermouth
Heavy cream
Finely chopped parsley

Pound the veal slices until thin. Season them lightly with salt and pepper. Make a sandwich of the veal, prosciutto, and cheese in the following order: veal, prosciutto, cheese, prosciutto, veal. Season lightly with salt and pepper between the slices.

Press them together firmly, then dust lightly with flour. Dip in beaten egg and then in bread crumbs. Refrigerate until needed. The Cordon Bleu may be frozen at this stage.

Melt butter in a heavy skillet, only enough to cover the bottom of the pan generously, and heat until foaming. Too much butter will "stew" rather than brown the veal. Cook the veal for four to five minutes on each side until healthily browned.

Lift the veal onto a baking sheet and keep the pieces warm in a low oven while deglazing the pan with three to four tablespoons vermouth. Scrape the pan bottom with a wooden spoon to loosen the brown crust. Stir in two to three tablespoons of cream and cook over high heat for a minute or two.

Add the veal and heat thoroughly. Serve with the sauce spooned over the Cordon Bleu. Garnish with finely chopped parsley. This is a suitable dish for cooking at the table in a chafing dish.

FRENCH CANADIAN VEAL

6 to 8 servings

This is an unusual way to cook the veal loin. Canadian bacon—it can be bought already sliced— together with the cheese, produces a wonderful flavor. Because the veal is cooked covered, braised, it is moist all the way through.

3 tablespoons butter
1 three-pound loin of veal, boned, rolled, and tied securely to hold its shape
1 tablespoon salt
4 to 5 twists of the pepper mill
2 carrots, chopped
1 onion, chopped

8 fresh tarragon leaves or 1 teaspoon dried tarragon
¾ cup parsley sprigs
¾ cup chicken stock
6 slices Canadian back bacon
¾ cup heavy cream
1 cup Gruyère cheese, grated

Heat oven to 325°F.

Melt butter in a casserole. Brown the veal on all sides and season it with salt and pepper. Add the chopped carrots and onion, the tarragon, parsley, and stock.

On top of the range, bring the casserole ingredients to a boil, then transfer it to the oven and cook for one and one-half hours, covered. Allow to cool.

Remove the veal, undo the strings, and cut the roast into one-quarter-inch slices, but not through to the base. Insert the bacon between alternate slices of veal and retie the roast.

Place it in the casserole, covered, and cook on top of the range for twenty minutes, adding water if necessary. Spoon the sauce from the casserole over the meat. Pour the cream over the roast, sprinkle grated cheese on the top, and slide the roast under the broiler until brown.

POITRINE DE VEAU FARCIE

8 to 10 servings

Breast of veal is the least expensive part of the animal, one not given the place it deserves. When boned with all the fat removed, it is a perfect cut for stuffing. The flavor is good and when the breast is cooked covered, it is moist and tender. It goes a long way.

Stuffing:

2 shallots, sliced
2 tablespoons butter
1 pound sausage meat

1 tablespoon chopped parsley
Pinch of thyme and marjoram

To make the stuffing, cook the shallots in butter until soft. Add the sausage meat, the parsley, and seasonings. Cook three to four minutes longer.

1 six- to eight-pound breast of veal, boned
2 tablespoons butter
¼ pound bacon, diced
2 carrots, sliced
1 onion, sliced
1½ cups veal stock

Bouquet garni: bay leaf, a few parsley
    stalks, a leaf or two of fresh sage or
    pinch of dried, 4 or 5 peppercorns, all
    tied together in cheesecloth
Salt and pepper to taste
Beurre Manié (see page 274)

Heat oven to 325°F.

Spread the stuffing over the flattened veal breast on the cut side. Roll and tie securely.

Heat butter in a casserole large enough to hold the rolled veal breast. Brown the veal all over. Set the veal aside and cook the bacon in the casserole until brown. Drain off all the fat except two tablespoons.

(Continued)

Add the carrots and onion. Cover the casserole with a lid and cook for five to six minutes.

Return the veal to the casserole, add the stock, the bouquet garni, and seasonings. Cover the casserole and cook for two to two and one half hours, or until tender. Remove the veal to a warm platter.

Strain the pan juices which may be thickened with beurre manié, if you wish, and serve as a sauce.

FRICASSEE OF VEAL

6 to 8 servings

Stock:

2½ to 3 pounds veal bones
1 carrot
1 rib of celery
1 small onion

1 bay leaf
A few peppercorns
Salt
Cold water

Cover the ingredients to a depth of two or three inches with cold water in a large pan and simmer for three to four hours, skimming the scum from the top at the start.

Strain the stock before using it and freeze what you do not need for the fricassee.

1 medium onion, peeled and diced
1 carrot, washed and diced
2 stalks celery, washed and diced
A few parsley stalks
A small piece of bay leaf
8 peppercorns

3 pounds stewing veal, cut into 2-inch
 cubes
6 cups veal stock (use chicken stock,
 homemade or canned, if you wish)
½ cup parsley sprigs, finely chopped

Tie the onion, carrot, celery, parsley stalks, bay leaf, and peppercorns in cheesecloth.

Place the veal in a heavy enamel-lined or stainless-steel pan. Cover with cold water. Bring to a boil and simmer for two minutes.

Drain the veal and wash it under cold running water to remove the scum. This eliminates the tiresome chore of skimming for thirty minutes. Rinse the pan and return the veal to it.

Add the stock, which should cover the meat by about an inch. If it is not enough, make up the difference with water. Add the vegetable-spice bag and a little salt.

(Continued)

Cover and simmer gently about thirty to forty minutes until the veal is almost tender when pierced with a fork.

Turn the veal into a colander set over a bowl. Reserve the cooking liquid. Remove the vegetable-spice bag.

Sauce:

4 teaspoons butter
5 teaspoons flour
3¼ cups liquid that
   veal has been cooked in

Salt and pepper
Lemon juice to taste
3 egg yolks
½ cup heavy cream

Melt butter in a heavy pan. Add the flour and cook over low heat for two or three minutes.

Off the heat, pour in the veal liquid and whisk until smooth. Simmer gently for ten to twelve minutes. Season with salt, pepper, and lemon juice.

Mix the egg yolks and cream in a bowl with a wire whisk. Beat one-half cup of the hot sauce into the cream mixture. Then pour the cream mixture back into the remaining sauce.

Place the veal in a clean casserole and pour the sauce over it. Heat very gently to avoid curdling. Sprinkle with finely chopped parsley before serving.

MEDITERRANEAN VEAL RAGOUT WITH OLIVES

12 or more servings

1 breast of veal with bones, approximately
   4½ pounds
1 three-pound boneless shoulder of veal
Salt and freshly ground pepper
1 cup oil
3 cups onion, coarsely chopped (about ¾
   pound)
½ cup flour
3 cloves garlic
6 whole cloves
4 cups dry white wine

2 cups water
1 can (1 pound 12 ounces) tomatoes
1 bay leaf
6 sprigs fresh parsley
2 sprigs fresh thyme or 1 teaspoon dried
   thyme
Salt and pepper to taste
24 stuffed green olives
24 imported pitted black olives (see note
   next page)

Heat oven to 375°F.

Cut, or have the butcher cut, the breast of veal and the boneless shoulder into two-inch cubes. Sprinkle them with salt and pepper.

(Continued)

Heat oil in one or two skillets and brown the meat all over, a few pieces at a time. As the cubes are browned, transfer them to a large casserole. Continue browning the meat until all of it is used.

Sprinkle the meat with the onion and flour and stir until the meat and onions are evenly coated with flour. Add the garlic, cloves, wine, and water.

Drain the tomatoes, reserving separately both juice and tomatoes. Add the juice to the meat and stir. Set the tomatoes aside.

Bring the veal to a boil and add the bay leaf, and the parsley and thyme, tied together in a bundle if fresh sprigs are used. Add salt and pepper to taste.

Bake in the oven, uncovered, for one and one-half hours, stirring occasionally.

Chop the reserved tomatoes and add them. Add the green and black olives and bake, skimming the surface of excess fat, for about thirty minutes longer. Serve with boiled rice.

Note: It is imperative that imported black olives be used in this recipe for the sake of authenticity. Preferably use those cured in liquid brine rather than "oil cured" olives.

BLANQUETTE DE VEAU

6 servings

2 pounds stewing veal	1 quart boiling water
1 large onion, studded with cloves	12 small onions
¼ cup carrots, chopped	5 tablespoons butter
1 bay leaf	¼ pound mushrooms, sliced
1 sprig thyme	¼ cup flour
2 sprigs parsley	2 tablespoons lemon juice
4 peppercorns	2 egg yolks, slightly beaten
2 teaspoons salt	1 tablespoon parsley, chopped

Cut the veal into two-inch pieces. Wipe the meat with a cloth. If veal is not perfection—in other words, too old and red—cover it with cold water, add two tablespoons of salt, and bring it to a boil. Boil for one minute. Drain and rinse the veal under running water.

Tie the onion, carrots, herbs, and peppercorns in a piece of cheesecloth. Add salt to the water and bring it to a boil.

Simmer the veal and herb bag in the salted water for about one hour, or until tender. Drain the veal, reserving the stock; discard the herb bag.

(Continued)

Drop the small onions into a pan of boiling water. After one minute, drain them and remove their skins when they are cool enough to handle. Sauté the onions gently in two tablespoons of butter until golden.

Cook the mushrooms in a double boiler with a little of the veal stock for five minutes, or until tender.

Melt the remaining three tablespoons of butter in a saucepan, stir in the flour, and when well-blended, add three cups of strained stock. Cook over medium heat, stirring constantly, until the mixture thickens and boils.

Add lemon juice to the slightly beaten egg yolks. Stir a little of the warm sauce into the egg mixture, then add it to the remaining sauce in the pan. Add the veal and parsley, and reheat.

Serve on a hot platter with the onions and mushrooms. Rice is the ideal accompaniment.

VEAL MARENGO

6 to 8 servings

3 tablespoons oil
3 pounds boned shoulder of veal, cut into
  2-inch cubes
1 medium onion
½ cup tomato purée
1 tablespoon potato flour
2 cups veal or beef stock
1 cup dry white wine
1 clove garlic, crushed with 1 teaspoon salt

2 bay leaves
1 teaspoon dried thyme
Salt and pepper to taste
12 small white onions
¼ pound mushrooms
3 tomatoes
Black pitted olives
Parsley, finely chopped

Heat oven to 350°F.

Heat the oil in a heavy casserole with a cover. Add the pieces of veal, and cook, uncovered, over medium heat for four to five minutes.

Peel and chop the medium onion, add it to the meat, and cook for three minutes.

Stir in the tomato purée and potato flour and mix thoroughly. Gradually pour in the stock and white wine. Add the garlic, bay leaves, thyme, salt, and pepper.

Cover the casserole, and transfer it to the oven for fifteen minutes.

(Continued)

Peel the small onions. (To do this easily, put them in boiling water for two minutes first.) Cook the onions until tender in enough reserved stock to cover, and add them to the casserole.

Wipe the mushrooms clean with a damp cloth and slice. Peel the tomatoes and cut them into quarters. Add the mushrooms and tomatoes to the casserole and cook, covered, for another thirty minutes, or until the veal is tender. The cooking time will depend upon the quality of the veal.

Just before serving, add the olives, and sprinkle the surface of the casserole with parsley.

OSSO BUCO

6 to 8 servings

Osso Buco is as Italian as Chianti and a wonderful way to use the shank or knuckle of veal. With the addition of pasta or potatoes it is a one-dish course. Serve a salad later.

6 to 8 veal shanks, 2½ to 3 inches thick
Flour
Clarified butter (see page 345)
1 can (1 pound) whole tomatoes, drained
1 small clove garlic, crushed
Salt and pepper
White wine

Veal or chicken stock
Gremolata: chop together 1 handful parsley sprigs; 1 small clove garlic, peeled and sliced; rind of 1 lemon, peeled and sliced; 1 teaspoon coarse salt

Heat oven to 350°F.

Dust the shanks with flour and brown them on all sides in clarified butter. In a casserole with a lid stand the shanks on their bones so that the marrow will not fall out. Choose a casserole that will hold them with no room to spare.

Chop the tomatoes coarsely and add them to the casserole along with the crushed garlic. Sprinkle with one tablespoon of salt and four or five twists of the pepper mill.

Add enough wine and stock—using three parts wine to one part stock—sufficient to reach two-thirds of the way up the shanks. Cover and cook in the oven for one and one-half hours. The meat should be ready to fall off the bone.

If you like the sauce a little thicker, remove the shanks to a warm serving dish and keep them hot while you reduce the liquid in the pan. Pour the sauce over the shanks and sprinkle with gremolata.

STUFFED SHOULDER OF VEAL

8 to 10 servings

1 shoulder of veal, boned

Stuffing:

1 cup fresh bread crumbs
2 or 3 mushrooms, chopped
2 tablespoons parsley
1 tablespoon fresh rosemary
¼ cup chopped onion

2 teaspoons salt
¼ teaspoon pepper
3 tablespoons melted butter
Salt and pepper for dusting
1 cup chicken or veal stock

Heat oven to 375°F.

Place the bread crumbs in a bowl. Add the mushrooms and all the remaining ingredients, except the stock.

Spread the stuffing over the fleshy side of the veal, roll the roast loosely, and tie it with string. Dust the shoulder with additional salt and pepper. Place it in a roasting pan and bake for one and one-half hours, basting occasionally.

Remove the roast from the pan. Pour off all but two tablespoons of the fat and scrape the bottom of the pan. Add the stock and cook the liquid at high heat until thickened. Cut the roast in thin slices and serve the sauce separately.

Variety Meats

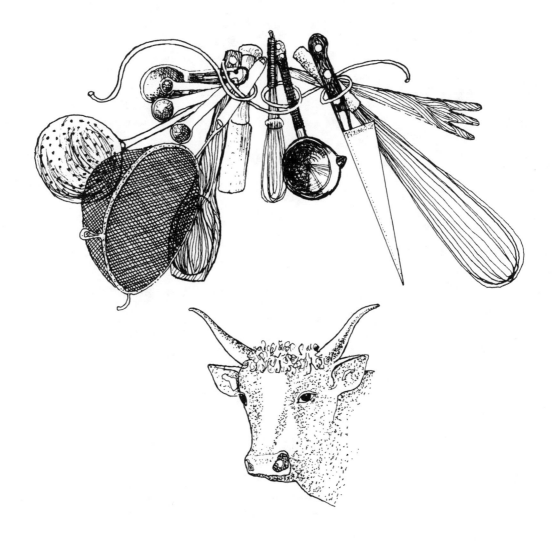

Variety Meats

Shakespeare used the word "offal" when he said, "What is Rome? What rubbish and what offal."

Variety meats have been classed as waste—not worth using—in America, and I imagine the reason is the abundance of meats of all kinds. There has been no need to make use of what is left over after the butchering has been completed. When I first came to live here, my butcher gave me kidneys for the asking. I could scarcely believe my good fortune.

At long last, America is overcoming this prejudice and actually appreciating the variety meats it has been overlooking for years.

All edible parts of an animal after dressing come under the heading of variety meats: entrails, heart, liver, kidneys, sweetbreads, tripe, and the small intestine of the pig called chitterlings. In Europe offal, the medieval name, is still used.

SMOKED TONGUE

Smoked tongue is low in calories and delicious. For those who are squeamish about the odds and ends of animals such as tongue, brains, sweetbreads, liver, and kidneys, start with a slice or two of tongue. I can assure you, you will like it so much that you won't care what part of the animal it came from. It is delightful cold with a tossed salad or julienned and mixed with other ingredients for a Salade du Chef.

2 ribs of celery, chopped
2 carrots, chopped
1 bay leaf
8 peppercorns

3 tablespoons salt
1 smoked tongue, approximately
   5 to 6 pounds
Sauce Cumberland (see page 285)

Put the chopped vegetables, herbs, and seasonings in a large pot. Lay the tongue on top of the vegetables and add sufficient cold water to cover.

Bring to the boil. Reduce the heat, and simmer, covered, for two and one-half to three hours. Turn off the heat and leave the tongue in the stock until you are ready to skin and dress it.

To serve, remove the tongue from the stock. Reserve the stock. Skin the tongue; it will come off easily. Remove the bone, cartilage, and fat from the thick end. Carve the tongue horizontally from the thin end.

Reheat the slices in a little of the reserved stock. Serve with Sauce Cumberland. *A*

RIS DE VEAU ESPAGNOLE

6 to 8 servings

Sweetbreads, like liver, kidneys, and brains, are not recommended for those who suffer from arthritic and allied complaints. I am not free from arthritic or rheumatic afflictions; nevertheless, I cannot resist sweetbreads braised with a Sauce Madeira and served with rice. It is so good that I'm quite prepared to put up with a twinge of pain once in a while.

3 pairs sweetbreads, approximately
   5½ pounds
¼ pound white mushrooms

Clarified butter (see page 345)
Sauce Madeira (see page 276)
2 tablespoons finely chopped parsley

Heat oven to 375°F.

Soak the sweetbreads in cold water with two tablespoons of salt for three to four hours. Drain.

In a heavy pan, cover the sweetbreads again with cold water containing two tablespoons of salt and bring to a boil. Boil for one minute, drain, and run under cold water.

Remove the membranes, sinews, and veins. Compress the sweetbreads under weights—between two chopping boards or two plates with a heavy pan on top—for one hour. If the sweetbreads are large, cut them in half lengthwise and then in half again.

Slice the mushrooms. Heat a little clarified butter in a heavy skillet and brown the sweetbread slices. Add more butter, as needed.

In an oven-proof casserole with a lid, combine the mushrooms, Sauce Madeira, and sweetbreads. (This dish may be prepared ahead of time to this point. Refrigerate until needed.) Bring the casserole ingredients to a boil on top of the range, then transfer to the preheated oven and cook for ten to fifteen minutes. Sprinkle with finely chopped parsley and serve with plain boiled rice.

A

KIDNEYS, BACON, AND BROWN RICE

Kidneys, or any other offal, euphemistically called "variety meats," are very much an acquired taste. But once it has been acquired, there is no shedding it. The kidney—whether it be lamb or veal—needs little cooking time, but requires care in preparation. The outer filament or skin should be removed and the inner fat core cut out. Kidneys should not be washed, and definitely not overcooked; there should be a trace of inner pinkness. Overcooking toughens them and the kidneys then resemble small leather buttons. If you feel like putting a new restaurant to the test, order kidneys. If they are leather-like, don't honor the establishment again with your patronage.

Allow 2 to 3 kidneys per serving
Unsalted butter
Flour for dusting
Brown rice, cooked (½ cup per serving)
Grilled bacon (see page 345)

½ cup chicken, veal, or beef stock (may be made from bouillon cubes)
¼ cup dry white wine
Salt and pepper to taste
1 bunch watercress

Skin the kidneys, cut them in half, and cut out the fatty core. Heat enough butter to coat a heavy skillet generously.

Dust the kidneys lightly with flour and cook over moderate to high heat for two to three minutes on each side.

Pile cooked rice in the middle of a warm serving dish. Arrange the kidneys on top and grilled bacon around the sides.

Raise the heat under the skillet; add the stock and white wine. Cook, while scraping, until the pan liquid is about as thick as heavy cream. Correct the seasoning and strain the liquid over the kidneys. Garnish the dish with watercress.

CALVES LIVER AND BACON

8 servings

The liver of the calf is less nutritious than that of other animals, but I prefer its delicacy, color, and texture. Served with grilled bacon, and perhaps sautéed onions and a purée of potatoes, it is one of my favorite quick supper dishes.

Unsalted butter
2 pounds calves liver, outer skin removed
   and sliced ¾-inch thick
Flour for dusting
Salt and pepper

½ cup chicken stock, or stock made from
   a bouillon cube
¼ cup Madeira
Lemon wedges
Grilled bacon (see page 345)

Heat sufficient butter to coat the bottom of a heavy skillet. Dust the liver slices lightly with flour and brown them quickly over medium-high heat, about one minute on each side.

Transfer to a heated serving dish. Sprinkle the liver lightly with salt and pepper.

Add the stock and Madeira to the pan, raise the heat, and scrape with a wooden spoon to loosen the browned bits on the pan bottom.

Cook, stirring, until reduced to the thickness of heavy cream. Season to taste with salt and pepper. Pour the sauce through a fine strainer over the liver. Serve wth lemon wedges and grilled bacon.

OXTAIL AND WHITE GRAPES

4 to 6 servings

After World War II in London, when almost everything was rationed, I managed quite frequently to acquire oxtails. It was the perfect, satisfying dish to serve on cold, dark winter days when there wasn't all that much around to brighten our lives except gratitude—and oxtails.

4 ounces fat bacon, diced
2 medium onions, coarsely chopped
2 carrots, scraped and sliced
3 pounds white seedless grapes,
   approximately
2 oxtails, disjointed (ask the butcher
   to do this for you)

Bouquet garni: 2 cloves garlic, peeled and
   crushed; 2 bay leaves; 6 to 7 parsley
   stalks; ½ teaspoon allspice; all tied
   together in cheesecloth
Salt and pepper
Finely chopped parsley

Heat oven to 325°F.

Spread the diced bacon on the bottom of a heavy pan with a lid. Add the chopped onions and carrots. Cook slowly, covered, for about ten minutes.

Crush the grapes and mix them with the oxtails and cooked vegetables in the casserole. Add the bouquet garni.

Cover the casserole first with a double thickness of wax paper and then the lid. Bring the casserole to a boil on top of the range. Transfer it to the oven and cook for three to three and one-half hours.

Place the oxtails in a serving casserole. Force all the other ingredients through a sieve and chill the liquid so that the fat can be removed. Pour the sauce over the oxtails and reheat the casserole.

Correct the seasoning and sprinkle with the chopped parsley. Serve with plain steamed or puréed potatoes.

PIGS' FEET

4 to 6 servings

Pigs' feet, commonly known as trotters, are much appreciated in Europe but rarely seen in the United States. What a loss! I feel quite certain that if the trotters were served under another name and their shape disguised, they would appear on the table of the most fastidious diner. Sometimes the slang used by the youth of today is more effective than the formal tongue; so, in this case, "Don't knock it, if you haven't tried it."

The trotters must first of all be cooked in an aromatic liquid for at least six hours, no matter how you plan to serve them later. If you have time, let them steep in a strong solution of salt water for twelve hours or so.

6 pigs' feet
3 carrots, peeled and sliced
3 medium onions stuck with 2 cloves each
1 large leek washed and cut in two
    (optional)
3 ribs celery, washed and sliced

1 small bunch of parsley
1 bay leaf
¾ cup white wine
¼ cup white wine vinegar
8 peppercorns
Sauce (see next page)

Singe the pigs' feet over an open flame and scrape clean. Rinse them well.

Tie them firmly with cheesecloth to a small wire roasting rack, one that will fit into a large pot. Some cooks tie them to wood slats, one on either side, but I prefer metal. Whether wire or wood, the rack will hold the trotters' shape while cooking. The pigs' feet will look more presentable, and be easier to handle.

(Continued)

Fit the rack of pigs' feet into a large pot; add all the other ingredients and cover with cold water. Bring to a boil and cover tightly. Simmer gently for six to eight hours. When cool enough to handle, untie the pigs' feet.

Sauce:

Vinaigrette Sauce (see page 290)
1 teaspoon prepared Dijon mustard
1 additional tablespoon olive oil
3 to 4 twists of the pepper mill

Finely chopped parsley
1 clove garlic, crushed to a smooth paste
2 tablespoons green onions, chopped

Prepare one mixing of Vinaigrette Sauce. Add all the other ingredients. Mix well. Serve the pigs' feet on a bed of potato purée and pass the sauce.

Odds and Ends

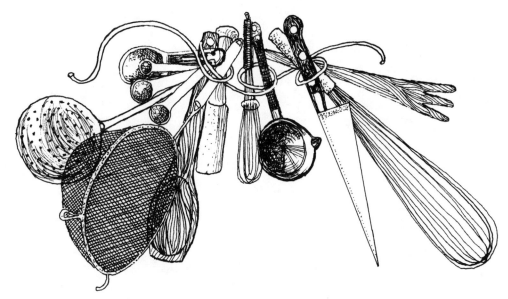

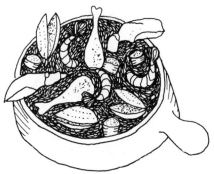

Odds and Ends

There are times when recipes I dearly love are "neither fish, fowl, nor good red herring." Rarely are they sufficient in number to warrant a chapter of their own. The only solution is to lump them together under the heading Odds and Ends. When I am undecided about what to serve—something simple, and anything but run-of-the-mill—I turn to Odds and Ends and usually I find the answer.

TOMATO TART

Makes 2 tarts

Tomato Tart is best made in the early autumn when tomatoes are plentiful and almost overripe. I have had no success with the commercially grown fruit that is trucked across the continent; it has little color and less flavor. The tart makes a very good luncheon or supper dish.

3 pounds ripe tomatoes
4 tablespoons olive oil
1 medium onion, peeled and chopped
3 or 4 sprigs of fresh basil, chopped

Salt and pepper to taste
2 All-Purpose Pastry shells,
 (see page 300)

Drop the tomatoes into boiling water; count to ten, then lift them out. Cool and peel. Remove the seeds; chop and drain the pulp in a colander.

Heat the oil in a heavy skillet. Add the onion and cook slowly, taking care it does not burn. It should be golden and soft.

Add the tomatoes and cook slowly for an hour or so, stirring from time to time, until almost all moisture has evaporated. Stir in chopped basil and season well with salt and pepper.

Filling:

8 to 10 tomatoes, not more than an inch
 and one-half in diameter
1 pound ricotta cheese, sliced thin and cut
 in 2-inch squares

2 cherry tomatoes
Butter for brushing
Salt and pepper

Spread the cooked tomato mixture over the bottom of the pastry shells. Slip the whole tomatoes into boiling water and count to ten. Remove with a slotted spoon and skin them. Slice vertically in one-quarter-inch slices.

Arrange the tomato slices and cheese slices alternately in rings on tomato base. Fill in the gap that will be left in the center of each tart with some end slices of cheese and a small cherry tomato. Brush with melted butter and dust lightly with salt and pepper.

Broil for about five minutes, or until cheese bubbles lightly and takes on a light tan. Serve hot or at room temperature.

A

GREEN RICE

Prepare the rice according to package directions. For each cup of cooked rice, mix in one tablespoon of finely chopped parsley.

CD

RICE AND MUSHROOMS

5 to 6 servings

3 tablespoons butter
2½ cups hot cooked rice (¾ cup
    uncooked, approximately)
½ pound fresh mushrooms

½ cup parsley sprigs, chopped
2 tablespoons lemon juice
Freshly ground black pepper
Coarse salt

Stir butter into the rice while still hot. Wipe the mushrooms clean with a damp cloth. Cut off the stems flush with the caps and discard. Dice the mushroom caps.

Stir the mushrooms, parsley, and lemon juice into rice. Season to taste with freshly ground black pepper and coarse salt. This dish goes well with escalopes of veal or chicken in any form. *C*

PILAF WITH RAISINS AND PISTACHIOS

5 to 6 servings

Like shashlik, pilaf is designed to be cooked over an open fire. Cooking is begun over very high heat, then the pilaf bakes more slowly as the fire dies down.

3 tablespoons oil
1 cup rice, uncooked
2 to 2½ cups chicken stock
Salt and pepper to taste

½ cup raisins
½ cup shelled pistachio nuts
3 to 4 scallions, sliced

Heat oven to 350° F.

In a casserole, heat the oil and fry the rice gently until the grains are transparent. Pour in two cups of stock, bring to a boil, cover, then bake in the oven for fifteen minutes.

Stir in the salt and pepper, raisins, pistachios, and scallions. Add a little more stock if the rice seems dry. Cover and continue baking the pilaf for five to seven minutes, or until all the liquid is absorbed and the rice is tender. Let stand ten minutes before removing the cover and stirring the rice. *C*

PAELLA

6 to 8 servings

1 two- to two-and-one-half-pound
  chicken, cut in 16 pieces
18 shrimp
3 medium tomatoes
24 green beans
4 ounces salt pork
2 chorizo sausages
1 small green pepper

4 to 6 tablespoons olive oil
Salt and freshly ground black pepper
2 teaspoons paprika
5 cups hot water
½ teaspoon saffron
2 cups rice, uncooked
½ cup frozen green peas, thawed

Cut the legs from the chicken and separate the thigh from the drumstick. Cut off the wings by slicing along the breast from back to neck, removing some of the breast with the knife. Divide the breast in two along the bone. With a cleaver, cut each piece in half again.

Shell, wash, and devein the shrimp.

Bring a small pan of water to a boil and drop the tomatoes in one at a time for ten seconds. Lift them out with a slotted spoon. Remove the stem end with a small knife and peel. Cut each tomato in quarters and chop coarsely.

Remove both ends of the beans and cut them into one-inch pieces. Cut the salt pork into one-inch cubes and the sausages into one-half-inch slices.

Slice the pepper in half; remove the white pith and all the seeds. Cut the pepper first into strips and then into one-inch pieces.

Heat four tablespoons of olive oil in a large pan over moderate heat. Dust the chicken pieces with salt and freshly ground black pepper. Cook them gently in the oil for about twelve minutes until they are golden brown. Remove the chicken and set aside on a plate.

In the same oil, fry the diced salt pork for three minutes, then add the chopped tomato. Stir in the paprika and cook a minute or two longer. Add five cups of hot water. Return the chicken pieces to the pan and simmer for ten minutes.

Remove one-quarter cup of the hot liquid and soak the saffron in it for about fifteen minutes.

Add the rice, shrimp, sausage, green beans, and green pepper to the pan; stir with a fork and cook gently, but steadily, for fifteen minutes.

Strain the saffron liquid and add it to the pan. Stir briefly and cook six to seven minutes longer. By then the rice should be cooked. Do not stir during this time. If the water has evaporated, add a little more. If there is too much water, just before the rice is finished, increase the heat and cook quickly until the rice is finally dry.

Before serving, stir in the thawed peas and correct the seasoning with salt and pepper.

C

CHOU FARCI

6 to 8 servings

Stuffed cabbage is not exactly haute cuisine to the so-called gourmet, but, believe me, it is a wonderful creation in more ways than one. It is reasonably economical, nutritious, and good for the "waist-watcher."

2 tablespoons butter
2 carrots, sliced
1 medium yellow onion, chopped
1 bay leaf
Pinch of thyme

1 can (1 pound) Italian plum tomatoes, drained
1 cup beef stock
1 large curly Savoy cabbage

Heat oven to 350°F.

Melt two tablespoons of butter in a pan large enough to hold the cabbage. Add the two sliced carrots, chopped onion, bay leaf, thyme, tomatoes, and stock (do not add the cabbage yet). Simmer together for a few minutes.

Filling:

1 pound chopped veal
¾ pound chopped pork
5 shallots, chopped
2 cloves garlic, minced

4 parsley sprigs, finely chopped
1 tablespoon salt
½ teaspoon ground pepper
½ cup white bread crumbs

To make the filling, thoroughly mix together all the above ingredients.

Blanch the cabbage by placing it in boiling salted water. Lift the cabbage out and drain upside down in a colander. When cool enough to handle, turn right-side up. Open the leaves gently, and, following their pattern, carefully place the stuffing between the leaves. Re-form to resemble the original shape.

Spread a piece of double cheesecloth (about four inches larger than the cabbage) around the cabbage and tie securely at the top with a string. Place the cabbage on the vegetable sauce in the pan, cover, and cook in the oven for approximately one hour.

Lift out the cabbage carefully and hold it over the dish in which it is to be served. Cut the cheesecloth from the bottom and allow the cabbage to drop gently onto the serving dish.

Strain the liquid into a bowl standing in ice. Remove the fat. Reheat, and boil to reduce the liquid. Correct the seasoning, if necessary. Spoon a little over the cabbage and serve the remainder in a warmed sauceboat.

FRIED PARSLEY

Select parsley sprigs that are large, fresh, and crisp. Wash and dry them thoroughly. The slightest drop of moisture causes alarming spattering.

Heat vegetable oil to 375° or 380° F. Drop the sprigs in by the handful and lift out almost immediately with a slotted skimmer. Drain them on paper towels.

ENDIVES MORNAY

6 servings

6 Belgian endives
4 cups chicken stock
2 cups Mornay Sauce (see page 276)

6 thin slices smoked ham
Finely chopped parsley

Heat oven to 350°F.

Blanch the endives in chicken stock for four minutes. Let the endives cool. Then cut out the bitter core from the bottom in a V-shape. Squeeze out the excess moisture from the endives.

Roll each endive up in a slice of ham. Lay in a buttered casserole seam-side down, and cover with the Mornay Sauce.

Bake for about twenty-five minutes, or until golden brown on top. Sprinkle parsley over the top before serving.

CURRIED VEGETABLES

This is one of my favorite vegetarian dishes. Once you have made the Curry Sauce—it freezes—do not be tied to the vegetables listed below. Use the best of what is available.

4 medium carrots
3 stalks celery
4 small zucchini
½ small cauliflower
¼ pound green beans

Curry Sauce (see page 287)
1 teaspoon fresh lime juice
1½ cups cooked rice
1 cup parsley sprigs, chopped

Wash the vegetables under cold running water. Scrape the carrots and cut them into one-inch pieces on the bias. Scrape the celery with a vegetable peeler to remove the coarse fibers. Cut into pieces to match the carrots.

Remove the ends from the zucchini and cut into quarter-inch rounds. Divide the cauliflower into small buds. Cut the ends off the green beans.

Bring one quart of water to a boil to which one tablespoon of salt has been added. Cook the vegetables and drain them, with the exception of the zucchini, in this order: the beans for four to five minutes, depending on their age; the carrots for four to five minutes; the celery for three to four minutes; and the cauliflower for four to five minutes. Test each vegetable while cooking; they should be crisp.

Simmer the zucchini in the Curry Sauce for three to four minutes. Add the other vegetables and heat thoroughly for six to seven minutes. Stir in the lime juice.

Pile the curried vegetables in the middle of a serving dish with rice at either end. Sprinkle with chopped parsley.

A

SPINACH CASSEROLE

6 to 8 servings

6 packages (10 ounces each) frozen
  chopped spinach
6 tablespoons butter
1 cup finely chopped onion
2 cups sour cream

Freshly ground nutmeg
Salt and freshly ground black pepper
½ cup bread crumbs
2 tablespoons grated Parmesan cheese

Heat oven to 350°F.

Defrost the spinach and drain thoroughly.

Melt four tablespoons of the butter in a skillet; add the chopped onion and sauté gently until transparent.

Purée the spinach with a little of the sour cream in a blender, or force it through a sieve or strainer. Add the onion and the butter in which it has been sautéed, and continue to purée, using more of the sour cream as it is needed.

Scrape the puréed spinach into a bowl, and stir in the remaining sour cream. Season with grated nutmeg, salt, and pepper.

Melt the remaining two tablespoons of butter in the skillet and stir in the bread crumbs, coating thoroughly.

Spoon the spinach mixture into a two-quart oven-proof, buttered dish. Sprinkle the top with buttered bread crumbs and then with the grated Parmesan cheese. Bake for thirty minutes, or until hot.

AC

CASSEROLE OF VEGETABLES

6 servings

3 medium carrots
4 ribs celery
1 pound fresh green beans
½ pound small mushrooms
12 small white onions, peeled
½ cup parsley sprigs, chopped

1 tablespoon butter
1½ cups Béchamel Sauce, lightly seasoned
with celery salt, white pepper, and
nutmeg (see page 275)
¼ cup grated Parmesan cheese

Heat oven to 325°F.

Scrape the carrots and cut on the bias into slices one-quarter inch thick. Remove the fibers from the celery with a vegetable scraper and cut into slices one-quarter inch thick on the bias. Remove the ends from the green beans and cut them in half. Wipe the mushrooms clean with a damp cloth and remove the stems.

Cook the beans in boiling salted water for three to four minutes. They must be crisp. Remove with a slotted spoon to a bowl.

Cook the carrots and celery together in the bean water for no more than two minutes. Add them to the beans. Cook the onions in the same water for three to four minutes.

Mix together all the vegetables with the mushrooms and half the parsley. Butter a casserole or oven-proof dish and fill with the vegetables.

Pour Béchamel Sauce on top of the vegetables; sprinkle with Parmesan cheese, and bake in the middle of the oven for twenty minutes, until lightly browned and bubbling. Sprinkle with the remaining parsley and serve hot.

A

CHEESE CASSEROLE

6 to 8 servings

I am told that this Cheese Casserole is a mock soufflé and much appreciated at ladies' luncheons. I can see no reason why it should be reserved for the fair sex alone.

4 tablespoons butter, melted
8 thin slices white bread, crusts removed
1½ cups grated cheese, Parmesan or
Romano

3 eggs
1 teaspoon salt
½ teaspoon dry mustard
2 cups milk

Butter the bread on one side. Place a layer of bread on the bottom of a one-quart oven-proof or soufflé dish, buttered-side down, and cut to fit the dish. Sprinkle with cheese. Add a layer of bread, buttered-side up.

Beat the eggs, salt, and mustard together. Add the milk and beat again. Pour over the bread. The top slices will float. Place the dish overnight in the refrigerator. Remove from the refrigerator an hour before baking.

Heat oven to 375°F.

Bake thirty-five to forty minutes and serve immediately.   C

WELSH RAREBIT

2 servings

4 ounces sharp Cheddar cheese, grated
6 tablespoons beer (milk may be
  substituted)
2 to 3 teaspoons English prepared
  mustard, fiercely hot

2 tablespoons unsalted butter
Salt
Freshly ground pepper
2 slices bread, toasted

Place the cheese and beer or milk in a small, heavy pan over low heat. Allow the cheese to melt slowly, stirring from time to time. It will look like thick cream. Add the mustard, the butter, salt, and pepper to taste. Reheat until very hot.

Place the toast slices on a heat-proof serving plate and pour the cheese mixture over them. Run under the broiler until the cheese bubbles and browns lightly. The cheese will spread and run over the toast. Serve right away with a good red wine or beer.

GEORGE SIMPSON'S LUNCHEON DISH

6 servings

My friendship with George Simpson goes back to World War II. He entertained royally, and royalty, when no one else seemed capable of doing so. The food was not "black market," and yet one never felt that rationing was still in existence. A lot of thought and planning went into the menus, and the hospitality was generous. This was one of his favorite luncheon dishes.

2 pounds onions
12 hard-boiled eggs

4 tablespoons butter
¼ cup grated Parmesan cheese

(Continued)

Peel and cut the onions in half. Slice. Sauté the onion slices in butter until golden. Slice the eggs.

Sauce:

6 tablespoons butter
4 tablespoons flour
4 cups milk

Salt, pepper, and nutmeg or curry
   powder

Heat the butter in a heavy pan. Add the flour; cook for three to four minutes over low heat, taking care it does not take on color.

Heat the milk; off the heat pour it on the *roux*, stirring until smooth. Add the salt, pepper, and nutmeg or curry powder to taste. Return to the heat and cook until thickened.

Butter an oven-proof dish and arrange an even layer of onion, followed by a layer of hard-boiled eggs and one of sauce. Continue alternating the layers, ending with the sauce. Sprinkle with grated cheese. Bake for thirty minutes until browned and bubbling.   *A*

Vegetables

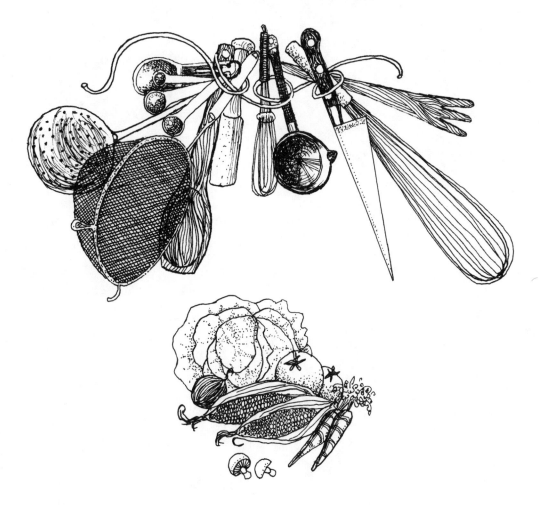

Vegetables

At long last vegetables are taking their rightful place in our diet. Gone, even in English boarding houses, are the days when a garden-fresh vegetable—England produces some of the best vegetables in the world—was cooked to an unrecognizable pulp and cabbage, when served, closely resembled a mound of damp green tissue paper.

Many European countries make greater use of the vegetable than we do. A dish of very small, very fresh peas, carrots, or beans served separately or together as a first course is a common occurrence. In the British Isles and America the artichoke and asparagus have been the only members of the vegetable family to be given that place of honor on the menu.

Undercooking and steaming are methods now widely used, and what a difference they make to the finished dish. There are few vegetables that when handled with loving care, and suitably seasoned, do not provide us with a delightful beginning to any meal or can become a luncheon or supper dish.

BRAISED ENDIVE

1 head endive per serving, or
  2 if they are small
Butter

½ cup chicken stock
Juice of 1 lemon
Salt and pepper

Heat oven to 325°F.

Remove any damaged outer leaves. Parboil endive head for one minute in boiling salted water. Drain. When endive is cool enough to handle, squeeze out the surplus water. Cut out a triangle of the thick stalk.

Butter a shallow glass, porcelain, or earthenware dish with a cover. Arrange the endive in the dish, slightly overlapping, if necessary.

Pour chicken stock over the endive, sprinkle with lemon juice, and dot with small pieces of butter. Dust lightly with salt and pepper. Cover. If the lid does not fit securely, cover first with wax paper and foil, then the lid.

Bring to a boil on top of the range. Transfer to the middle of the oven and cook for an hour and a half until the endive is tender and the liquid is almost the consistency of syrup. *AC*

BRAISED LETTUCE

6 to 8 servings

Braised Lettuce is one of the vegetables equally good served as a separate course or as a side dish with main courses, such as roast lamb or loin of veal. Choose very firm and mature heads rather than those with delicate leaves.

4 heads Boston lettuce
2 carrots
2 stalks celery
3 leeks

4 tablespoons butter
½ cup chicken stock
Salt and pepper
2 tablespoons chopped parsley

Heat oven to 350°F.

Remove the outer leaves from the lettuce. Rinse the heads under cold running water and plunge them whole into boiling water for two to three minutes.

Remove and drop them into a bowl of ice water. Drain thoroughly and squeeze gently to remove excess water. Cut each head in half lengthwise, starting from the stem end. Fold each half to resemble a closed fist.

Peel the carrots and cut them into one-and-one-half-inch pieces; slice each piece into thin strips lengthwise. Cut the celery into one-and-one-half-inch pieces and slice like the carrots. Cut the leek into one-and-one-half-inch pieces, then in half lengthwise, and slice thinly lengthwise.

Melt the butter in a frying pan and sauté the vegetables for five minutes without browning.

Butter an oven-proof dish. Cover the bottom of the dish with the vegetables, then place each piece of lettuce, folded-side down on the vegetables, tucking in the edges to make neat bundles.

Pour in the stock, season with a little salt and pepper; cover with foil.

Cook in oven for forty to forty-five minutes. Sprinkle with chopped parsley and serve hot.

A

BRAISED CELERY

Braised Celery is not one of the most economical vegetables. Half a head, or four ribs per person, is the usual serving. It is the perfect vegetable to serve with the Thanksgiving or Christmas turkey, and it can be prepared ahead of time.

½ celery heart per serving or 4 celery
   stalks
Softened butter
Salt and pepper

¼ cup chicken stock
Juice of 1 lemon
Finely chopped parsley

Heat oven to 350°F.

Prepare the celery hearts by scraping the outside with a vegetable peeler. If celery stalks are used, treat in the same way, but cut them into two-inch pieces on the bias.

Boil the celery in plenty of boiling salted water for twenty minutes. Lift out the celery and drain.

Butter an oven-proof dish with a cover. Arrange the hearts or stalks in the dish; dot with butter, and season lightly with salt and pepper. Pour in one-quarter cup of chicken stock.

Cover and cook in the oven for thirty minutes. Before serving, sprinkle with the juice of one lemon and finely chopped parsley.

ACD

CHOU CHINOIS

4 to 6 servings

1 small head cabbage
2 tablespoons butter
2 tablespoons oil
1 clove garlic

2 teaspoons salt
½ teaspoon caraway seeds
2 tablespoons fresh lemon juice

Cut the cabbage in half and remove the core. Wash and shred the cabbage very finely.

In a heavy pan, melt the two tablespoons of butter with the oil. Add the crushed garlic clove and the salt. Heat until very hot, but do not allow to brown.

Add the cabbage and stir over medium to high heat until the cabbage is wilted, two to three minutes at the most. Stir in the caraway seeds and lemon juice.

Lift out the cabbage with a slotted spoon and serve on a heated serving dish.   *D*

CARROTS VICHY

5 to 6 servings

6 to 8 medium carrots
3 tablespoons unsalted butter
1 tablespoon water
1 teaspoon salt

3 or 4 twists of a pepper mill
1 tablespoon sugar
Finely chopped parsley

Wash, scrape, and slice the carrots thinly on the bias.

Melt the butter in the water in a heavy saucepan with a close-fitting lid. Add salt, pepper, and sugar. Stir in the sliced carrots, coating well with the butter mixture.

Cook, covered, over a low flame for four to five minutes. Test for doneness; carrots should be crisp. Cook two minutes longer with the cover off. (If the lid is not close-fitting, it may be necessary to add additional water to prevent the carrots from burning.)

Correct the seasoning and serve with finely chopped parsley sprinkled over the top.

D

BRUSSELS SPROUTS AND CHESTNUTS

½ pound fresh Brussels sprouts per
   serving, approximately
¼ pound chestnuts

1 tablespoon salt
2 tablespoons butter
Salt and pepper

Remove the outside leaves and hard stalks from the Brussels sprouts. Wash in salted water.

Boil the chestnuts for five minutes. Peel and quarter them. Cook for five minutes more in salted water.

Add one tablespoon of salt to the Brussels sprouts in a heavy pan. Pour boiling water over them and boil briskly for five to six minutes. They should be crisp. Drain.

Melt butter in a heavy pan. Add the sprouts and chestnuts. Toss until they are heated through; season to taste with salt and pepper.   *D*

SUCCOTASH

5 to 7 servings

Succotash goes well with grilled, broiled, or roasted chicken. It is particularly useful in the summer when there is outdoor cooking, because it can be made in advance and is not harmed by being kept.

2 cups frozen corn
2 cups frozen
   baby lima beans
1 small red bell pepper, diced, seeds and
   white pith removed

1 small green bell pepper, diced, seeds
   and white pith removed
3 tablespoons unsalted butter
Salt and pepper
Chopped parsley

Combine all the ingredients, except seasoning and parsley, in a pan and heat to melt the butter. Cook the vegetables for three to four minutes, while stirring.

Season to taste with salt and pepper. Sprinkle with parsley before serving.   *ACD*

GREEN BEANS AND WATER CHESTNUTS

5 to 6 servings

1½ pounds green beans
1 small can water chestnuts
2 tablespoons butter

Salt
3 or 4 twists of the pepper mill

Remove ends from the green beans; cook the beans in boiling salted water for three to four minutes. They must be crisp.

(Continued)

Drain the water chestnuts; slice and cut them into matchstick-sized pieces. Stir them into the beans for the last two minutes of cooking time.

Heat the butter in a heavy pan. Add the beans and sliced chestnuts; stir over moderate heat until heated through. Season to taste with salt and pepper.

D

WATERCRESS AND GREEN PEAS

5 to 7 servings

This is an unusual combination of flavors. Small green peas have a sweetness all their own that is counteracted, but not overwhelmed, by the fresh mustardy-hot watercress. To remove most of the peppery flavor, blanch the watercress—pour boiling water over it.

I, personally, prefer a distinctly watercress character. This dish goes well with the roasted chicken in the poultry chapter.

2 packages (10 ounces each) frozen
   green peas
1 bunch watercress

2 to 3 tablespoons butter
Salt and pepper

Cook the peas in boiling salted water for two to three minutes.

Pick over the watercress, discarding coarse stalks.

Purée the peas and watercress with the butter in a food processor; season with salt and pepper.

CD

BOSTON BAKED BEANS

Boston Baked Beans are hearty winter fare and well worth the time and trouble involved. They go well with cold meats of all kinds and are useful for Saturday or Sunday night suppers.

4 cups dry white pea beans or
   Great Northern beans
¾ pound salt pork
1 large onion, peeled
2 tablespoons tomato paste
2 tablespoons cider vinegar

Pinch of ground cloves
½ cup dark molasses
2 teaspoons salt
1 teaspoon freshly ground black pepper
1 cup dark brown sugar

Soak the beans overnight in enough cold water to cover them generously. Drain; place them in a large kettle and cover with fresh water by two inches.

Bring to a boil slowly; reduce heat to simmer, and cook gently until the beans are almost tender. If the water boils away, add more boiling water to keep beans well-covered. Drain, saving any cooking water.

Meanwhile, scald the pork in boiling water. Cut half of the pork into pieces about one inch square; leave the other half whole.

Heat oven to 250°F.

Place the onion in the bottom of a large earthenware casserole or bean pot with a lid. Add half the drained beans, then the cubes of pork; top with the remaining beans. Place the whole piece of pork on top.

Mix together all the remaining ingredients and pour them over the beans. Heat two cups of the remaining bean liquid and pour it over the casserole.

Cover and bake in the oven for six to eight hours. Keep an eye on the beans. If the liquid boils away, add any remaining bean liquid heated to the boiling point, or boiling water. The beans must always be covered with liquid.

During the last hour, uncover the pot and allow the beans to finish cooking. Do not add more liquid during this time. Serve with hot rolls or brown bread.   *AC*

VEGETABLE MELANGE

6 to 8 servings

This is one of the many ways to serve vegetables as a separate course when they are small and young. You will get the full benefit of the flavor without competition from meat, fish, or fowl.

3 to 4 zucchini
¾ pound fresh green beans
2 to 3 small carrots
3 ribs celery
1 quart water
1 tablespoon salt

4 tablespoons unsalted butter
2 tablespoons salad or olive oil
4 to 6 tablespoons coarsely
   chopped parsley
1 tablespoon lemon juice

Scrub and cut off the ends of the zucchini and the green beans. Slice all vegetables on the bias, about one-eighth inch thick. They should all be the same thickness.

Bring one quart of water and one tablespoon of salt to a rolling boil. Drop in the beans and cook for three to four minutes, depending on their age and freshness. They must be crisp. Remove; drain, and freshen with cold water.

Heat the butter and oil in a heavy skillet or large, deep saucepan or wok, over medium heat. Cook the carrots for three to four minutes, the celery for another three minutes, approximately, and the zucchini. Cook all the vegetables together for another two minutes.

Stir in the cooked beans, parsley, and lemon juice. Correct the seasoning.

MACEDOINE OF VEGETABLES

6 to 8 servings

½ cup diced carrots
¾ cup green beans
½ cup diced celery
½ cup corn
½ cup small frozen green peas

½ cup small frozen lima beans
2 to 3 tablespoons butter
Vinaigrette Sauce (see page 290), (optional)
Sour cream (optional)
Freshly chopped parsley

Cook the diced carrots in boiling salted water. Drain, reserving the liquid.

Cut the beans into half-inch pieces and cook quickly in the carrot water. Cook the celery very lightly in the same water.

Drop the frozen vegetables into boiling salted water; lift out immediately and drain.

To serve hot, toss in butter. Sprinkle with chopped parsley.

To serve cold, prepare the Vinaigrette Sauce; whisk in one tablespoon of sour cream, if desired, and toss the vegetables. Sprinkle with chopped parsley.

VEGETABLES VINAIGRETTE

5 to 7 servings

½ pound green beans
4 carrots
3 stalks celery
½ small head cauliflower
1 tablespoon salt

¼ pound mushrooms
½ cup parsley sprigs, finely chopped
Vinaigrette Sauce (see page 290)
Lettuce leaves

Wash and cut the ends off the beans. Peel, scrape, and slice the carrots thinly on the bias. Wash the celery stalks and peel off any tough fibers with a vegetable peeler. Slice them on the bias. Break up the cauliflower into small heads. Put all vegetables in cold water.

Bring one quart of water to a boil with one tablespoon of salt. Add the green beans and cook at a rolling boil for three to four minutes. They should remain crisp. Lift them out with a slotted spoon. Drop the carrots and the celery in the same water; cook for four minutes. Lift them out with a slotted spoon. Add the cauliflower to the same water and cook at a rolling boil for four minutes. Remove with a slotted spoon.

Wipe the mushrooms clean with a damp cloth; slice them very thinly. In a bowl combine all the drained vegetables, the mushrooms, and the parsley. Toss well with Vinaigrette Sauce. Serve on lettuce leaves.

ACD

RATATOUILLE

6 to 8 servings

2 large onions
2 medium eggplants
3 to 4 tomatoes
2 red or green peppers
1 clove garlic
1 teaspoon salt

⅓ cup olive oil
Salt and pepper to taste
Paprika
A pinch of dried marjoram or 1 teaspoon
  of fresh marjoram

Heat oven to 350°F.

Slice the onions in thin rounds. Score the eggplants; slice, and sprinkle them with salt. Leave under a weighted plate for half an hour or so to remove excess moisture.

Peel and slice the tomatoes. Remove the pith and seeds from the peppers and slice the peppers thinly.

Peel the garlic clove and mash it to a paste with one teaspoon of salt. Sauté the onions and garlic in oil until the onions are golden. Reserve the oil.

Spread a layer of onions on the bottom of an earthenware casserole with a lid. Dust lightly with salt, pepper, and paprika. Follow with a layer of eggplant, a layer of sliced pepper, and a layer of sliced tomatoes, and more onions. Continue until the casserole is full. Dust lightly between each layer with the salt, marjoram, pepper, and paprika. Add the reserved oil.

Cook for one and one-half hours. Do not overcook or the result will be a purée. Serve hot or cold. *ACD*

STUFFED EGGPLANT

4 servings

2 small eggplants
4 tablespoons oil
2 tablespoons butter
2 onions, finely sliced
6 large tomatoes, skinned, seeded, and
  chopped
1 clove garlic, finely chopped

1 teaspoon chopped parsley and thyme,
  mixed
Salt and pepper
2 tablespoons bread crumbs, tossed in
  1 tablespoon melted butter
½ cup grated Parmesan cheese

Cut the eggplants in half lengthwise; score the pulp with a knife. Sprinkle with salt and leave for one hour upside down to drain.

(Continued)

Wipe the eggplants dry and fry them in the oil on both sides for ten minutes. Remove from the pan. Scoop out the inside without breaking the skins, reserve the skins, then chop the pulp.

Melt the butter in a pan and cook the onion gently, without browning. Add the tomatoes, garlic, chopped eggplant, and herbs. Correct the seasoning with salt and pepper, and simmer for five minutes. Spoon the mixture into the eggplant cases, and sprinkle with the bread crumbs and cheese. Brown them under the grill.

A

CHOU-FLEUR PANACHE

6 servings

This is a very useful dish of vegetables. It may be prepared well ahead of time and is a good stand-by for those who toil all day in an office. It can be made the evening before, requires only heating up, and it waits without spoiling.

1 large cauliflower
2 tablespoons salt
1 large bunch broccoli
2 tablespoons butter

¼ cup sour cream
3 tablespoons grated Parmesan cheese
⅓ cup bread crumbs

Heat oven to 350°F.

Wash the cauliflower and break it into small heads. In a large pan bring two quarts of water with two tablespoons of salt to a boil. Cook, covered, until tender, about ten minutes. Drain the cauliflower and reserve the water. Place the cauliflower in a deep one-and-one-half-quart pie dish or casserole.

Wash the broccoli; break it into small pieces, and peel the stalks down to the tender pith. Chop coarsely. Cook the broccoli and stalks in the cauliflower water, uncovered, for eight to ten minutes. Do not overcook or the fresh, green color will be lost.

Purée the broccoli in a blender with the butter and sour cream. Season to taste with salt and pepper.

Spoon the purée evenly over the cauliflower. Sprinkle with grated cheese, and bread crumbs. Bake in the oven for twenty minutes.

ACD

ZUCCHINI AU GRATIN

6 to 8 servings

7 tablespoons butter
6 to 8 small zucchini
Salt and pepper
Lemon juice

1 cup bread crumbs
¼ cup grated Parmesan cheese
¼ cup parsley sprigs, finely chopped

Heat oven to 350°F.

Butter a shallow oven-proof dish generously with one tablespoon of butter. Wash the zucchini and cut off both ends. Slice in half lengthwise and arrange them on a dish, cut-side up. Dust lightly with salt and pepper, and sprinkle with lemon juice.

Melt four tablespoons of butter in a small pan and stir in the bread crumbs. Mix well to coat them evenly with butter. Stir in the grated cheese and a pinch of salt and pepper. Sprinkle this mixture over the zucchini. Melt the remaining two tablespoons of butter in the same small pan and dribble it over the bread crumbs.

Bake in the center of the oven for thirty-five minutes, until the zucchini is tender and the crumbs well-browned. Serve, sprinkled with finely chopped parsley.

COURGETTES RAPEES

4 to 6 servings

2 pounds small zucchini
2 teaspoons salt
3 to 4 tablespoons butter
3 to 4 tablespoons oil

2 tablespoons lemon juice
Freshly ground black pepper
3 tablespoons parsley sprigs, minced

Wash the zucchini thoroughly under cold running water. Using the coarsest side of the grater, grate into a colander. Sprinkle the grated zucchini with two teaspoons salt. Mix thoroughly and allow to stand for ten minutes or more.

Squeeze the zucchini dry with your hands; taste. If it seems too salty, rinse in cold water and squeeze dry again.

Heat the butter and oil in a wok or a large, heavy skillet. Add the zucchini and cook, stirring with a wooden spoon for two to three minutes. It should be cooked only to the crisp stage.

Stir in the lemon juice. Taste again for seasoning. A few twists of the pepper mill is usually necessary. Stir in the parsley. Serve hot.

ZUCCHINI, CELERY, AND MUSHROOMS

4 to 6 servings

3 medium zucchini
2 ribs celery
4 firm mushrooms
2 tablespoons butter

1 tablespoon oil
Salt and pepper to taste
½ teaspoon sugar (optional)

Wash and slice the zucchini in rounds approximately one-eighth inch thick. Do not peel. Wash the celery and cut into slices one-eighth-inch thick on the bias.

Cut off the stems of the mushrooms flush with the caps. Wipe the caps clean with a damp cloth and slice thinly.

Heat the butter and oil in a heavy skillet; add the sliced celery and cook for two minutes. Add the zucchini and cook for four to five minutes, turning and stirring. While the celery and zucchini are still crisp, add the mushrooms and cook for two minutes longer. Season with salt, pepper, and sugar.

PUREE OF LIMA BEANS

6 to 8 servings

3 packages (10 ounces each) frozen baby
   lima beans
4 tablespoons sweet butter

½ cup sour cream
Salt and pepper
Chopped parsley

Cook the lima beans in boiling salted water for two minutes. Drain.

Purée the beans in a food processor with the butter and sour cream. Season to taste with salt and pepper.

Reheat in the top half of a double boiler when needed. Garnish with chopped parsley. *ACD*

PUREE PARMENTIER

4 to 6 servings

The last two years have been the years of the purée. No doubt it has been overdone to some extent, but the purée has been around for a long time and will continue to be long after the mania for puréeing everything in sight has died down.

A purée of leeks and potatoes is one of the best, and one of the most useful. There is little it quarrels with whether it be beef, pork, lamb, or poultry, and it lends itself to advance preparation.

4 to 5 medium leeks
2 small potatoes
2 tablespoons butter

Salt and pepper
Finely chopped parsley

Wash the leeks thoroughly in warm water to remove sand and grit. Cut off one-third of the green leaves and set them aside for the stockpot. Chop the remaining two-thirds of each leek coarsely.

Peel and dice the potatoes. Cook the potatoes and leeks together with the butter and about one-half cup of water in a heavy pan with a tight-fitting lid for fifteen minutes, or until tender.

Purée the potatoes and leeks in a food blender or processor, and season to taste. Keep the purée hot until needed in the top half of a double boiler over hot water. To serve, stir in a couple of tablespoons of chopped parsley.   *AC*

PARSNIP PUREE

4 to 6 servings

The parsnip is an almost forgotten vegetable, seemingly belonging to the root-cellar days. I use it frequently in the winter months when root vegetables are at their best. Serve it in place of almost any purée.

3 to 4 pounds parsnips, approximately
4 tablespoons butter
1 teaspoon powdered cinnamon
Grated rind of 1 lemon

2 to 3 tablespoons heavy cream
Salt and pepper to taste
Finely chopped parsley

Peel the parsnips; cut into manageable lengths, and quarter. Cut out the woody center. Chop coarsely. Cover with cold water in a heavy pan and add one tablespoon of salt for every quart of water. Boil gently until tender.

(Continued)

Drain and purée the parsnips in a food processor or blender with the butter. (If you have neither, use a food mill or a fine strainer and wooden spoon.)

Stir in the cinnamon, grated lemon rind, and cream. Season to taste with salt and pepper. Keep hot in the top half of a double boiler.

Sprinkle with finely chopped parsley before serving.

AC

VEGETABLE HARLEQUIN

6 to 8 servings

Vegetable Harlequin is a mélange of purées, a very colorful one and highly suitable for that special occasion when one has ample time for preparation and little for last-minute chores. Ideally, it should be put together the day before and refrigerated until about an hour before it goes into the oven for reheating. It goes well with roasts, lamb, pork, poultry, or beef, but can also be given a place on the menu as a separate course.

1 pound white turnips, peeled and sliced
¼ pound (about 2) small potatoes, peeled and sliced
1 bunch carrots, peeled and sliced
1 small head cauliflower, chopped
2 packages (10 ounces each) frozen spinach, thawed and drained, or 2 pounds fresh spinach, cooked

2 cups Béchamel Sauce (see page 275)
Salt
Freshly ground pepper
Nutmeg
1 pound Gruyère cheese, coarsely grated
½ cup buttered bread crumbs

Heat oven to 350°F.

Cook the vegetables separately in boiling salted water until tender. Purée each vegetable separately with a small amount of Béchamel Sauce. Season the vegetable purées with salt, pepper, and nutmeg to taste.

Butter a two-quart glass soufflé dish.

Spread the turnip and the potato mixture on the bottom of the dish and sprinkle with Gruyère. Add a layer of the spinach mixture; sprinkle with Gruyère and continue with the cauliflower and carrots in the same manner. Sprinkle the top with bread crumbs and bake for twenty-five minutes, or until mixture is browned on top and heated all the way through.

TOMATO HALVES AND POTATO PUREE

6 servings

Halved tomatoes filled with a purée of potatoes is a good accompaniment to serve with grilled lamb chops.

3 medium tomatoes
Potato Purée (see below)
1 tablespoon finely chopped parsley

Heat oven to 350°F.
Cut the tomatoes in half horizontally and with a spoon scoop out the center, being careful not to break the skin. Drain.

Potato Purée:

2 pounds potatoes
1 tablespoon butter

1 cup hot milk
Salt and pepper to taste

Peel and boil the potatoes in salted water until tender. Drain.
Force the potatoes through a sieve or *moule*. Beat in the butter and gradually add the hot milk. Whip until light, and season with salt and pepper. I find a wire whisk produces the best results.
With a forcing bag fitted with a large star tube, fill the tomato halves, mounding the purée. Bake for approximately twenty minutes. Sprinkle with parsley before serving.   *AD*

POMMES DE TERRE NORMANDE

4 to 6 servings

1 pound potatoes, peeled
2 leeks
Butter

2 tablespoons chopped parsley
Salt and pepper to taste
Milk

Heat oven to 350°F.
Slice the potatoes and the white part of the leeks. Butter an oven-proof dish and arrange the potatoes in layers alternating with the leeks. Sprinkle a teaspoon of parsley, and salt and pepper between each layer. Dot the top layer of the potatoes with butter. Pour in enough milk to come two-thirds of the way up the potatoes. Bake in the oven for forty-five minutes.   *A*

FLORENTINE IDAHOES

1 potato per serving
6 packages (10 ounces each) frozen
  chopped spinach (enough for eight
  potatoes)
4 tablespoons butter

½ cup sour cream
Grated nutmeg
Salt and pepper
Grated Parmesan cheese

Heat oven to 425°F.

Prick the potatoes with a fork and bake for about forty minutes. Cut a slice off the top and scoop out most of the inside, leaving a substantial shell. Set aside the pulp for another use.

Thaw the spinach. Squeeze out all the water and cook for two to three minutes with butter. Purée in a blender or food processor until smooth. Stir in sour cream; season with grated nutmeg, salt, and pepper.

Fill each potato shell and dust the spinach filling with grated cheese. Bake in the oven for twenty minutes, or until heated through.

AD

POMMES DE TERRE BOULANGERE

6 to 8 servings

2 pounds medium potatoes
3 tablespoons butter
2 tablespoons oil

2 medium onions, thinly sliced
Butter
Salt and pepper

Heat oven to 375°F.

Peel and cut the potatoes into slices approximately one-eighth inch thick.

Heat the butter and oil in a skillet and add the onions. Cook until golden and soft, not brown. Shake the pan occasionally. Drain the cooked onions, saving the liquid from the pan.

Butter a two-quart baking dish. Place a layer of potatoes at the bottom of the dish. Arrange a layer of onions on top of the potatoes. Season with salt and pepper. Continue the layers of potatoes and onions, seasoning each layer and ending with the potatoes on top.

Add more salt and pepper and dot with butter. Pour in the liquid from the onions and just enough water to reach the bottom of the top layer of potatoes.

Bake in the middle of the oven until most of the liquid has been absorbed and the potatoes are tender when tested with a fork, about thirty to forty minutes.

AC

SWISS POTATOES

6 to 8 servings

1¾ pounds potatoes, approximately
2 eggs, slightly beaten
2 tablespoons flour
Pinch of nutmeg

Salt
½ cup finely diced Gruyère cheese
4 tablespoons oil

Peel the potatoes and grate them using a fine blade. Squeeze the grated potatoes in a cheesecloth bag to extract the water. There should be about one and three-quarter cups potatoes.

Add the eggs, flour, nutmeg, and salt to taste. Stir in the cheese and blend well.

Heat the oil in a skillet and drop about three tablespoons of the potato mixture into the skillet at a time. Cook until golden on one side; turn and cook on the other.

STEAMED POTATOES

Steamed potatoes are excellent with almost every kind of fish: poached, baked, or grilled.

Peel and quarter small potatoes. Shape them to look like olives if you wish, but do have them as uniform in size as possible. Place the potatoes in a colander over a pan of boiling water, sprinkle them with salt and cover with a lid to fit. The lid will keep most of the steam in. Steam until tender, roughly twenty minutes depending on the size of the potatoes.

To keep them hot, remove the lid from the colander and cover with a clean kitchen towel.

POMMES DE TERRE DUCHESSE

Pommes de Terre Duchesse is used as a decorative garnish for platters and as a border for scallop shells to be filled with seafood.

1½ pounds potatoes
1 tablespoon butter
2 egg yolks

¼ cup hot milk, approximately
Salt and pepper

Boil the potatoes in their jackets in salted water until done.

Peel and rub them through a sieve. Mix the sieved potatoes with the butter in a heavy pan.

(Continued)

Beat in one egg yolk and enough hot milk to make a firm purée. Season to taste with salt and pepper.

Fit a forcing bag with a large star or rose tube. Pipe shapes to your liking onto a greased baking sheet.

Brush the potato purée with the remaining egg yolk mixed with one tablespoon of cold water. Brown under the broiler or in a 450°F. oven.

Eggs

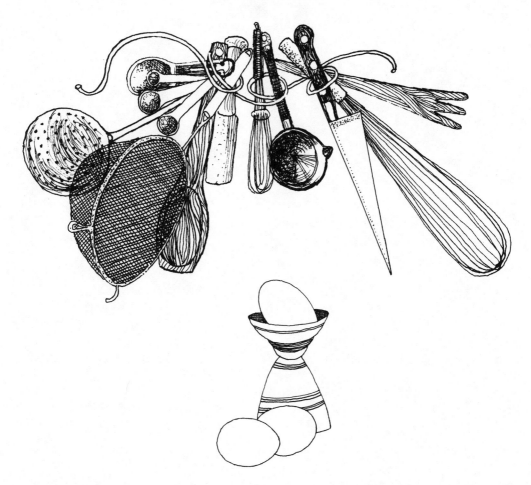

Eggs

The egg is the most ingenious piece of packaging I know of—shaped not to roll out of the nest, and coated to ensure its freshness for a long time. It is a thing of beauty and a valuable source of energy. Nancy van Sweringen, whom I have already mentioned in this book, once announced rather grandly that she could keep a man alive for an indefinite period on eggs and orange juice. I do not doubt her.

Every so often one of my friend's ability as a cook is summed up by the phrase "not able to boil an egg." Indeed, this so-called simple task is not a fair test for the non-cook. The egg is a delicate and temperamental commodity. It must be handled with care and treated with respect. If shocked by sudden heat, or deluged by oil or melted butter, it will most definitely misbehave and either curdle or reject the liquids. On the other hand, if gently coaxed and given time to take up the fat, a minor miracle happens, and one yolk will absorb as much as one to one and one-half cups of oil.

There are few facets of the culinary art from soups to nuts, where the egg does not feature. Life without it would be a duller roost; it is so incredibly adaptable. The simple, yet sophisticated, bouché, filled with scrambled eggs seasoned and raised to the pinnacle of perfection by a sliver of fresh truffle, is an hors d'oeuvre I shall remember all my life. This was invariably the first course on the train from Calais to Paris in those far-off days before World War II when one traveled at a measured pace from London to the Cote d'Azur. Incidentally, it is a dish that can be created at home with very little trouble with a baker's bouché, and, unless you are in a wildly extravagant mood, an herb such as parsley or tarragon can take the place of the truffle.

There are few times when the egg fails to come to the rescue. An unexpected visitor, when the cupboard is practically bare, might be offered a splendid omelet, a glass of wine, and fruit with the utmost confidence.

The egg is a subject more fitting for a book than a line or two.

CODDLED EGGS

To "coddle" means to treat an invalid tenderly, to boil gently, and to undercook, as with Overbury's semi-educated grammar school boy: "Hee is tane from grammar-schoole halfe coddled."

Whatever interpretation you put on the word, apply it to cooking the egg. It is a delicate morsel and demands the same nursing as the invalid.

Pierce the broad end of the egg and place it in a small pan of cold water. Bring to a boil; turn off the heat immediately and let it stand in the water for four and one-half minutes. Lift it out and crack it on the broad end with a spoon to stop the cooking.

An alternate method is to pierce the broad end of the egg and start cooking it in cold water. Bring it to a boil, then lower the heat and simmer gently for exactly three minutes.

BOILED EGGS

The egg is "boiled" when cooked until hard. But again I remind you to start the process slowly.

Place the egg in cold water and simmer it for approximately fifteen minutes after the water comes to the boil. Roll it on a hard surface as soon as it can be handled and drop it into a bowl of cold water to prevent the yolk from discoloring.

POACHED EGGS ON TOAST

4 servings

4 eggs, pierced at broad end with a needle
1 teaspoon vinegar

4 slices hot buttered toast, preferably whole-wheat

Roll the eggs, one by one, ten times across a skillet three-quarters full of simmering water to which one teaspoon of vinegar has been added. This helps to set the white very slightly so it does not spread all over the skillet.

Break each egg—two at a time if you are handy—into gently simmering water. The water should just about cover the yolk; if it does not, spoon a little of the water over the yolk to produce a film, or cover the pan with a lid. The trapped steam will produce the same effect.

Poach the eggs for three to four minutes until the whites are just set, longer if you dislike a runny yolk. Lift the eggs out with a slotted spoon. Allow to drain. Serve on slices of hot buttered toast.

SCRAMBLED EGGS

1 tablespoon butter
Allow 2 eggs per person

Salt and pepper
Parsley, finely chopped (optional)

Melt butter in a heavy pan.

Break all the eggs but one into a bowl and mix. Do not beat. Stir lightly; season with salt and pepper. Stir eggs into melted butter in the pan. Over low heat, cook, while stirring, until the eggs are creamy and still moist.

Serve right away. If there is a delay, stir in an uncooked egg which will help to keep the mixture moist. If you like, stir in finely chopped parsley as the eggs cook.

OEUFS INDIENS

6 to 8 servings

¼ cup chicken stock, homemade or made
    with bouillon cube
1 teaspoon curry powder, or to taste
1½ cups mayonnaise (see page 277)

Salt and pepper
Lemon juice to taste
6 to 8 eggs, hard-boiled and peeled
Parsley sprigs, freshly chopped

Heat the chicken stock in a small pan and add the curry powder. Mix and simmer for a minute or two. Simmering tones down the spices. Cool and stir into the mayonnaise. Season to taste with salt, pepper, and lemon juice.

Slice the eggs in half. Arrange them on a serving dish. Spoon the sauce over the eggs and sprinkle with the chopped parsley before serving.   *A*

EGGS MIMOSA

6 to 8 servings

6 large or jumbo eggs, hard-boiled and
    peeled
2 cups chicken liver pâté or foie gras
1 cup heavy cream, whipped

Salt and pepper
2 cups mayonnaise (see page 277)
Lemon juice
Parsley sprigs, whole or finely chopped

(Continued)

Cut the eggs in half horizontally. Remove and reserve the yolks. Cut a thin slice from the bottom of each egg half so that it will stand upright.

Beat the pâté, adding a little cream if necessary, to make a smooth paste. Correct the seasoning with salt and pepper. Force the paste through a forcing bag and with a large tube mound it in the egg whites. Place the filled egg halves in a serving dish.

Whip the cream and mix it with the mayonnaise; season with lemon juice, salt, and pepper. Spoon over the eggs.

Sieve the yolks and scatter them over the sauce-coated stuffed eggs. Garnish the edges of the dish with parsley.

DEVILED EGGS WITH MUSHROOMS

8 servings

¼ pound mushrooms
2 tablespoons finely chopped onion
2 tablespoons butter
8 eggs, hard-boiled and peeled
2 tablespoons mayonnaise (see page 277)

2 tablespoons dry mustard
1 tablespoon lemon juice
½ teaspoon celery salt
⅛ teaspoon white pepper
1 bunch watercress for garnish

Chop the mushrooms and sauté with the onion and butter.

Cut the eggs in half, remove the yolks, and sieve them. Combine the yolks with all the other ingredients except the watercress.

Pile the mixture into the egg halves. Garnish with watercress.

EGGS A LA RUSSE

12 servings

2 cups mayonnaise (see page 277)
6 tablespoons chili sauce
2 tablespoons chopped onion
2 tablespoons chives
2 tablespoons parsley

2 tablespoons green olives, pitted and chopped
12 eggs, hard-boiled, peeled, and sliced in half lengthwise
½ cup parsley sprigs, finely chopped

Mix all the above ingredients together, except for the eggs and the parsley, and chill well.

Arrange the egg halves on a suitable platter, cut-side down. Spoon the sauce evenly over the eggs. Garnish with chopped parsley.

OEUFS AUX CREVETTES

10 servings

2 pounds cooked shrimp
Generous scraping of nutmeg
1 cup heavy cream

10 whole eggs
Parmesan cheese, grated
Parsley, finely chopped

Heat oven to 425°F.

Chop the shrimp into medium-fine pieces. Line the bottom of ten one-half-cup ramekins with shrimp.

Add nutmeg to the cream and bring to a boil. Add one tablespoon of cream to each ramekin. Make a small well in the center of the shrimp with the back of a spoon. Break an egg over the shrimp, taking care not to puncture the yolk. Spoon two tablespoons of cream over the eggs. Sprinkle with grated Parmesan cheese.

Stand the ramekins in a baking dish. Add enough hot water to come half-way up each ramekin, and bake for ten to fifteen minutes, until the white is set.

Sprinkle with chopped parsley before serving.

OEUFS VERTS EN COCOTTES

6 to 8 servings

4 tablespoons butter, unsalted
2 packages small frozen peas,
   (10 ounces each), thawed
Salt and pepper

6 eggs
1 cup heavy cream, heated to almost
   boiling point
Finely chopped parsley

Heat oven to 350°F.

Melt butter in a pan. Add the peas and cook over low heat for five or six minutes. Purée the peas in a blender and season to taste with salt and pepper.

Spoon enough purée into one-half-cup ramekins to come one-third of the way up each. Break an egg over the purée, taking care not to puncture the yolk. Spoon in sufficient cream to cover.

Bake, covered with a baking sheet, for ten minutes, or until the egg white is set, longer if you like the yolk hard. Serve sprinkled with a little chopped parsley.

OEUFS A LA CREME

1 slice broiled bacon per serving,
  crumbled
Butter
2 tablespoons heavy cream per serving

1 large egg per serving
Paprika
Finely chopped parsley

Heat oven to 350°F.
Broil the bacon until crisp, then crumble.
Lightly butter one-half-cup ramekins.
Place one tablespoon of cream in each ramekin; add the crumbled bacon and one egg. Cover with one tablespoon of cream, and dot with butter.
Place the ramekins in a shallow baking pan with one inch of boiling water and bake for fifteen minutes, longer, if you like the yolks well-set. Serve hot, garnished with paprika and parsley.

EGGS FLORENTINE

8 servings

2 packages (10 ounces each)
  frozen spinach, thawed
  and squeezed almost dry
2 tablespoons butter
½ cup sour cream

Salt and pepper
Nutmeg
8 eggs
1 cup heavy cream
Parmesan cheese, grated

Heat oven to 400°F.
Cook the spinach with the butter over gentle heat. Purée in a blender with the sour cream. Blend the puréed spinach with salt, pepper, and nutmeg to taste. Place about two table-spoons of puréed spinach in the bottom of each of eight one-half-cup ramekins. Make a hollow in the center of the spinach and slide a raw egg in each.
Heat the heavy cream to boiling. Spoon one tablespoon of boiling cream and a generous sprinkling of Parmesan cheese over each ramekin. Place them in a baking pan. Pour boiling water into the pan, sufficient to come half-way up the ramekins.
Bake eight to ten minutes in the middle of the oven until the egg whites are set.   *A*

EGG MOUSSE

6 servings

1 cup Quick Aspic (see page 290)
5 hard-boiled eggs
3 or 4 twists of the pepper mill
1 teaspoon salt
¼ teaspoon paprika

1 teaspoon anchovy paste
1 teaspoon Worcestershire sauce
1 cup heavy cream
Parsley or watercress for garnish
Mayonnaise (see page 277)

Prepare the aspic according to the recipe and cool.

Shell and halve the eggs; press the yolks through a fine sieve into a mixing bowl. Chop the egg whites coarsely and set aside.

To the egg yolks in the bowl, add the pepper, salt, paprika, anchovy paste, and Worcestershire sauce. Stir in the cooled aspic.

Whip the cream to soft peaks and combine with the aspic mixture. Add the chopped egg whites and mix lightly. Chill until the mousse thickens slightly.

Spoon the mousse into an oiled one-quart mold or soufflé dish and chill for at least two hours.

Garnish with parsley or watercress and serve with freshly made mayonnaise.

OEUFS EN GELEE

Up to 8 servings

Vinegar
1 egg per serving

Tarragon sprigs or slices of truffle
Quick Aspic (see page 290)

Bring a skillet of water to a gentle boil. Add a few drops of vinegar; vinegar will help to prevent the egg white from spreading. Roll each egg ten times across the skillet in the gently boiling water. Lift it out with a slotted spoon. This operation tends to partly set the egg white.

Crack each egg into a cup and slide it carefully into the simmering water or, if you are courageous, three or four at a time.

Poach for three to four minutes until the white is set. A little of the poaching water spooned over the yolk will produce a white film. Have a bowl of ice water handy. Lift out the eggs with a slotted spoon and place them in the cold water until needed.

(Continued)

Prepare the aspic according to the recipe.

Cool the aspic until almost thick. Spoon a little into one ramekin or cocotte for each serving and chill it to set. Put an egg on top. You may need to shape the white with a knife. Spoon the aspic over each egg to cover and allow to set. Decorate with sprigs of tarragon dipped in aspic or with truffles sliced thin and cut in shapes that take your fancy. Pour aspic over the cutouts. Chill.

If the egg is to be turned out of the ramekin for serving, decorate the bottom of the ramekin first by spooning in a thin coating of aspic, followed by the decoration with more aspic over it to set it. Remember, what is now the bottom becomes the top. *A*

OMELETS

The omelet creates the same cloud of mystery as the soufflé. I wonder if it has anything to do with the French name? Both are straightforward, provided you give your attention to the methods and principles.

The omelet pan generates discussion. There are purists who claim a special pan must be set aside for the sole purpose of making omelets and never washed or scoured. (I once knew a fanatical cook who banished his wife for using steel wool on his omelet pan.) However, I have found that an omelet can be produced with a great variety of pans as long as they are the right size for the number of eggs being used. I prefer a pan measuring seven inches across the bottom and ten across the top with a gently sloping curved side.

Begin by using two to three eggs mixed lightly in a bowl with a fork. Heat the pan until a drop of water on the bottom bounces off. Add one tablespoon of unsalted butter. When it foams and dies down, pour in the eggs. Right away start shaking the pan back and forth with the left hand, lifting the eggs with a fork to allow the mixture to cook. Almost immediately begin rolling the omelet from the handle-end down, keeping the pan at a steep angle. Change the grip of the left hand—so that the fingers face upward—and grab a warm, not hot, plate with the right hand.

Tilt the pan almost to the vertical with the plate's edge meeting the pan's edge. A sharp knock and the omelet will roll out, folded, onto the plate. Glaze with a little butter.

Fillings should be added hot, almost as soon as the eggs hit the pan. Speed is the keynote. Fifty seconds is all that is needed for a "weeping" omelet, longer if you like it drier. Avoid salt in the eggs as it tends to toughen them.

SOUFFLE OMELET

2 servings

3 eggs, separated
2 tablespoons superfine sugar
Grated rind of half an orange

4 tablespoons rum or cherry brandy (or
  half cherry brandy and half cognac)
1 tablespoon unsalted butter

Heat oven to 425°F.

Beat the egg yolks with one tablespoon of sugar until light yellow in color. Add the grated orange rind and two tablespoons of liqueur. Beat the egg whites until stiff but not dry and grainy. Fold the yolks into the whites.

Melt the butter in a nine-inch omelet pan or an oval gratin dish approximately the same size. Pour in the egg mixture and press it down in the middle with the back of a knife.

Bake on the middle shelf of the oven for about ten minutes. Sprinkle lightly with the remaining sugar and put it back into the oven for another minute or two. Heat the remaining liqueur; pour it around the omelet, light, and send the omelet to the table in flames.

Salads

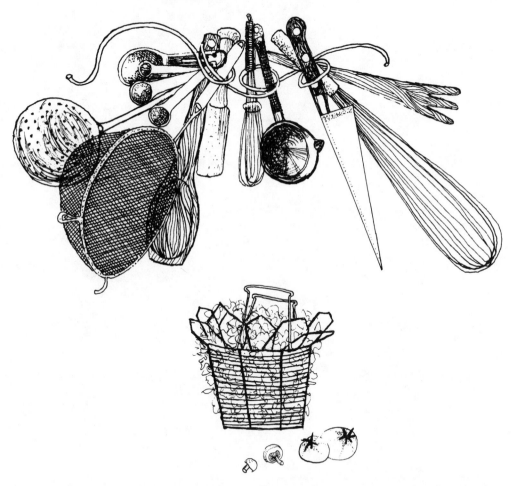

Salads

"Salad" is about as elastic a word in culinary language as any. Salads may contain vegetables—cooked or uncooked—poultry, fish, meats, cheese, or fruit. They may consist of everything from a handful of plastic-like iceberg lettuce leaves tossed with a mouth-puckering dressing, to an elaborate Salade du Chef made up of almost all of the above ingredients.

Salads can be simple or intensely elaborate, but whatever you choose to make, take the greatest possible care with the dressing. It should bring out the character of the salad, not overpower it. Use the dressing sparingly, only enough to coat the ingredients thoroughly. There should never be a puddle of dressing in the bottom of the bowl.

Salads can take the place of a first course. In my household that is where, more often than not, you will find it, except for the simple tossed green salad.

THE SIMPLE GREEN SALAD

8 to 10 servings

The straightforward tossed green salad is hard to beat. It serves two purposes: It refreshes one's palate after the entrée—on rare occasions it is served with the entrée—and it provides a welcome break in the service, rather like the sorbet that was served between courses in lengthy menus around the turn of the century.

1 head Boston lettuce
1 head romaine lettuce

Vinaigrette Sauce (see page 290)
2 tablespoons sunflower seeds

Wash and dry the lettuce leaves. Tear them into bite-sized pieces. Toss with just enough dressing to coat them and sprinkle with sunflower seeds. Toss again.

GREEN SALAD, PIGNOLI NUTS

Bib, Boston, and romaine lettuce
1 tablespoon pignoli nuts per serving
Vinaigrette Sauce (see page 290)

Wash, dry, and tear the lettuce leaves into bite-sized pieces.

Mix the nuts with the salad greens as they are being dressed with the vinaigrette. The amount of nuts used is up to you. I personally like just enough to be surprised by the crunch every now and again.

WATERCRESS SALAD

Watercress is delicate and needs support. No sooner is it tossed with a dressing than it wilts before your eyes. Combine it with a more robust salad green, such as romaine or iceberg, to hold it up.

SPINACH SALAD QUEEN MARY

6 to 8 servings

Years ago I was served this spinach salad on the **Queen Mary.** *It is the best I've ever had. I've never forgotten the pleasure of sailing on the* **Queen Mary** *nor her spinach salad. A small portion may be served as a first course or a larger one as a main course with French bread for luncheon, followed by fruit.*

1 pound fresh spinach leaves, without
    stems, washed and dried

2 hard-boiled eggs, chopped
6 slices bacon, cooked and crumbled

Dressing:

1 egg
1 teaspoon Parmesan cheese
Salt
Freshly ground pepper
2 tablespoons Dijon mustard

3 tablespoons fresh lemon juice (about 1
    medium lemon)
1 teaspoon Worcestershire sauce
1 teaspoon sugar (optional)
¼ cup salad oil

In a bowl combine the raw egg, Parmesan cheese, salt, pepper, mustard, lemon juice, Worcestershire sauce, and sugar. Mix well, then whisk in the salad oil.

Twenty minutes or so before serving, pour the dressing over the spinach and toss until the leaves are thoroughly coated with the dressing. Just before serving, sprinkle with chopped egg and crumbled bacon and toss again.

CUCUMBER SALAD

6 to 8 servings

2 medium cucumbers
1 teaspoon salt
1 small white onion

½ cup sour cream
Finely chopped dill
Freshly ground pepper

Scrub the cucumbers with a stiff vegetable brush. Cut off the ends and score the full length of each cucumber all around with the tines of a sturdy fork. Slice the cucumbers very thinly into a large plate.

Sprinkle the slices with salt. Place a second, smaller plate on top of the cucumbers and press down. Allow the cucumbers to stand for half an hour. Squeeze out the water that will result.

(Continued)

Peel and slice the white onion paper-thin.

Mix the cucumbers, onion, sour cream, and dill together and add three or four twists of the pepper mill. When served with a cold fish, salmon for example, a second sauce for the fish, such as mayonnaise, is unnecessary.

CUCUMBER AND DILL

6 to 8 servings

2 cucumbers, or 1 English hothouse
   cucumber if possible
½ cup Vinaigrette Sauce (see page 290)

3 tablespoons sour cream
2 tablespoons chopped dill
Salt and pepper

Peel the cucumbers, slice lengthwise, scoop out the seeds, and dice. If English cucumber is used, score and slice it. Dust the pieces lightly with salt and place them in a colander to drain for half an hour.

Mix the dressing with the sour cream and chopped dill in a bowl. Stir in the diced or sliced, drained cucumber. Add pepper, then test for seasoning. A little more salt may be needed.

MUSHROOM SALAD

6 to 8 servings

2 pounds very fresh mushrooms
1 small bunch fresh chives, or a
   tablespoon of fresh tarragon, chopped

½ cup parsley sprigs, chopped
2 white onions, thinly sliced
Vinaigrette Sauce (see page 290)

Wipe the mushrooms clean with a damp cloth and cut off the stems flush with the caps. Slice the mushrooms very thinly.

Cut the chives with scissors; chopping by knife bruises the chives.

Toss the mushrooms, chives or tarragon, parsley, and onion slices with the Vinaigrette Sauce. Mushrooms soak up dressing, so the amount of dressing must be left to your judgment.

SALADE DE HARICOTS VERTS

4 to 6 servings

1½ pounds cooked green beans
2 small white onions, finely sliced
2 tablespoons sour cream

Vinaigrette Sauce (see page 290)
Parsley, finely chopped

Mix the beans with the sliced onion.
Stir the sour cream into the Vinaigrette Sauce.
Pour the dressing over the beans and onions, and toss them with chopped parsley.

BEAN SALAD

10 to 12 servings

I would not think of serving this bean salad any other way except on its own; it is hearty and makes a splendid one-course luncheon dish. I have used it for a buffet when there were several other dishes and I had little or no control over how or with what it was eaten.

2 cups fresh green beans
1 cup canned
   cooked black beans
1 cup canned cooked garbanzo beans
   (chick peas)

1 cup canned cooked white beans, Great
   Northern
1 cup canned cooked red kidney beans
½ cup green onions, sliced thin
½ cup white onions, sliced in thin rings

Cut the fresh green beans into half-inch-long pieces and cook them in boiling salted water for five minutes. Drain and chill. Drain and chill all the canned beans.

Dressing:

1 small clove garlic
1 teaspoon salt
3 tablespoons red wine vinegar
4 tablespoons prepared mustard

4 teaspoons lemon juice
Freshly ground black pepper
12 tablespoons salad oil

(Continued)

To prepare the dressing, peel and crush the clove of garlic with the salt to make a smooth paste. In a screw-top jar combine the vinegar, garlic-salt paste, prepared mustard, lemon juice, and three to four twists of a black pepper mill. Shake well to mix.

Add the oil and mix again. Store the dressing, covered, in the refrigerator.

Combine all the salad ingredients in a large bowl, add only enough dressing to coat the beans, and toss to mix. Store the remaining dressing in the refrigerator.   *AC*

BEET AND ENDIVE SALAD

4 to 6 servings

1 pound fresh Belgian endive
½ cup cooked beets, cut in julienne slices

Vinaigrette Sauce (see page 290)
1 tablespoon finely chopped parsley

Wash the endive thoroughly and slice it on the bias. Drain the beets and mix with the endive in a salad bowl. Just before serving, add the dressing, toss, and sprinkle with finely chopped parsley.   *A*

POTATO AND BEET SALAD

Approximately 4 servings

Before I reached the age of ten and was packed off to a boarding school, I spent the greater part of my time away from my parents and teachers on the lakes and in the hills not far from where I grew up. I took food for three or four days. When the wind was in the right direction and her temper at its best, my parents' cook would put up this salad in a one-gallon jar. It lasted for two or three days and went with anything—sausages, eggs, bacon—that I happened to have with me. I have reproduced it to the best of my ability, using a vinaigrette and sour cream dressing in place of mayonnaise.

2 cups diced cooked potatoes
½ cup Vinaigrette Sauce (see page 290)
   mixed with 2 tablespoons sour cream
½ cup diced cooked beets

3 or 4 scallions or green onions, thinly
   sliced
½ cup parsley sprigs, chopped
Salt and pepper

Use small, waxy red potatoes. Boil them in their jackets. Peel, dice, and mix them with the Vinaigrette Sauce while they are still hot.

Stir the diced beets, sliced scallions or green onions, and parsley in with the potatoes before serving. Adjust the seasoning.   *A*

TOMATO SALAD

6 to 8 servings

5 to 6 tomatoes, not overripe
2 teaspoons salt
2 teaspoons sugar
2 tablespoons lemon juice

4 tablespoons salad or olive oil
Freshly ground black pepper
½ cup chopped parsley sprigs
Small bunch fresh mint, chopped

Drop the tomatoes into boiling water. Count to ten. Lift them out and when cool enough to handle, slip them out of their skins. Slice the tomatoes and lay them flat on a large platter or in a shallow dish. Sprinkle them with two teaspoons of salt and two teaspoons of sugar, and allow them to stand for half an hour.

Mix the lemon juice and oil together with three or four twists of the pepper mill. Dribble the oil mixture over the tomatoes, and sprinkle them with chopped parsley and mint.   *A*

SALAD TENNESSEE

6 to 8 servings

¾ pound Tennessee, Smithfield, or
    Westphalian ham
4 hard-boiled eggs
1 head Boston lettuce
1 cup finely sliced sweet gherkins
6 firm tomatoes

Butter
1 can Italian anchovy fillets, drained
Vinaigrette Sauce (see page 290)
2 tablespoons catsup
½ cup parsley sprigs, finely chopped

Slice the ham, cut it into strips, and then dice. Remove the yolks from the eggs and press them through a fine sieve. Cut the egg whites into strips and arrange them on lettuce leaves. Scatter the diced ham on top and sprinkle with the sieved egg yolks. Top with the sliced gherkins.

Peel the tomatoes and sauté them gently and lightly in butter. Cut them in half. Arrange the tomato halves on top of the salad, cut-side down. Cut the anchovies in half lengthwise and arrange them on top of the tomatoes in a lattice pattern.

Mix the vinaigrette and catsup, and spoon over the salad just before serving. Sprinkle with finely chopped parsley.   *A*

APPLE, GRAPEFRUIT, AND BELL PEPPER SALAD

6 servings

1 large grapefruit
2 to 3 hard, crisp eating apples

1 green bell pepper or 1 red bell pepper
½ cup parsley sprigs, finely chopped

Stand a colander or strainer in a bowl. Peel the grapefruit over the colander, removing all the white pith. Cut out the sections. Reserve the juice. Transfer the grapefruit sections to a clean bowl.

Peel, core, and quarter the apples. Cut into thin slices and mix with the grapefruit sections to prevent discoloring.

Quarter the bell pepper. Cut out all the white pith and remove the seeds. Seeds are extremely hot. Slice the pepper very thinly. Mix with the apple and grapefruit.

Dressing:

½ cup grapefruit juice
¼ cup vegetable salad oil

Salt and pepper
Finely chopped parsley

Mix one-half cup grapefruit juice with the oil. Season with salt and pepper. Spoon over the fruit and toss.

With a slotted spoon arrange the fruits and pepper on a serving dish or individual dishes. Sprinkle with finely chopped parsley before serving. *A*

Soufflés

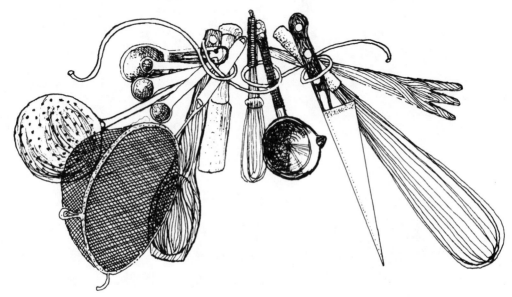

Soufflés

The soufflé is looked upon as a fearsome confection by many people, perhaps because of its French name or the fact that attention must be paid to timing. Reasons for fear are groundless if you study the recipe beforehand and remember that the hot soufflé waits for neither man nor God. Unless there is a reasonably competent cook in the kitchen to complete the preparation and assemble the soufflé, do not attempt it for formal dinner parties. Reserve this wonderful creation for your intimate friends who will not think it odd that you have to leave the table to complete its preparation and pop it in the oven. The formula for the savory soufflé is, in fact, quite simple. Once you have the hang of soufflé-making, you will find there is an infinite variety of ingredients to be used as a base—ingredients that are rarely found in an ordinary cookbook.

Cold soufflés are another matter. They can be made well in advance, and when the soufflé is made with fresh citrus juice, in my opinion, there is little that can beat this light and refreshing dessert. The "waist-watchers" will complain that half a pint of cream is used in the making. My answer is that half a pint of cream divided between eight or ten mouths does not amount to much. Forego a martini instead or that third glass of wine, if the thought really bothers you.

Do not push the soufflé aside or class it as "haute cuisine" and, therefore, beyond the skill of earth-bound mortals. Forget its French title and give it its proper place in your culinary repertoire. It is a splendid dish, hot or cold, sweet or savory, to set before your family or friends.

SAVORY SOUFFLES

Here is a basic formula for savory soufflés that works and is well worth trying. It is both fun and creative, and often solves the question of what to do with a small amount of leftovers. Follow general instructions for making soufflés in the other recipes.

Béchamel Sauce (see page 275)
1 cup liquid (milk, chicken stock, veal
   stock, or beef stock)
Salt and pepper
Nutmeg (optional)

4 egg yolks
1 cup diced or ground chicken, fish,
   cheese, or vegetables
6 egg whites
½ teaspoon cream of tartar

SOUFFLE SURPRISE

4 servings

Soufflé Surprise is one of my favorite luncheon dishes, served with a good salad and fresh fruit to follow. Here is a tip: So that you will know where to find the poached eggs, mark their positions on the outside of the dish and chances are you will serve them intact.

5 tablespoons butter
4 eggs
2 ounces finely chopped mushrooms
1 tablespoon flour
½ cup hot milk

Salt and pepper
3 eggs separated, plus 1 additional
   egg white
2 ounces grated Parmesan cheese
Cream of tartar

Heat oven to 425°F.

Prepare a one-quart soufflé dish by brushing with one-half tablespoon of soft butter. Refrigerate until needed.

Poach the four eggs until *just* set and slip them into a bowl of cold water until needed. Sauté the mushrooms in two tablespoons of the butter until just soft. Drain and season well.

Melt two and one-half tablespoons of butter in a small, heavy pan. Add the flour, stir to mix, and cook for three to four minutes over gentle heat. Off the heat, pour in the hot milk and whisk until smooth. Return to the heat and cook, stirring, until thickened. Add salt and pepper to taste. Remove from the heat and stir in the three egg yolks, one at a time, and grated cheese.

Beat the four egg whites until they foam. Add a pinch of cream of tartar; continue beating until they hold definite peaks. Fold in the stiffly beaten egg white.

Place about one-third of the mixture in the prepared soufflé dish and sprinkle with the mushrooms. Arrange the well-drained poached eggs on top and cover with the rest of the soufflé mixture.

Cook in the oven for about twenty minutes. You will find the poached eggs are still soft.

SMOKED HADDOCK SOUFFLE

4 to 6 servings

When I was young, Sunday night suppers at home were usually cold: cold meats, salads, and a cold dessert. The one exception was a hot smoked haddock soufflé that one member of the family put together, all the ingredients having been previously prepared and arranged. And how good it was!

1½ pounds smoked haddock
3 cups milk
6 tablespoons butter
6 tablespoons flour
¼ teaspoon nutmeg, freshly scraped
Pinch of cayenne pepper
Salt and pepper to taste

Grated rind of 1 lemon
8 eggs, separated plus 2 additional
  egg whites
Cream of tartar (optional)
Butter
4 tablespoons grated Parmesan cheese

Heat oven to 450°F.

Butter the inside of an eight-cup soufflé dish and sprinkle with sufficient grated cheese to coat the sides of the dish.

In a heavy pan, cover the fish with milk and bring slowly to a boil. Watch carefully, because it can boil over very quickly. Simmer gently for five minutes. Drain; set aside one and one-half cups of the milk. If there is not enough, make up the difference with water.

Cool, then flake the fish, removing all large and small bones, until you have one and one-half cups of fish.

Melt the butter in a one-quart saucepan. When foaming, stir in the flour and cook over low heat for three to four minutes, taking care it does not brown. Heat the reserved milk; off the heat, add it to the butter and flour. Whisk until smooth. Cook over moderate heat, stirring, until thickened.

Stir in the flaked fish, nutmeg, cayenne, salt, pepper, and lemon rind. Stir in the eight egg yolks one at a time.

Beat the ten egg whites with a pinch of salt, if you are using a copper bowl. If the bowl is porcelain or stainless steel, use a pinch of cream of tartar. Beat until definite peaks are formed.

(Continued)

Fold the egg whites into the fish mixture quickly and firmly, and spoon into the prepared pan. Run a thumb around the edge to form a ridge. Sprinkle the top with the remaining cheese.

Bake the soufflé in the lower third of the oven for fifteen minutes. Reduce the temperature to 350°F. and bake twenty minutes more for a wet soufflé, longer if you like it dry. Serve immediately.

CHEESE SOUFFLE

4 servings

A perfectly straightforward cheese soufflé is the ideal first course. Preparing and serving it in individual soufflé dishes eliminates the worry of there not being enough to go around.

Melted butter and grated Parmesan
  cheese
3 tablespoons butter
3 tablespoons flour
1 cup milk
¾ cup grated Parmesan and Gruyère
  cheese in equal parts

4 eggs, separated plus 1 additional
  egg white
½ teaspoon salt
Dash of nutmeg
Dash of cayenne pepper
Cream of tartar

Heat oven to 400°F.

Brush the inside of a one-quart soufflé dish or four one-cup dishes with melted butter and dust lightly with finely grated Parmesan cheese.

Melt the three tablespoons of butter in a heavy pan. Add the flour and cook gently while stirring, being careful not to burn the *roux*. Heat milk and, off the heat, add it to the *roux*. Whisk until smooth and cook until thickened.

Add both the cheeses; mix until they are thoroughly dissolved. Cool slightly. Beat in the egg yolks one at a time. Add the salt, nutmeg, and cayenne. This is your soufflé base and may be made ahead of time.

Beat the egg whites until foaming. Add a pinch of cream of tartar and continue beating until definite peaks are formed. With a metal spoon fold two spoonfuls of egg white into the soufflé base; then fold in the remainder, gently but firmly. Spoon the soufflé mixture into prepared dishes. Dust lightly with Parmesan cheese.

Reduce the heat to 375°F. immediately after placing soufflé in the oven. Bake for fifteen minutes, if using individual one-cup dishes, and for thirty minutes, if using a one-quart dish. Serve immediately.

TWO-CHEESE SOUFFLE

4 servings

3½ tablespoons butter
¾ cup grated Parmesan cheese
3½ tablespoons flour
1 cup milk, heated
4 eggs, separated plus one additional
  egg white

Salt and pepper
Pinch of cayenne pepper
1 teaspoon Dijon mustard
Cream of tartar
2 to 3 ounces Gruyère cheese, cut in small
  cubes

Heat oven to 425°F.

Prepare a one-quart soufflé dish by brushing it with one-half tablespoon soft butter and dusting with one-quarter cup grated Parmesan cheese. Refrigerate until needed.

Melt three tablespoons of butter in a small, heavy pan. Add the flour; stir to mix, and cook for three to four minutes over gentle heat. Off the heat, pour in the hot milk and whisk until smooth. Return to the heat and cook, stirring, until thickened.

Add the egg yolks one at a time, stirring after each addition. Add the salt, pepper, and cayenne to taste. Go lightly with the cayenne. Stir in the mustard. Stir in the remaining grated Parmesan cheese only.

Beat the egg whites until they foam. Add a pinch of cream of tartar and continue beating until they hold definite peaks. Stir cubed Gruyère into the egg and cheese base and quickly fold in the egg whites before the cubes have time to melt.

Spoon the soufflé mixture into the prepared dish. Reduce the temperature to 400°F. immediately after placing soufflé in the oven. Bake for twenty-five minutes in the middle of the oven. Serve at once.

SPINACH SOUFFLE

4 to 6 servings

2½ tablespoons butter
¼ cup grated Parmesan cheese, plus
  2 tablespoons
½ cup milk
½ cup strong chicken stock
2 tablespoons chopped shallot
3 tablespoons flour

4 eggs, separated plus 2 additional
  egg whites
¾ cup chopped or puréed spinach
Scraping of nutmeg
Salt and pepper
4 strips bacon, broiled crisp and crumbled
Cream of tartar

(Continued)

Heat oven to 375°F.

Prepare a one-quart soufflé dish and an aluminum collar by brushing the dish with one-half tablespoon butter and dusting with one-quarter cup grated Parmesan cheese. Tie the buttered foil collar around the dish, to stand two or three inches above the rim.

Heat the milk and chicken stock together.

Melt the butter in a heavy one-quart saucepan. Add the shallot and cook very gently for three to four minutes. Stir in the flour and continue to cook very gently three minutes longer. Off the heat, pour in the warm milk and chicken stock mixture. Whisk and return to the heat; cook slowly for two to three minutes. Allow to cool slightly. Stir in the egg yolks one at a time.

Season the spinach with nutmeg, salt, and pepper to taste. Stir the spinach into the sauce and add the crumbled bacon. Correct the seasoning so that it is pronounced.

Beat the egg whites until they foam. Add a pinch of cream of tartar. Continue beating until they hold stiff peaks. Stir a couple of large spoonfuls of the egg whites into the spinach mixture. Fold in the remainder of the egg whites.

Gently, but firmly, spoon the mixture into the prepared soufflé dish. Sprinkle with two tablespoons of grated cheese. Bake for thirty minutes. Serve immediately.

MUSHROOM SOUFFLE

6 to 8 servings

Mushroom Soufflé is another good luncheon dish, and this particular soufflé is superb. To ensure success, take your time when slicing the mushrooms—they definitely must be paper-thin—and delay stirring them into the sauce until you are ready to put the soufflé together. The sauce contains salt which will draw out the mushrooms' moisture if they sit in it too long and will thin the sauce.

5½ tablespoons butter
1 cup grated Parmesan cheese
½ pound white, fresh mushrooms
5 tablespoons flour
1 teaspoon salt
¼ teaspoon paprika

Dash of cayenne pepper
1½ cups hot milk
6 eggs, separated plus 2 additional
   egg whites
Cream of tartar

Heat oven to 400°F.

Prepare a two-quart soufflé dish by brushing with one-half tablespoon of butter and dusting it with one-quarter cup grated Parmesan cheese.

Wipe the mushrooms clean with a damp cloth. Cut off the stems flush with the caps and slice very thinly.

Melt five tablespoons of butter in a heavy pan. Add the flour, salt, paprika, and cayenne. Cook for three minutes.

Add the hot milk gradually to the *roux*, whisking vigorously. Stir in three-quarters cup of Parmesan cheese, and cook for one or two minutes more. Stir the egg yolks, one at a time, into the *roux*.

Beat the eight egg whites until they foam. Add a pinch of cream of tartar and continue beating until they hold definite peaks.

Fold the mushrooms into the *roux* and fold the entire mixture into the beaten egg whites. Spoon gently into the prepared two-quart soufflé dish.

Bake on the center shelf of the oven for twenty minutes. Open the door very gently and with a small sharp knife make a circular cut about two inches from the edge of the dish. This allows the center to rise separately and avoids the danger of the soufflé being top heavy. Bake for twenty minutes more. Serve immediately.

CAULIFLOWER CHEESE SOUFFLE

4 to 5 servings

Cauliflower Cheese Soufflé is on the solid side, so do not be disappointed if it turns out not to be a cloud of lightness. It is an excellent accompaniment for roast leg or shoulder of lamb.

3½ tablespoons butter
1 small cauliflower
Salt and pepper
3 tablespoons flour
1½ cups hot milk
Scraping of nutmeg

3 eggs, separated plus one additional
  egg white
½ cup grated Parmesan cheese
Cream of tartar
¼ cup browned bread crumbs

Heat oven to 400°F.

Prepare a one-quart soufflé dish by brushing it with one-half tablespoon soft butter. Refrigerate until needed.

Remove the leaves and hard stalk from the cauliflower, break into small pieces, and cook in a little boiling salted water until quite soft. Mash to a fairly smooth purée and season with salt and pepper.

Melt three tablespoons of butter in a small, heavy pan. Add the flour, mix, and cook for three to four minutes over gentle heat. Off the heat, pour in the hot milk and whisk until smooth. Return to the heat and cook, stirring, until the milk mixture is thickened. Season with salt and pepper; add nutmeg to taste.

(Continued)

227

Remove from the heat and stir in the egg yolks one at a time, one-half cup grated cheese less one tablespoon, and the cauliflower.

Beat the egg whites until they foam. Add a pinch of cream of tartar and continue beating until they hold definite peaks.

Fold the egg whites into the cauliflower mixture and turn into the prepared soufflé dish. Sprinkle the top with bread crumbs and with the rest of the Parmesan cheese. Bake for about thirty-five minutes.

APRICOT SOUFFLE

6 servings

Bill van Nortwick, one of my oldest American friends, gave me this recipe many years ago. It is perfect at any time of the year, but perhaps is best on a cold and dreary winter day. Most of the preparation can be done ahead of time and the cooked soufflé has the good manners to wait for as long as twenty minutes after the cooking time.

Apricot Pureé:

1 tightly packed cup of dried apricots,
   soaked overnight in sufficient water to cover
¼ cup sugar

In a pan with a cover, cook the apricots slowly until tender. If the water boils away, add a little more. Add the sugar and cook for two minutes, stirring. Cool and force the apricots through a wire strainer. The purée should be heavy and not liquid or runny. Cool.

Butter	⅓ cup sugar
Sugar	¼ teaspoon almond extract
3 egg whites	Whipped cream
Cream of tartar	

Butter the inside of a bowl or mold and sprinkle evenly with sugar, shaking out the surplus. Do the same with the lid or a piece of wax paper large enough to tie over the bowl in place of the lid.

Beat the egg whites until foaming. Add a pinch of cream of tartar and continue beating until soft peaks are formed. Add the sugar gradually and the almond extract and continue beating until stiff. Fold the egg white mixture into the apricot purée with a large metal spoon and pour the mixture into the mold or bowl. Tie the wax paper securely over the bowl or cover the mold with the lid. The mixture may now be refrigerated until needed.

When ready, place the bowl in a pan of boiling water sufficient to come two-thirds of the way up its sides. Reduce the heat until just simmering. Cook for forty minutes. Add more water if needed. Turn the soufflé out onto a warm platter and pass the whipped cream separately.

SOUFFLE A L'ORANGE

6 to 8 servings

2½ tablespoons softened butter
⅓ cup granulated sugar, plus 2 tablespoons
1 large orange
3 tablespoons sifted flour
¾ cup milk

4 eggs, separated plus 1 additional
  egg white
Cream of tartar
4 tablespoons Cointreau
Confectioners' sugar

Heat oven to 400°F.

Prepare a six-cup soufflé dish by brushing it lightly with one-half tablespoon of butter and rolling granulated sugar around the dish to coat it lightly. Shake out the excess.

Peel the orange with a vegetable peeler taking care not to include any of the white pith. Chop the peel and crush it with one tablespoon of sugar in a bowl, or use a pestle and mortar.

In an enamel or stainless-steel saucepan, mix the flour and one-third cup of sugar. Add a little of the milk to blend. Beat in the remaining milk and the orange peel. Stir over gentle heat until the mixture thickens and reaches the boiling point. Boil for thirty seconds only. Remove the pan from the heat and allow to cool slightly.

Beat the egg yolks into the sauce one at a time. Beat in one tablespoon of softened butter and dot the top of the sauce with the remaining tablespoon of butter.

In a bowl beat the egg whites and cream of tartar until soft peaks are formed. Sprinkle in one tablespoon of sugar and beat until stiff peaks are held.

Stir the Cointreau into the sauce base and add one-quarter of the egg whites. Fold in the remaining egg whites and turn the mixture into the prepared soufflé dish. Fill the dish only to within one and one-quarter inches of the top.

Place the soufflé dish on a baking sheet in the center of the oven. Reduce the heat to 375°F. and bake for twenty minutes. Quickly sprinkle the soufflé top with confectioners' sugar and bake ten to fifteen minutes longer. The top should be pleasantly browned. Rush to the table.

HOT LEMON SOUFFLE AND HOT ORANGE SOUFFLE

4 to 6 servings

These two citrus soufflés are made without a flour and butter base and are superb, light, and fresh.

Butter
Sugar
6 eggs, separated plus 1 additional
  egg white
½ cup granulated sugar

Pinch of salt
Grated rind of 1 lemon and juice of 2
  lemons (½ cup juice)
Cream of tartar
Sprinkling of confectioners' sugar

Heat oven to 375°F.

Prepare a two-quart soufflé dish by greasing it with butter and dusting with sugar. Refrigerate until needed.

Beat the egg yolks until they are thick and light yellow. Gradually add the sugar and salt and continue beating until the mixture is smooth. Beat in the lemon rind and juice.

Beat the egg whites until they are foaming, add a pinch of cream of tartar, and continue beating until they hold definite peaks.

Fold the beaten egg whites into the yolk mixture gently but thoroughly. Start by mixing in two spoonfuls of egg white and continue folding in the rest.

Spoon into the prepared soufflé dish and place the dish in a pan of boiling water. The water should reach three-quarters of the way up the dish. Bake for thirty-five to forty minutes. Sprinkle with confectioners' sugar and serve immediately.

To make the Hot Orange Soufflé, follow the directions for the Hot Lemon Soufflé, but substitute one six-ounce can of undiluted frozen orange juice concentrate plus the grated rind of one orange for the lemon juice and lemon rind.

CHOCOLATE SOUFFLE

8 to 10 servings

A hot chocolate soufflé, so chocolaty that it can satisfy almost any "chocoholic," is a luxury that should come out of hiding for special occasions only.

6 tablespoons butter
4 tablespoons flour
8 ounces Maillard chocolate, or another
  semisweet chocolate
2 cups milk
1 cup sugar

8 egg yolks
½ teaspoon vanilla extract (optional)
14 egg whites
½ teaspoon cream of tartar
  or ½ teaspoon salt
Confectioners' sugar

Heat oven to 450°F.

Prepare a three-quart soufflé dish by buttering it, dusting with sugar, and tying a long strip of aluminum foil, buttered on the inside, around the mold to stand three inches above the top.

In a heavy pan, melt the butter and stir in the flour. Cook for two minutes. Grate or chop the chocolate and stir it in. Heat the milk and add it to the pan, stirring quickly until smooth.

Stir in the sugar and cook, stirring until thickened. Beat with a whisk for a minute or two. Stir in the egg yolks, two at a time, and the vanilla. Preparation up to this point may be done ahead of time. Stir the chocolate base from time to time to prevent a skin from forming. Alternatively, a light dusting of sugar will prevent this.

Beat the egg whites slowly at first to incorporate as much air as possible. Add the cream of tartar if the bowl is not copper, or salt if copper is used. Beat until definite peaks are formed. Thin the chocolate mixture with two large spoonfuls of egg white, then fold in the rest.

Spoon into the prepared dish. Place in a pan of hot water and bake for forty to forty-five minutes. Remove the collar, dust with confectioners' sugar, and rush to the table.

SOUFFLE A L'AVOCAT

8 servings

A soufflé of avocados came to me as quite a surprise. I had never been quite able to make up my mind as to whether the avocado was a fruit or vegetable. I have now decided it can be either. It is unusual and well worth a try.

Almond Crunch:

½ cup butter
½ cup sugar
1 tablespoon water

½ tablespoon light corn syrup
⅓ cup finely chopped blanched almonds

Butter a baking sheet.

Melt butter in a one-quart saucepan over low heat. Add the sugar and heat to the boiling point, stirring constantly. Stir in water and corn syrup. Boil over medium heat, stirring constantly, to 290°F. on the candy thermometer for about seven minutes, or until a small amount of mixture dropped into cold water separates into hard but not brittle threads.

Remove from the heat. Stir in the almonds. Spread the mixture over the baking sheet about one-quarter inch thick. Cool. When firm, break into pieces and crush with a rolling pin.

(Continued)

1½ cups granulated sugar
⅓ cup water
1 cup heavy cream, whipped

8 egg whites
3 tablespoons Kirsch
1½ cups avocado purée

Place a four-inch band of double-thickness aluminum foil around the top of a one-quart soufflé dish. Fasten it with tape so the foil stands about two inches above the rim of the dish.

Place the sugar and water in a heavy one-quart saucepan. Over medium heat, simmer the sugar to 200°F. on a candy thermometer, approximately five minutes. *Do not stir.*

Meanwhile, whip the cream and refrigerate it.

With an electric mixer, beat the egg whites in a large bowl until stiff, but not dry. Continue beating while slowly adding the syrup to the egg whites. Whip until mixture is completely cool, about ten minutes. Beat in the Kirsch. At a very low speed, slowly add the avocado purée and then the whipped cream.

Spoon one-third of the mixture into the prepared soufflé dish. Sprinkle one-third of the almond crunch mixture in an even layer. Repeat with a second layer of one-third of the avocado mixture and another one-third of the almond crunch. Spread the remaining one-third of the avocado mixture and top with the remaining almond crunch. Place in the freezer overnight.

Remove the foil and serve with a cold Sabayon (see page 292) or strawberry sauce.

ST. JOHN'S ICED LIME SOUFFLE

6 to 8 servings

The Connaught Hotel in London served a very good hot lime soufflé at one period in its history, and I could see no reason why an iced lime soufflé would not be equally as good. It is more than equally as good, since it can be made eight hours before or even a day ahead of time.

1 envelope unflavored gelatin
¼ cup water
¾ cup milk
4 eggs, separated plus 3 additional whites

½ cup sugar
½ cup fresh lime juice (about 6 limes)
1 cup heavy cream
3 drops of green food coloring

Fold over lengthwise a long strip of aluminum foil and oil it on one side. Tie it around a one-quart soufflé dish, oiled side in, to make a collar standing three inches above the top.

Sprinkle the gelatin over the one-quarter cup water to soften it. Heat the milk in the top of a double boiler.

Beat the egg yolks with the sugar until they are light and lemon-colored; pour the hot milk over them. Return the mixture to the top of the double boiler and add the gelatin.

Cook the mixture over hot water, stirring or whisking constantly, until it is thick and creamy; be careful that it does not boil. Remove the pan from the heat, let the mixture cool, then add the lime juice. Refrigerate the mixture until it begins to thicken.

Whip the cream until it is thick but not stiff, and fold it into the lime mixture, adding three drops *only* of green food coloring. Refrigerate the mixture until it is just beginning to set.

Beat the egg whites until they are stiff but not dry, and fold them gently into the mixture with a metal spoon. Spoon the soufflé into the prepared mold and chill it for at least three hours, or longer if desired. Remove collar carefully before serving.

Variation: For those of you who live in Florida, here is a variation of St. John's Iced Lime Soufflé. In my opinion, the Key lime is a quite different fruit from the green lime that is sold in every greengrocer.

In place of one-half cup regular fresh lime juice, substitute one-half cup chilled Key lime juice (about six limes). Follow the directions for preparation given in the recipe for St. John's Iced Lime Soufflé. Before serving, remove the foil collar and pat one-half cup of macaroon or cake crumbs onto the sides of the soufflé.

CHAPEL CLEEVE COLD LEMON SOUFFLE

6 to 8 servings

Chapel Cleeve is a house in Sommerset, England. One wing dates back to the Middle Ages and is inhabited by bats, but the lived-in part that I know is late-Victorian in the grand manner.

When the French chef was away, Mrs. Beck, the cook, took great pride in her Cold Lemon Soufflé. She gave me the recipe many years ago, leaving out just one ingredient and an all-important part of the method. This is the way of many cooks and something I fail to understand. Many soufflés later, I brought it to perfection. It answers to all and every cliché given to the soufflé.

1 envelope unflavored gelatin	½ cup sugar
¼ cup water	½ cup lemon juice
¾ cup milk	3 tablespoons grated lemon rind
4 eggs, separated plus 3 additional whites	1 cup heavy cream

Fold over lengthwise a long strip of aluminum foil and oil it on one side. Tie it around a one-quart soufflé dish or mold, oiled side in, to make a collar three inches above the top.

Sprinkle the gelatin over one-quarter cup water to soften it. Heat the milk in the top of a double boiler.

(Continued)

Beat the egg yolks with the sugar until they are light and lemon-colored; pour the hot milk over them. Return the mixture to the top of the double boiler and add the gelatin.

Cook the mixture over hot water, stirring or whisking constantly until it is thick and creamy; be careful that it does not boil.

Remove the pan from the heat, let the mixture cool, then add the lemon juice and rind. This is important to preserve the freshness of the lemon. Refrigerate the mixture until it begins to thicken.

Whip the cream until it is thick but not stiff, and fold it into the lemon mixture. Refrigerate the mixture until it is just beginning to set.

Beat the egg whites until they are stiff but not dry, and fold them gently into the mixture wth a metal spoon. Spoon the soufflé into the prepared mold and chill three hours or longer.

ICED RASPBERRY SOUFFLE

8 to 10 servings

If you have the good fortune to grow your own raspberries, or if you can buy them locally when they are in season and inexpensive, replace the frozen berries in this recipe with fresh ones and sweeten to taste. Either berry makes a marvelous soufflé to look at and an even better one to taste.

3 packages (10 ounces each) frozen raspberries, defrosted
1½ tablespoons unflavored gelatin
4 eggs, separated
2 to 3 tablespoons superfine sugar, if needed

¼ cup Framboise
1½ cups heavy cream
Pinch of salt
½ cup whipped cream for decoration (optional)

Prepare a four-cup soufflé dish by tying a lightly oiled collar of aluminum foil around it to stand about two inches above the rim. Chill until needed.

Drain the raspberries and set aside two-thirds cup of juice and an additional one-quarter cup of juice. Purée the raspberries and set aside one and one-half cups of purée.

Sprinkle the gelatin over the one-quarter cup of juice to soften it. Beat the egg yolks until they are thick and yellow.

Bring two-thirds cup of the raspberry juice to a boil and simmer for three to four minutes. Pour the hot liquid in a fine stream over the yolks while beating. Add the softened gelatin and continue beating until the mixture is cool. To accelerate the operation, stand the bowl in a larger one filled with ice and water. Stir in the purée and Framboise.

Beat the heavy cream over ice until it holds a ribbon. Stir into the egg and purée mixture. Chill over ice until about to set.

Beat the egg whites with a pinch of salt until they hold stiff peaks. Fold the whites into the raspberry mixture with a large metal spoon, lightly and thoroughly.

Spoon the mixture into the prepared dish and chill for at least four hours. Remove the collar and serve, garnished with whipped cream rosettes.

SOUFFLE MONTE CRISTO

6 to 8 servings

I have no idea how this soufflé got its name. The name is unusual and so is the soufflé. The combination of flavors and textures, surprisingly enough, go well together.

4 large eggs, separated plus 1 additional egg white	1 cup heavy cream
⅓ cup sugar	2 squares unsweetened chocolate, grated
1 envelope unflavored gelatin	1 pint fresh strawberries
¼ cup water	Sugar
4 to 6 tablespoons Kirsch	Whipped cream for decoration

Fold over lengthwise a long strip of aluminum foil, and oil it on one side. Tie it around a one-quart soufflé dish, oiled-side in, to make a collar standing three inches above the top. Remove both ends of a twelve-ounce soft drink can and oil the outside, placing it in the center of the mold.

Beat the egg yolks with one-third cup of sugar until they are thick and lemon-colored. Sprinkle gelatin over one-quarter cup water, let it stand for ten minutes, and dissolve it over gentle heat. Do not let it boil. Stir the gelatin into the egg yolk mixture, and add the Kirsch.

Whip the cream until it is thick but not stiff, and fold it into the egg yolk mixture.

Beat the egg whites until they are stiff, and fold them into the yolk mixture. Pour half of the soufflé mixture into the prepared dish, and sprinkle it with the grated chocolate. Pour in the remaining soufflé mixture. It should come one-half inch above the dish. Refrigerate the soufflé for at least four hours.

Wash the strawberries or wipe them with a damp cloth. Hull and sprinkle them with sugar and Kirsch to taste.

Gently run a knife around the soft drink can and carefully remove it. Fill the cavity immediately with the strawberries, packing them in tightly; reserve a few for decoration.

Remove the collar before serving. Garnish with rosettes of sweetened whipped cream and strawberries cut in quarters.

ICED CHOCOLATE SOUFFLE

10 to 12 servings

The chocolate soufflé, hot or cold, makes a big hit at any dinner party. It is rich, so choose the rest of the menu with care, working up to the dessert's richness.

8 squares (8 ounces) semisweet chocolate
2 cups half-and-half
2 envelopes unflavored gelatin
¼ cup cold water
6 eggs, separated
½ cup sugar

2 teaspoons vanilla
½ teaspoon salt
¼ cup dark rum
2 cups heavy cream
½ cup dry cake crumbs

Fold over lengthwise a long strip of aluminum foil, and oil it on one side. Tie it around a one-quart soufflé dish, oiled-side in, to make a collar standing three inches above the top.

In the top of a double boiler over hot water, melt the chocolate in the half-and-half. Sprinkle the gelatin over the one-quarter cup cold water to soften it.

Beat the egg yolks with one-quarter cup sugar until they are light and lemon-colored. To the chocolate mixture, add the vanilla, salt, egg yolk mixture, and softened gelatin.

Cook the mixture over low heat, stirring constantly, until it is the consistency of very heavy cream. Cool. Add the rum; chill the mixture until it begins to thicken.

Beat the cream with one-quarter cup of sugar until it is thick but not stiff. Beat the egg whites until they hold firm peaks.

Combine the chocolate mixture with the whipped cream and fold in the egg whites with a large metal spoon. Spoon into the soufflé mold and chill for at least three hours. Remove the collar before serving. Pat dry cake crumbs or crushed macaroons onto the side of the soufflé.

ICED COFFEE SOUFFLE

6 to 8 servings

1 envelope unflavored gelatin
¼ cup cool water
3 eggs, separated plus 2 additional
   egg whites
½ cup sugar

1½ cups milk
8 tablespoons dry instant coffee
½ pint heavy cream
½ cup macaroon crumbs or lightly
   browned cake crumbs

Prepare a one-quart soufflé dish by tying a collar of oiled aluminum foil around it to stand two inches above the rim. Refrigerate until needed.

Sprinkle the gelatin over one-quarter cup cool water to soften it.

Beat together the egg yolks and sugar until stiff and creamy. Heat the milk until almost boiling. Spoon a little of the milk into the egg yolks, then pour the egg yolk mixture into the remaining hot milk, whisking vigorously. Return to the top of the double boiler.

Add the gelatin and coffee; cook until the mixture reaches the thickness of heavy cream, whisking all the time. Allow to cool.

Watch the coffee mixture carefully. When it begins to set, whip the cream until thick. Fold it into the coffee mixture.

Whip the egg whites until stiff and fold them in. Pour the mixture into the soufflé dish and chill for at least two hours. Remove the collar before serving. Pat cake or macaroon crumbs onto the sides of the soufflé.

Desserts

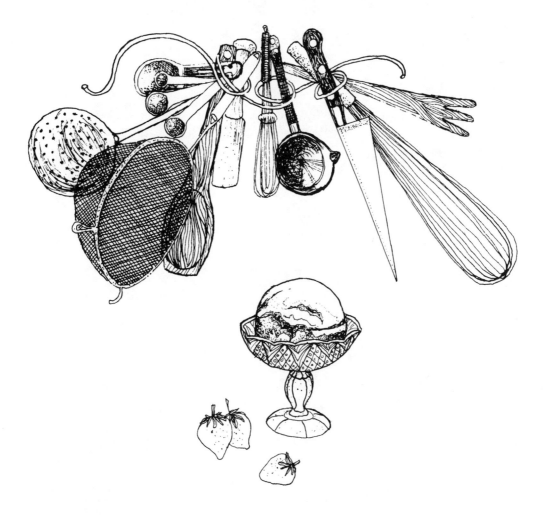

Desserts

It may come as a surprise to learn that I consider the dessert the most important item on the menu. It is the last to be served and the one by which the meal is remembered. I can already hear cries of anguish: "How could he possibly make such a statement when we are one and all following the advice of the wise men and turning our faces the other way when desserts are offered!" Well, my advice is, if you really crave a portion of something wickedly rich, have it by all means, but cut down on your eating the following day. It is better to indulge yourself now and again than to spoil your otherwise good nature. Yet another cry is: "We can't possibly allow ourselves the iced lime soufflé; there's a whole cup of cream in that!" Quite true, but divided between ten it does not amount to much. Consider what you are shunning before you do so.

The dessert covers a wide field from a single piece of fresh fruit, or a small bunch of grapes, to the excitingly rich, luxurious frozen chocolate mousse.

Choose your dessert carefully and, if you are "waist-watching," have no more than one small helping, no matter how strong the craving.

BREAD-AND-BUTTER PUDDING

6 to 8 servings

Bread-and-Butter Pudding seems to have taken a back seat in the culinary repertoire in America, yet it appears with monotonous regularity on the menus of good French restaurants in this country and in Europe. When I was a child, it was lumped together with Rice Pudding, Queen of Puddings, and simple snow eggs as nursery food.

7 to 8 slices white bread	2 cups milk
½ tablespoon butter	2 tablespoons golden raisins
2 large eggs	2 tablespoons currants
3 tablespoons sugar	

Heat oven to 350°F.

Remove the crusts from the bread and cut each slice in half horizontally to make fourteen to sixteen very thin slices. Butter them on one side.

Beat the eggs and sugar together in a bowl. Add the milk and beat again.

Grease the inside of the soufflé or pie dish with butter. Lay two slices of bread on the bottom, buttered-side up, and sprinkle them with a quarter of the raisins and currants. Lay two more slices of bread on the top, buttered-side up, and sprinkle with raisins and currants. Continue until all but four slices are used. Add the remaining raisins and currants.

Cut the remaining bread slices in half diagonally. Slide two slices of bread between each side of the dish and the layered bread, long-end down and point up. Fold the points down so that they form a sort of lid.

Pour the eggs and milk over the layered bread in the dish and wait for one-half hour before baking in the middle of the oven. Bake for forty minutes, at which time the top will be brown and crisp. Serve at room temperature. *A*

RICE PUDDING

4 to 6 servings

Rice Pudding is not considered "gourmet" by those who use that extraordinary word. But, how wrong they are. Well-made, it is delicious and can be found on the menu of many good French restaurants.

4 cups milk	½ teaspoon vanilla extract
¾ cup sugar, or less	⅓ cup raisins or currants
Pinch of salt	Powdered cinnamon
2 tablespoons butter	Freshly grated nutmeg
3 tablespoons rice, uncooked	Heavy cream

Heat oven to 300°F.

Mix milk, sugar, salt, butter, and rice in a five- to six-cup, shallow oven-proof dish. Stir the mixture three or four times.

Bake for two hours, uncovered.

Add the vanilla and raisins. Stir and sprinkle with the spices.

Bake for another hour without stirring so that a skin forms on the top. When the pudding is taken out of the oven, it will sink a little. Loosen the pudding from the edge of the dish with a small knife so that the skin sinks with the rice.

Serve slightly warm or at room temperature with very cold heavy cream. *A*

QUEEN OF PUDDINGS

4 to 6 servings

Queen of Puddings is a creamy custard-like mixture, covered with a layer of preserves—raspberry, strawberry, or a jelly of sorts, should you prefer it—and topped with a soft meringue, lightly browned. It is an old-fashioned dessert much beloved by Victorians and Edwardians.

5 ounces white or whole-wheat fresh
    bread crumbs (about 9 slices, crusts
    removed)
4 tablespoons vanilla sugar, or
    4 tablespoons granulated sugar and
    1 teaspoon vanilla extract

2 cups milk
4 tablespoons unsalted butter
4 large egg yolks
4 tablespoons black or red currant jelly,
    melted

Heat oven to 350°F.

Put the bread crumbs and sugar in a mixing bowl. Heat the milk to just below its boiling point. Dissolve butter in the milk and add the vanilla extract, if vanilla sugar is not used.

Pour the milk over the bread crumbs lightly and mix. Leave for about ten minutes. Beat the egg yolks and mix them into the crumbs and milk.

Butter a shallow one-quart oven-proof dish—a deep pie dish is ideal. Pour in the custard and bake in the oven for about twenty minutes. Cooking time will depend on the depth of the dish. The custard must not overcook.

Spread the melted jelly over the baked custard, taking care not to break the surface.

Meringue:

4 egg whites
Pinch of salt

½ cup superfine sugar, plus 1 tablespoon
    for dusting

(Continued)

Beat the egg whites until peaks are formed. Add a pinch of salt. Continue beating while adding half the sugar. Fold in the other half of the sugar and pile the meringue on top of the custard.

Sprinkle with the remaining tablespoon of sugar and return the pudding to the oven for fifteen minutes, or until the meringue browns. Serve hot or at room temperature.   *A*

PULLMAN PUDDING

6 to 8 servings

A steamed pudding is good winter fare and this is one of the best. The flavor is sharp, and once all the ingredients are assembled your troubles are over, provided you don't allow the pot to boil dry. Unlike a soufflé, it will wait for you.

2 ounces dried prunes
2 ounces dried apricots
2 ounces glacé cherries
1 ounce angelica or candied fruits
1 tablespoon flour
½ cup unsalted butter
½ cup granulated sugar
Grated rind of 1 orange
3 eggs

2 ounces fresh white bread crumbs
   (3 slices, crusts removed)
⅔ cup flour, sifted
1 teaspoon double-acting baking powder
⅓ cup orange juice
1 tablespoon butter for greasing mold
3 tablespoons light corn syrup
6 dried apricot halves, soaked
Whipped cream

Cut up the prunes, apricots, cherries, and angelica in small pieces and mix thoroughly with one tablespoon of flour. Set aside.

Cream the butter and sugar; stir in the orange rind. Beat eggs lightly and stir them into the butter and sugar mixture.

Mix the bread crumbs with the flour and baking powder. Fold into the batter. Stir in orange juice and fold in flour-coated chopped fruits.

Butter a three-cup pudding steamer or bowl thoroughly and pour in the corn syrup. Arrange the apricot halves on the bottom of the bowl and spoon in fruit mixture, tapping the bowl to eliminate air pockets. Cover. (If you are using a bowl, cover it first with buttered wax paper and then two layers of foil, tied securely with string.)

Stand the pudding container in a pot with enough boiling water to come two-thirds up its sides. Steam for one and three-quarters to two hours, covered. Check the water level now and again; keep it at a gentle simmer.

Unmold the pudding and serve with whipped cream.

GINGER PUDDING

6 to 8 servings

Butter for greasing mold
½ cup unsalted butter
½ cup dark brown sugar, tightly packed
2 eggs, lightly beaten
1 cup flour, sifted

½ teaspoon bicarbonate of soda
1 tablespoon powdered ginger
2½ ounces crystallized ginger, chopped
1 tablespoon flour for dusting
Whipped cream

Grease with butter a one-quart mold or bowl, or a special mold with a lid for steamed puddings.

Cream the butter and brown sugar until light. Stir in the beaten eggs and beat thoroughly.

Sift together flour, bicarbonate of soda, and powdered ginger. Dust the chopped ginger with flour. Mix the flour and egg mixture thoroughly and stir in the chopped ginger.

Spoon into the prepared mold or bowl. If a bowl is used, tie a piece of wax paper and then foil securely over the bowl to make a lid. Stand the pudding container in a large pot with hot water halfway up its sides and simmer for one and one-half hours.

Turn out the pudding on a warm serving plate. Serve with whipped cream. The pudding will come to no harm if it has to wait half an hour or so.

PLUM PUDDING

To the best of my knowledge, this recipe for Plum Pudding has been in my family for four generations, mine being the fourth. Christmas would seem odd without it.

In the tropics or frigid north it is equally good and, in whatever part of the world I happened to be, one or two always arrived in the nick of time for Christmas. Plum Pudding is one of the best examples of the British passion for heavy heat-generating puddings, made with quantities of dried fruits, and is a genuine boost to the dried fruit-producing regions of the Mediterranean, the Peloponnesus in particular.

1¾ pounds beef suet
1 pound white bread crumbs, made from
    stale bread
¾ pound currants
¾ pound large raisins
¾ pound golden raisins

4 cups all-purpose flour
1 teaspoon baking powder
8 large eggs
½ cup brandy
¼ cup brandy for flaming
Hard Sauce (see page 292)

(Continued)

Have ready two twenty-four-inch squares of clean cloth.

Chill the beef suet thoroughly. Remove the membrane and grate it on the coarsest side of your grater. Prepare the bread crumbs from stale bread. Wash and dry the currants and raisins.

Sift the flour and baking powder together, then mix all the dry ingredients in a large bowl.

Beat the eggs lightly and add the one-half cup of brandy to them. Pour the egg mixture into the bowl with the dry ingredients and mix thoroughly.

Flour each square of cloth generously and pile half of the pudding mixture on each piece of cloth. Gather up the edges and tie them securely with heavy string.

Bring to a boil a pot of water large enough to hold both, or a pot for each, and boil for five hours. Drain the pudding and hang it up by its string. It will keep in this way for a year.

To serve the pudding, boil for one hour and unwrap from its cloth onto a serving dish. Pour warm brandy over the pudding and carry it to the table in flames with a sprig of holly stuck in the top. Serve with Hard Sauce.   *A*

SUMMER PUDDING

6 to 8 servings

Summer Pudding is made in England when there is a glut of soft fruits, and sufficient preserves already have been made to see the household through the year. Traditionally, raspberries and red currants are the fruits used. The uncomplicated fresh flavor is unforgettable and, served with rich heavy cream, it is a dessert fit for a king.

6 to 8 thin slices white bread, crusts removed	1 tablespoon water
4 cups red currants	Sugar to taste
4 cups fresh raspberries	Whipped cream, unsweetened

Line the bottom and sides of a mixing bowl with slices of bread, cutting them to fit the bowl. Set aside enough slices to cover the pudding.

Remove the stems from the currants and combine with the raspberries in an enamel-lined or stainless-steel pan. Add a tablespoon or so of water and cook for about two minutes, stirring to mix. Stir in sugar to taste; chill.

Pour the berries into the bread-lined bowl and cover with the remaining slices of bread. Place a plate to fit on top (slightly smaller than bowl rim), then add a heavy weight. Chill in the refrigerator overnight.

Turn out the pudding on a serving dish, preferably a deep one so that the juices will not spill over. Serve with unsweetened whipped cream.   *A*

POACHED PEARS WITH RASPBERRY SAUCE

6 servings

Fruit compotes are much neglected in this country. The pear is one of our best fruits. Served with or without a sauce, it is a most suitable ending to any meal, rich or light.

6 pears, Anjou or Comice, not too ripe
3 cups sugar
2 quarts water

4 sticks cinnamon, 8 whole cloves,
    1 lemon cut into quarters, all tied
    in a cheesecloth bag

Peel the pears. Cut a thin slice from the bottom of each so that the pears will stand upright.
To prepare the poaching syrup, in a large pan with a lid dissolve the sugar in the water. Add the spice bag. Simmer for half an hour with the lid on.
Add the pears and simmer gently until they feel soft when pierced with a toothpick. Do not overcook. Cool the pears in the syrup; then drain. (Freeze the syrup for future use.)

Raspberry Sauce:

1 package (12 ounces) frozen raspberries, drained
½ cup black currant preserves

Rub both through a fine sieve and mix thoroughly.
To serve, arrange the pears on a serving dish. Spoon enough sauce over them to coat completely and pass the remainder in a sauceboat.
        A

COMPOTE OF RED PLUMS

6 to 8 servings

3 pounds red or black plums, not overripe
½ cup sugar
¼ cup water

Crème Anglaise (see page 294), or
    heavy cream

Heat oven to 350°F.
Wash the fruit and remove the stems, if any. Place the plums in a two-quart casserole or a stainless-steel or enamel-lined pan with sugar and water, cover with a tight-fitting lid, and bring almost to the boil on top of the range.
Transfer to the oven and cook, lightly covered, for fifteen to twenty minutes. Add additional sugar to taste. Cooking time depends on the ripeness of the plums.
Serve cold with Crème Anglaise or heavy cream.
        A

COMPOTE OF APRICOTS

4 to 6 servings

2 pounds apricots
Sugar or honey to taste

Heat oven to 325°F.

Wash and halve the apricots. Remove the stones and put six aside. Crack the six stones with a hammer and take out the kernels. Place the apricots and kernels in an enamel-lined or stainless-steel pan with a lid.

Add two tablespoons of water and put in the oven for twenty minutes, or until tender but not falling apart. Stir in the sugar or honey to taste. Allow the apricots to cool in the pan. Remove the kernels before serving.

A

COMPOTE OF FRUITS

8 servings

¼ cup sugar
Juice of 1 large lemon
2 pears, peeled and sliced
⅓ cup seedless green grapes
⅓ cup red grapes, seeded
2 bananas, peeled and sliced
2 apples, peeled, cored, and sliced
4 dried figs, sliced
3 oranges, peeled and separated into wedges
⅓ cup water
½ cup apricot jam
⅓ cup Kirsch or cognac
1 cup fresh strawberries

Place the sugar in a large crock or earthenware bowl. Stir in the lemon juice and all the fruit, except the strawberries.

In a saucepan, combine the water and the apricot jam. Cook the mixture, stirring, until it is thick. Force it through a sieve, and stir in the Kirsch or cognac.

Pour the sauce over the fruit mixture and stir it well. Store the compote in the refrigerator. This may be made a day ahead of time.

Before serving, stir in the strawberries.

A

POACHED RHUBARB

5 to 6 servings

When I was young, rhubarb was used as a blood cleanser in the spring. I never could understand why blood got soiled in the winter and not at any other time of year. I liked rhubarb then and I like it now. The flavor is improved by root ginger, something unobtainable when I was growing up. Try rhubarb for breakfast instead of citrus fruit.

3 pounds rhubarb
1 tablespoon root ginger, peeled and finely chopped
½ cup sugar

Heat oven to 350°F.
Wash the rhubarb and trim both ends, making sure none of the green leaves remains. The leaves contain a highly efficient poison.
Cut the stalks into one-and-one-half-inch pieces. Mix the rhubarb pieces with chopped ginger and sprinkle them with one-half cup of sugar.
In a heavy stainless-steel or enamel-coated pan with a lid, cook the fruit on the center rack of the oven for thirty minutes. After twenty minutes check to see that it is not overcooked. Test for doneness. Cooking time varies according to the age of the rhubarb.
Stir in more sugar as it is needed. Serve cold. *A*

APPLE RINGS

4 servings

Baked apples are fall fare and there is nothing new about using alcohol in cooking them. In Normandy, Calvados and apples are not newcomers. So why not in our own country use that splendid bourbon that is nationally available?
For those who shun cream, the apple rings may be served without it, and they will not be disappointed. Do the baking in advance—don't refrigerate—and serve at room temperature.

Butter
4 hard, juicy apples
½ cup lemon juice

½ cup bourbon
¾ cup dark brown sugar
1 cup whipping cream

Heat oven to 350°F.
Butter lightly a shallow oven-proof dish. Peel, core, and slice the apples in rings, one-quarter of an inch thick. Arrange them in the dish. It may be necessary to overlap them slightly.

(Continued)

Pour lemon juice and bourbon over the apples and sprinkle with brown sugar.

Bake on the center rack in the oven for forty-five minutes or until the apple rings are tender and translucent.

Pour off the syrup. There should be at least three-quarters cup. Chill the syrup.

Whip the cream and add the chilled syrup gradually as you whip.

Serve the apple rings in the dish in which they were cooked or rearrange them in a fresh one. Brush with the remaining syrup and pass the cream separately.   *A*

DEEP-DISH RHUBARB PIE

5 to 6 servings

All-Purpose Pastry (see page 300)
3 pounds rhubarb
2½ cups granulated sugar
Rind of 1 lemon, grated

¼ teaspoon ground ginger
2 ounces fresh green ginger, diced
1 egg yolk mixed with 2 tablespoons milk
Superfine sugar for dusting

Prepare the pastry according to the recipe. Refrigerate for at least two hours.

Heat oven to 425°F.

Remove the leaves and root end of the rhubarb; the leaves are poisonous. Cut the stalks into one-and-one-half-inch pieces. In a bowl, mix together the rhubarb, sugar, grated lemon rind, ground ginger, and diced green ginger.

Pile the sugared rhubarb into a deep, one-quart pie dish and mound it high.

Mix egg yolk with the milk.

Roll out the prepared pastry, approximately one-eighth inch thick. Brush the rim of the pie dish with the egg yolk. Cover the mounded rhubarb with the pastry and trim it to fit the dish.

Gather the remaining fragments into a ball and roll out to the same thickness as before. Cut strips the same width as the rim of the dish. Brush the dough that is already on the dish with egg yolk. Lay the strips around the edge and press into place. With a fork, or fingers and thumb, imprint the edge with ridges.

With the remainder of the pastry, make cut-out decorations of your choice and place them on the pie top. Press them into place and brush with egg yolk. If the pie is not to be baked right away, it must be brushed again just before it is put into the oven. Egg yolk loses its effectiveness if not used immediately.

Bake the pie for fifteen minutes; reduce the temperature to 350°F. and bake thirty-five minutes more. If the crust is taking on too much color, cover it with foil for the last half hour of baking. Sprinkle with superfine sugar after removing it from the oven.   *A*

PLUM GRASMERE

5 to 6 servings

Plum Grasmere is very much like Early American fruit desserts—the Crumbles, Brown Betty, and so on—all splendid dishes. It has been much neglected. The same topping may be used on raspberries, apples, and gooseberries.

3 pounds black plums
1 cup softened butter
8 ounces flour, sifted with a pinch of
    bicarbonate of soda and 3 tablespoons
    powdered ginger

3 ounces light brown sugar
3 ounces granulated sugar
Butter for greasing baking dish
2 teaspoons granulated sugar

Heat oven to 350°F.

Wash the plums and remove the stems, if any. Cut the fruit in half and remove the pits.

Chip the butter into the flour that has been sifted with the bicarbonate of soda and ginger. Crumble the butter-flour mixture with the tips of fingers until it is the consistency of cornmeal. Add the sugars and continue to crumble.

Butter a one-and-one-quarter-inch-deep oven-proof dish generously. Arrange the plums in it and sprinkle them lightly with two teaspoons of granulated sugar. Spread the crumbled topping evenly over the plums; do not press down.

Bake for forty minutes. Serve at room temperature.   *A*

DEEP-DISH APPLE PIE

5 to 6 servings

All-Purpose Pastry (see page 300)
6 Greening apples, or any hard, juicy
    apple
½ cup sugar

8 cloves
2 sticks cinnamon, broken in half
Grated rind of 1 lemon

Prepare pastry dough according to the recipe. Chill in the refrigerator for at least two hours.

Heat oven to 425°F.

Peel, core, and slice the apples thinly. In a bowl, toss together the apples, sugar, cloves, cinnamon sticks, and grated lemon rind.

Fill a deep pie dish with the sliced apples, mounding them to form a dome.

(Continued)

Roll out the pastry, about one-eighth inch thick. Moisten the edge of the dish. Lay the pastry over the apples, pressing pastry to the rim of the dish. Cut a strip of dough the same width as the dish rim. Moisten the edge of the pastry and lay the strip neatly around the rim, pressing so that it makes a firm contact. Make deep indentations with the forefinger and thumb of left hand and the first finger of right.

Glaze:

1 egg yolk mixed with 2 tablespoons cold water
Superfine sugar for dusting

Mix the water with the egg yolk and brush the entire surface with the mixture. Make decorative cutouts with the remaining pastry and arrange them on top. Brush with the glaze.

Bake in the oven for one hour. A steam vent in the crust is unnecessary. If the pastry is taking on too much color, cover with a sheet of brown paper. Dust the crust with the sugar while hot.

A

APPLE CHARLOTTE

5 to 6 servings

3 pounds apples (preferably Greenings, but any hard, juicy apple will do)
16 tablespoons sweet butter, melted
Grated rind of 1 lemon
1 stick cinnamon

2 tablespoons lemon juice
1 loaf white bread, thinly sliced
Heavy cream
Apricot Sauce (see page 293)

Heat oven to 400°F.

Peel, core, and dice the apples. Cook them slowly with half of the melted butter, the grated lemon rind, and cinnamon for about half an hour, or until they are reduced to a thick purée.

Remove the cinnamon stick. Stir in the lemon juice.

Remove crusts from the bread. Cut the slices in half to resemble triangles with flat ends. Dip the pieces in melted butter and line the bottom and sides of a Charlotte dish, or any suitable one-quart bowl or mold, overlapping the bread slices to cover the sides completely.

Fill center of the mold with apples and cover with the remaining bread dipped in butter.

Place the mold on a baking sheet and bake at 400°F. for approximately forty minutes, or until the top is brown.

Unmold on a serving dish and serve hot, or at room temperature, with heavy cream or Apricot Sauce.

GERMAN APPLE PIE

6 servings

German Apple Pie is redolent of autumn and spice; and what could be less trouble to prepare or more suitable for fall days with a nip in the air?

5 hard and juicy apples, peeled, cored,
   and thinly sliced
Juice of half a lemon
1 cup sugar
½ teaspoon ground cinnamon

4 tablespoons butter
1 egg
½ cup flour
1 teaspoon baking powder

Heat oven to 350°F.

Sprinkle the apples with lemon juice and toss them with one-half cup of sugar and the cinnamon. Melt half the butter in a large oven-proof skillet and add the apples. Toss, shaking the skillet, until the apples are heated through.

Cream together the remaining butter and sugar and blend in the egg.

Sift the flour and baking powder together and stir this into the egg mixture. Drop the batter by spoonfuls over the apples. Bake forty-five minutes. Serve at room temperature.

LEMON MERINGUE PIE

6 servings

Lemon Meringue Pie is a hardy perennial. While it was once popular in this country, it has taken a back seat for no reason that I have been able to understand. The French cooks and chefs, who know a good thing when they see it, have taken it to their bosoms. It is to be found in many a multi-starred restaurant in France.

All-Purpose Pastry (see page 300)

Prepare and bake one nine-inch pie shell according to the recipe.

Lemon Filling:
3 eggs plus 1 egg yolk
1 cup sugar

8 tablespoons butter
Juice and grated rind of 2 lemons

In the top of a double boiler, combine the eggs, egg yolk, and sugar. Stir in the butter, lemon juice, and rind. Cook the mixture over hot water, stirring constantly, until it is thick.

Cool the filling and pour it into the pie shell.

(Continued)

Meringue:

4 egg whites
½ teaspoon salt
¼ teaspoon cream of tartar

1 teaspoon vanilla
1½ tablespoons superfine sugar

Heat oven to 500°F.

Beat the egg whites with the salt until they are foamy. Sprinkle the whites with the cream of tartar; add the vanilla and half of the sugar. Continue beating the egg whites until they are stiff. Fold in the rest of the sugar.

Spoon the meringue over the lemon filling and roughen the top with a spatula, or force the meringue through a pastry bag.

Bake the pie in the oven until the meringue is lightly browned, about five minutes.   *A*

FRUIT FLAN

6 servings

That extra pie shell you baked and froze comes into its own when, at the height of the summer, you have nothing for dessert but fresh fruits and there are five or six unexpected guests.

In recent years when I make fruit pies, instead of using pastry cream—which in any case I dislike—as a base for the whole fruit, I make a purée of the fruit itself. The advantages are no flour, no eggs, and no sugar unless you want it, and more fruit in the bargain.

1 All-Purpose Pastry shell, baked
  (see page 300)
6 peaches, approximately
¾ cup apricot preserves

1 tablespoon lemon juice
1 box strawberries
1 box blueberries

Skin and chop two peaches. Heat one-half cup of the apricot preserves with the lemon juice. Rub the preserves through a fine sieve with the chopped peaches to make a purée. Spread the purée evenly over the pastry shell.

Skin and slice the remaining peaches. Wash, dry, and hull the strawberries; wash and pick over the blueberries.

Arrange the fruits in a well-thought-out pattern in the pastry shell.

Mix the remaining one-quarter cup of apricot preserves with one tablespoon of water and press through a fine sieve. Brush the fruits with the purée to glaze them.   *A*

COFFEE GRANITA

6 to 8 servings

Lou Garten, a man of great talent and taste, is one of the foremost designers of needlepoint in America. He lives in a gingerbread house in Palm Beach, Florida, surrounded by his work. He tells me, and I am quite certain he exaggerates, that literally he can do nothing in the kitchen, and that he has two menus should anyone have the good fortune to share a meal with him. I have been one of the fortunates, and the superb Granita, beautifully served, was the finale to a meal of perfectly cooked shrimp and salads. Lou Garten hides this additional talent under a bushel.

3 cups strong coffee
1 tablespoon cognac
Superfine sugar to taste

½ cup heavy cream
1 tablespoon confectioners' sugar

Mix together the coffee, cognac, and superfine sugar.

Chill the coffee in a bowl large enough to allow for expansion. Freeze the coffee, scraping down the side of the bowl as ice forms. Do this occasionally to make a slush like wet snow.

Spoon into chilled glasses. Whip cream with confectioners' sugar; spoon on top.   *A*

SIMPLE SYLLABUB

10 to 12 servings

Syllabub is old and English, older than the eighteenth century when one could buy it in London's St. James Park. The warm milk would be directed straight from the cow into a bowl containing the wine. I doubt if that would go down very well in this day and age, but it must have been a charming sight.

A little goes a long way. Syllabub is superb with fresh berries—strawberries, blueberries, and raspberries—and is better made a day ahead.

¼ cup sugar
4 tablespoons lemon juice
Rind of 1 lemon
6 tablespoons dry white wine

4 tablespoons fine brandy
2 tablespoons medium-dry sherry
2 cups heavy cream
½ teaspoon grated nutmeg

Combine all the ingredients, except the cream and nutmeg, in a ceramic mixing bowl. Allow them to stand for at least two hours.

Strain them into a two-quart bowl. With an electric beater or a wire whisk, beat at medium speed, adding the cream slowly.

When all the cream is in and the mixture is holding soft peaks, add the grated nutmeg. Spoon into individual small glasses, or a one-quart glass dish.   *A*

CREME BRULEE MOCHA

4 to 6 servings

Crème Brûlée Mocha is a variation on a theme—a crème brûlée with a coffee-and-brandy flavor. The next time you make Praline Powder, make double the amount. Store the rest in an airtight container. It takes up little space in the refrigerator and keeps indefinitely. And it has many uses. Try it sprinkled on vanilla ice cream.

4 egg yolks
½ cup sugar
1¾ cups heavy cream

1 tablespoon instant coffee
1 tablespoon brandy
Praline Powder (see page 295)

Beat egg yolks, adding sugar gradually, until light in color and texture, about five minutes.

Heat the cream to near the boiling point. Stir in the instant coffee until it dissolves. Blend a little of the cream with the egg yolks, then pour in the remainder of the cream, whisking steadily.

In the top of a double boiler, over hot water, cook the mixture until it is heavy and coats the back of a wooden spoon. Add brandy to taste.

Pour the crème brûlée into molds or dishes. Chill. Before serving, sprinkle with Praline Powder. Run under broiler one minute, or until the praline melts.

A

CREME BRULEE AUX FRUITS

10 servings

Crème Brûlée:

4 egg yolks
¼ cup sugar

1 teaspoon vanilla
2 cups cream

Combine the egg yolks with the sugar and vanilla, and beat the mixture until it is light yellow and creamy.

In a saucepan, bring the cream almost to a boil and very gradually pour it over the egg yolk mixture, whisking constantly.

Pour the custard into the top of a double boiler and cook it over hot water, stirring until it is thick. Take care; custard curdles easily.

1 pineapple, peeled and cubed
4 tangelos, peeled and sectioned

1 bunch white seedless grapes, halved
Praline Powder (see page 295)

Put enough of the mixed fruits into ten small ramekins to come two-thirds of the way up each ramekin. Fill with Crème Brûlée and sprinkle Praline Powder on top to coat generously. Run the ramekins under the broiler for one minute to melt the Praline Powder. Chill. *A*

ILE FLOTANTE

5 to 6 servings

Île Flotante, Floating Island, is without a doubt the most popular dessert I offer guests, and it is one of the least complicated to serve. The island and the custard may be made the day before. In fact, the island may be frozen for future use. It is an impressive and, at the same time, a simple dessert.

Island:

3 large egg whites
Pinch of salt
¼ teaspoon almond extract
¾ cup confectioners' sugar, sifted

Soft butter
Granulated sugar
Crème Anglaise (see page 294)

Heat oven to 225°F.
Beat the egg whites until they hold soft peaks. Add a pinch of salt and the almond extract. Add the confectioners' sugar gradually and continue beating for five to six minutes.
Butter a six-cup soufflé dish thoroughly. Dust it with granulated sugar. Fill the dish with the meringue and stand it in a roasting pan with enough hot water to come halfway up the side. Bake for one hour.
Cool and unmold the meringue onto a dish deep enough to hold the Crème Anglaise. Pour the Crème Anglaise around the meringue island. It will float.

Caramel:

3 tablespoons hot water
½ cup granulated sugar

Add hot water to one-half cup of granulated sugar in a small, heavy pan. Use an old pan. Stir over very low heat until the sugar dissolves.
Raise the heat and boil, without stirring, until the syrup turns an amber shade. The darker the syrup, the sharper the flavor. I like it dark amber. Brush down the sides of the pan with a pastry brush dipped in hot water from time to time. Pour the syrup over the island in a steady stream. Allow it to run over the island and into the custard. *AB*

MERINGUES

4 egg whites
Pinch of cream of tartar
1 cup superfine sugar

Heat oven to 225°F.

Beat the egg whites with a pinch of cream of tartar. Continue to beat while gradually adding the sugar. Beat until egg whites are stiff, about five minutes.

Cover a baking sheet with nonstick or parchment paper. Arrange large spoonfuls of meringue on it and bake on the middle shelf in the oven for one hour and twenty-five minutes. Cool in the oven with the door slightly ajar.

APPLE MERINGUE

6 to 8 servings

6 to 7 large, hard, juicy apples
½ cup white wine
2 tablespoons butter, approximately

Grated rind of 1 lemon
½ cup red currant jelly

Heat oven to 375°F.

Peel, core, and slice the apples, not too thinly. Place them in a two-quart pan with a lid. Add the white wine and cook slowly over low heat for ten to fifteen minutes. Shake the pan every now and then, holding the lid firmly in place so that the apple slices will rotate in the pan. Do not overcook.

Butter a two-and-three-fourths-quart baking dish and spread the cooked apples gently over the bottom. The dish should be about two-thirds full. Sprinkle with the grated lemon rind. Dot with the red currant jelly.

Meringue:

6 egg whites
2 cups granulated sugar

1 teaspoon vinegar
1 teaspoon vanilla extract

Beat the egg whites in an electric mixer or with a hand beater until soft peaks are formed. Add the sugar gradually while continuing to beat. Add the vinegar and vanilla extract and continue beating for at least eight minutes.

With a star tube and forcing bag, pipe the meringue over the apples. Shell shapes are a good choice.

Bake in the oven for fifty minutes to one hour. After twenty minutes, look at meringue; if it is becoming too dark in color, lower the heat to 250°F. and cover with a sheet of brown paper or foil.

Do not refrigerate unless the weather is very humid. *A*

PECAN MERINGUE TORTE

5 to 6 servings

4 egg whites
1 cup superfine sugar
¼ teaspoon vinegar
1 teaspoon almond extract
1 cup chopped pecans

1 cup heavy cream
Confectioners' sugar
Fresh strawberries dusted with sugar for
  garnish

Heat oven to 350°F.

Cover a baking sheet with nonstick kitchen parchment. Mark two nine-inch circles on the paper.

Beat the egg whites until stiff. Continue beating thoroughly until egg whites are very stiff, adding sugar gradually. Then add the vinegar and almond extract. Fold in the chopped nuts carefully.

Divide the meringue into two parts and spoon one part over each circle. Smooth with a damp spatula, but do not press down. Bake for thirty-five minutes. Turn off the heat and allow the meringue to cool in the oven.

Filling:

1 cup heavy cream
1 cup raspberries or
  6 tablespoons apricot purée
Superfine sugar

Whip the heavy cream until spoonfuls hold their shape. Stir in the raspberries or the apricot purée. Sweeten to taste. I suggest three tablespoons superfine sugar.

Spread the filling over one meringue circle and place the other on top. Dust with confectioners' sugar. Garnish with fresh strawberries dusted with sugar.

ALMOND GATEAU

6 servings

This is a rich and toothsome little cake. A little goes a long way. It is a good substitute for petits fours after dinner.

Pastry:

8 ounces flour (2 cups less 2 tablespoons)
Pinch of salt
10 tablespoons butter

4 tablespoons iced water
2 tablespoons lemon juice
1 egg yolk

Sift together the flour and salt. Chip two tablespoons of butter into the flour and blend well with the fingertips.

Make a well in the center and add the iced water, lemon juice, and egg yolk, working the mixture to make a smooth paste. Add a bit more water if necessary.

Gather the pastry into a ball and roll it out into a rectangle about one-fourth inch thick.

Cut four tablespoons of butter into thin slices. Spread it evenly over the rectangle of dough, taking care not to put it too close to the edge.

Fold the pastry over in thirds, enclosing the butter. Chill for half an hour. Roll pastry out again into a rectangle and spread the remaining four tablespoons of butter as before. Fold again and chill.

Fold and roll the dough three additional times, chilling after each folding, to make a total of five times. (Mark the dough with your finger to indicate number of turns.)

Fold in thirds for the final time and place dough in the refrigerator to rest for one hour.

Filling:

8 tablespoons unsalted butter
½ cup sugar
1 teaspoon almond extract
3 egg yolks
¼ cup heavy cream

½ pound ground almonds
1 tablespoon grated lemon rind
Glaze: 1 egg yolk mixed with
    2 tablespoons milk

Heat oven to 425°F.

Cream the butter and sugar. Add the almond extract and egg yolks; beat thoroughly. Beat the cream, separately, until it holds peaks.

Stir the ground almonds and lemon rind into the butter-sugar mixture and fold in the whipped cream.

Roll out the refrigerated pastry and cut off one piece measuring approximately seven by nine inches. Transfer it to a greased baking sheet.

Roll out the remaining pastry to a rectangle about nine by eleven inches. Spread the almond mixture over the smaller rectangle to within an inch of the edges on all sides.

Moisten the edges with the egg and milk mixture and lay the larger rectangle on top. Pinch the edges to seal and turn them up with a fork and press all around. Make a lattice pattern with a small sharp knife, cutting the pastry not quite all the way through. Brush with the egg and milk mixture.

Place in the center of the oven. Reduce the temperature immediately to 400°F. and bake for thirty minutes. If the color is not rich enough, brush with a little more egg and milk glaze. Bake for a further ten minutes. Sprinkle with sugar; cool on a wire rack. *A*

VENETIAN CHOCOLATE ROLL

10 to 12 servings

This chocolate roll is one of the simplest to make and, in spite of being the richest, it is the most popular. Don't be put off by its richness; allow yourself a small portion and cut down on what you eat the following day.

7 eggs, separated, and 1 extra egg white
1 cup sugar
4 ounces semisweet chocolate
3 ounces unsweetened chocolate
4 tablespoons strong coffee
2 teaspoons vanilla extract

½ teaspoon almond extract
1 teaspoon ground cinnamon
1 teaspoon ground star anise
Filling (see next page)
Cocoa for dusting

Heat oven to 300°F.

Beat the egg yolks with the sugar until thick and yellow.

Chop or grate the chocolate. Melt the chocolate with the coffee in a bowl placed in a pan of warm water. Cool slightly. Mix with the beaten egg yolks, extracts, and spices.

Beat the egg whites until stiff peaks form. With a large metal spoon stir a spoonful or two into the chocolate mixture, then fold in the rest of the egg whites.

Pour into an eleven-by-sixteen-inch cookie pan, lined with oiled wax paper, and smooth the surface with a spatula. Bake in the middle of the oven for fifteen minutes. Turn off the heat and leave it in the oven seven to eight minutes more.

(Continued)

Filling:

1½ cups heavy cream
3 tablespoons sugar
4 tablespoons unsweetened cocoa

½ teaspoon almond extract
1 teaspoon star anise

Place the cream, sugar, and cocoa in a bowl and refrigerate while the cake roll is baking.

Remove the cake pan from the oven and cover with a clean towel wrung out in cold water. When cool, remove the cloth and loosen the cake from the sides of the pan. Dust generously with cocoa. Turn out on to wax paper. Remove the wax paper the cake was baked on.

When ready to fill the roll, beat the contents of the bowl until stiff. Stir in the almond extract and star anise.

Spread the filling evenly to within an inch of the edge. Carefully roll up lengthwise. Repair any tears with more cocoa.

RHUM BABA

About 1 dozen

Babas can be baked and frozen. To use them after freezing, thaw to room temperature, then warm gently in the oven for fifteen minutes or so at 250°F. Spoon the rum mixture over them while they are still warm.

1 envelope yeast
¼ cup lukewarm water
2 tablespoons sugar
½ teaspoon salt
¼ cup lukewarm milk
4 eggs, lightly beaten
2 cups sifted flour

⅔ cup soft butter
1 tablespoon golden raisins
1 tablespoon currants
¾ cup apricot preserves
Candied cherries or whole blanched
    almonds for decoration
Rum Syrup (see recipe next page)

Heat oven to 350°F.

Sprinkle the yeast over the lukewarm water. Combine it in a bowl with the sugar, salt, milk, and eggs.

Stir in the flour and beat the dough hard with a wooden spoon for at least eight minutes.

Cover the bowl with a clean towel; set it in a warm spot and let the dough rise until it is double in bulk.

Beat in the butter, raisins, and currants until the butter is completely incorporated.

Fill greased baba molds or muffin tins about one-third full with the dough and let the babas rise until they are almost double in bulk.

Bake the babas in the oven for twenty to twenty-five minutes, or until a toothpick inserted in the center comes out clean. Unmold the babas onto a shallow dish with a rim, and let them cool slightly.

Rum Syrup:

2 cups water
1 cup sugar
½ cup dark rum

In a saucepan bring to a boil the two cups of water and one cup of sugar. Remove from the heat; let the syrup cool to lukewarm, and stir in the rum.

Prick the tops of the babas in several places with a toothpick and gradually pour the syrup over them. Let them stand for about thirty minutes, basting them frequently with the syrup.

Heat the apricot preserves, press through a sieve, and spoon or brush the preserves over the babas. Decorate each baba with a candied cherry or whole blanched almond.   *AB*

PEACHES AND SAUCE DIJONNAISE

Allow 1 whole fresh peach per serving   ¾ cup sugar
2 cups water   Sauce Dijonnaise (see page 292)

If the peaches are ripe to perfection, I prefer them uncooked. Otherwise, poach them in a simple syrup of two cups water and three-quarters cup sugar, dissolved and simmered for five minutes.

To prepare, drop each peach into boiling water, roll it around, and lift out with a slotted spoon. The skin slips off easily. Cut in half and remove the stones.

To poach, drop the peach halves into the syrup and cook for eight to ten minutes with the syrup barely simmering. Cool them in the syrup, if possible. Drain, if serving with the sauce.

If the peaches are to be served raw, spoon a little Sauce Dijonnaise over them right away to prevent them from turning brown.   *A*

STRAWBERRIES RUE DU BAC

6 to 8 servings

One of the best luncheons I have ever had in Paris in a friend's house was unbelievably simple: Oeufs en cocottes, a beautifully roasted chicken, watercress salad, cheese (the name of which I can't remember), followed by these delicious strawberries. Food does not have to be complicated to be good.

2 pints strawberries, perfect and
    unblemished
¼ cup Cointreau or orange Curaçao

½ cup shelled pistachio nuts, coarsely
    chopped
Superfine sugar for dusting

Wash, wipe, and hull the strawberries.

In a mixing bowl, sprinkle the strawberries with liqueur. Mix in the chopped pistachio nuts. Allow the ingredients to stand for fifteen to twenty minutes.

Spoon the strawberries into a glass serving bowl and dust with fine sugar.

RASPBERRY FOOL

6 servings

In England, half heavy cream and half pouring custard is often used instead of all cream, because heavy cream in most of Europe is almost solid. The addition of custard gives the Fool a lightness. A recipe for pouring custard, Crème Anglaise, is on page 294. Fold into the fool, at end, if desired.

2 packages (10 ounces each) frozen raspberries
1 cup heavy cream

Defrost and drain the raspberries. Reserve the juice.

Press the fruit through a fine sieve, taking care not to allow any of the seeds to get through. The result should be one cup of heavy purée. If it is too thick, add a little of the juice. It is unlikely that additional sugar will be needed.

Whip the cream until it is thick and holds very stiff peaks.

Fold the fruit purée into the whipped cream and spoon into small wineglasses, or serve in a glass bowl. Chill before serving.

STRAWBERRIES CARDINAL

6 to 8 servings

Strawberries

One pint of strawberries will satisfy three average appetites.

Wash, then hull the strawberries. If the berries are hulled first, water will fill the hole left by the stem. Drain the strawberries on paper towels.

Sauce Cardinal:

2 packages (10 ounces each) frozen raspberries
½ cup red currant jelly

Sieve the raspberries by pushing them through a fine strainer with a wooden spoon.

Melt the red currant jelly in a saucepan over low heat and mix with the strained raspberries. Chill the sauce.

Pour Sauce Cardinal over the strawberries in their serving dish before serving.   *A*

SORBET AU CHAMPAGNE

4 to 6 servings

This is James Beard's recipe and it is as good as he is. You may do this in an electric freezer or in trays in the refrigerator, as you wish. If you are making it for a large group, you should double the recipe.

½ cup sugar
2 cups water
Grated rind of 1 orange

½ cup orange juice
½ bottle champagne

Bring the sugar and water together to a rolling boil. Boil hard for six minutes.

Remove from the heat and stir in the orange rind, orange juice, and champagne.

Bring to a boil again. Cool slightly, pour into freezing trays, and place in the freezer. When there is a solid one-inch layer of frozen sherbet in the tray, transfer the sherbet to a bowl, and stir with a fork until mushy.

Return to the tray and refreeze. The sorbet may also be frozen in an electric freezer packed with salt and ice. Serve small quantities in chilled glasses.   *A*

STRAWBERRY SORBET

6 to 8 servings

2 pints strawberries
3 cups sugar
1 cup hot water

4 tablespoons lemon juice
2 egg whites

Wash, then hull the strawberries. Purée them in a food mill or force them through a wire sieve or strainer. Do not use a blender.

In a heavy pan, dissolve the sugar in one cup of hot water. When the sugar is completely dissolved, bring it to a boil over high heat. When it reaches a rolling boil, the temperature will be 216°F. Take the pan off the heat immediately and chill the syrup over iced water.

When cold, mix the syrup with the strawberry purée and lemon juice and pour into a two-quart ice-cream maker.

Pack the space around the container with ice and freezing salt. Layer them in proportions of three parts ice to one part salt, using a two-cup measure as the unit. Put the dasher and lid in place, start up the motor and freeze for twenty minutes.

Beat the egg whites with a pinch of salt until they form soft peaks. Remove the cover from freezer and take out the dasher. Stir in the beaten egg whites and replace the dasher and lid of the ice-cream maker. Freeze the sherbet for another twenty minutes.

RASPBERRY SORBET

6 to 8 servings

With inexpensive ice-cream makers available, sorbets and ices are simple and quick to prepare. Fresh fruits make the best sorbets, but I use frozen when fresh fruits are not available. Treat yourself to an ice-cream maker.

4 cups water
1½ cups sugar
4 cups fresh raspberries or 2 packages
   (10 ounces each) frozen raspberries

2 tablespoons fresh
   lemon juice
2 egg whites

In a small enamel-lined or stainless-steel pan, dissolve the sugar in the water over low heat. When it is completely dissolved, turn up the heat and boil rapidly for five minutes exactly (or bring to a temperature of 216°F. on a candy thermometer). Remove the syrup from the heat and cool.

Rub the fresh raspberries through a fine wire sieve or strainer; there should be no seeds in the purée. If you must use frozen fruit, defrost it first, then drain and force it through a sieve or strainer. (A large metal spoon is the best forcer.)

Add the lemon juice and mix the purée with the cooled syrup. Pour the mixture into the canister of an electric ice-cream maker and follow the manufacturer's directions.

Freeze for twenty minutes. Stop the motor and open the canister. The mixture should be of the consistency of wet snow. If it is too soft and watery, continue freezing for another five minutes.

Beat the egg whites and fold them into the mixture in the canister by removing the dasher and stirring very gently with a long-handled spoon. Replace the dasher.

Put the lid back on and freeze for another twenty minutes. The ice should be well-formed, pliable but not solid. Store in the freezer compartment of the refrigerator for at least one hour before using.

Note: Use half these quantities if using Waring Ice Cream Parlor and follow the manufacturer's directions.   *A*

CRANBERRY ICE

6 to 8 servings

1 quart cranberries
1½ cups water
1¾ cups sugar

1 cup water
2 teaspoons gelatin
2 egg whites

Wash the cranberries, then cook them in one and one-half cups of water until they are soft. Force the berries through a strainer and add one and three-quarter cups of sugar and the one cup of water to the strained juice. Discard the pulp. Boil for five to six minutes.

Soften the gelatin in a little of the juice, then stir it into the remainder of the juice until it dissolves. Chill.

Freeze in an electric ice-cream maker or hand-cranked machine until the mixture becomes a mush, about ten to fifteen minutes.

Beat the egg whites until they are fluffy but not stiff. Fold them into the partly frozen cranberry ice and continue freezing until firm enough to lift out on a spoon.

Clean the dasher. Pack down the cranberry ice in its container. Store the cranberry ice in the refrigerator freezer.   *A*

CINNAMON ICE CREAM

6 to 8 servings

2 cups heavy cream
½ cup granulated sugar
2 tablespoons powdered cinnamon

4 egg yolks
1 cup milk
Pinch of salt

Heat the cream with the sugar and powdered cinnamon in the top half of a double boiler.

Beat the egg yolks with the milk and a pinch of salt in a mixer and add them to the cinnamon-cream mixture.

Cook the ingredients, stirring with a wooden spoon, until the mixture is thick and heavy. Take care not to overcook or the mixture will curdle.

Strain it into a bowl and chill before freezing in the electric ice-cream maker. Follow the manufacturer's instructions.

This ice cream is extremely rich. I would advise its use the day it is made, since it becomes very solid if kept for any length of time. *A*

COFFEE ICE CREAM

6 to 8 servings

½ cup sugar
4 egg yolks
⅛ teaspoon salt
2 cups milk
1 envelope unflavored gelatin

¼ cup water
½ cup dry instant coffee
½ pint heavy cream
1 teaspoon brandy

Beat the sugar, egg yolks, and salt until lemon-colored. Heat the milk almost to the boiling point. Add the scalded milk and cook until the mixture coats the back of a spoon. Strain, if necessary.

Soften the gelatin by sprinkling it over one-quarter cup water. Add the softened gelatin. Add coffee, then cool the mixture.

When the mixture has cooled completely, add the heavy cream and brandy.

Pour into the ice-cream maker and freeze approximately forty-five minutes, according to manufacturer's directions. *A*

TORTONI

Tortoni is one of my favorite stand-bys and this one is better than any that comes from the store. I make it, in quantity, and there is seldom a time when there are not at least a dozen sitting in the freezer.

1 cup heavy cream
¼ cup confectioners' sugar
2 tablespoons Marsala

½ cup crushed and sieved macaroons,
   approximately 5 to 6
1 egg white, beaten

Whip the cream with the sugar until it is light and holds soft peaks. Fold in the Marsala and macaroons.

Beat the egg white until stiff. Fold them into the cream.

Spoon the mixture into glasses or ramekins. Freeze. If the Tortoni are frozen and covered, they may be kept for several weeks.

Note: Use the hard Italian variety of macaroons for best results.   *AB*

Sauces

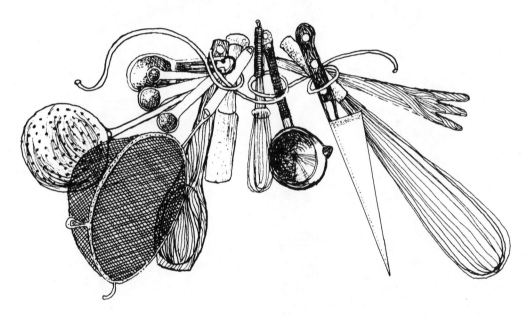

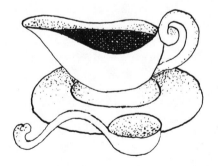

Sauces

What is good for the goose is not necessarily good for the gander. Sauces must be used with discretion and on no account should play a dominant role. The sauce is the counterpart of the setting for a precious stone—there to complement but not steal the scene.

Unless a recipe calls for the main ingredient to be masked—completely coated—by the sauce, serve the sauce separately so that everyone can help himself. One of the most glaring faults of restaurants—and I might add private houses as well—is to produce a plate on which an island of meat gyrates in a sea of sauce.

The sauce may be rich or simple: heavily laced with cream, butter, or liqueurs; or pan juices mixed with a strong, appropriate stock. Set your sights on the latter, and you and your waistline will be the beneficiaries.

BEURRE MANIE

Beurre manié is used as a thickening agent for sauces, stews, and so on.

Blend equal parts of flour and unsalted butter. I roll the mixture into balls, each roughly one teaspoon, and freeze them , securely wrapped, for future use. *AB*

TARRAGON BUTTER

16 tablespoons unsalted butter, softened
A good handful of fresh tarragon leaves

In a food processor or blender, mix half the butter and all the tarragon leaves by turning on the motor for thirty to forty seconds. Turn into a bowl and mix with the rest of the softened butter.
Chill, then shape into balls for freezing. It keeps indefinitely. *AB*

MINT BUTTER

8 tablespoons unsalted butter, softened
2 large handfuls fresh mint leaves
1 teaspoon salt
2 or 3 twists of the pepper mill
Sugar to taste
Lemon juice

In a food mill or blender, purée the butter and mint leaves. Season the mixture to taste with salt, pepper, sugar, and lemon juice.
Chill, then roll into sausage-shaped portions, and freeze. *AB*

SAUCE ESPAGNOLE (BROWN SAUCE)

1 quart

Brown Sauce is one of the "mother" sauces. It is a useful base to keep frozen in small portions.

6 tablespoons cooking oil, bacon fat, or
   clarified butter (see page 345)
⅓ cup finely chopped carrot
⅓ cup finely chopped onion
⅓ cup finely chopped celery
½ cup chopped lean bacon or ham
4 tablespoons flour

6 cups beef stock
2 tablespoons tomato paste
8 peppercorns
1 bay leaf
1 small bunch parsley
Salt and pepper

Place the oil or butter in a heavy, two-quart pan and cook the vegetables with the ham or bacon for fifteen minutes.

Stir in the flour and cook slowly eight to ten minutes more, or until the flour turns brown. Do not be concerned when it turns dark; that is what you want.

Off the heat, stir in the beef stock and blend with a wire whisk. Stir in tomato paste and add peppercorns, bay leaf, and parsley.

Simmer slowly for two hours longer. Season with salt and pepper. Strain.　　　*AB*

SAUCE BECHAMEL

1 cup

Sauce Béchamel is another "mother" sauce, a base for a great many white sauces. When properly made, it is a far cry from the white or cream sauce made without care that bears a striking resemblance to billboard poster paste.

1 cup milk
1 slice onion
1 small piece bay leaf
6 peppercorns

1 tablespoon butter
1 tablespoon flour
Salt

Combine the milk, onion, bay leaf, and peppercorns in a saucepan; cover and simmer gently five to six minutes. Strain.

(Continued)

Melt butter in a heavy pan. Add flour and cook five minutes, taking care it does not brown. Add half of the strained warm milk, mix, and add the remaining milk. Boil quickly for two minutes. Season with salt.

Note: By holding the quantity of the liquid constant and increasing the flour and butter, the result will be a thicker sauce. For a thin sauce, use one cup of liquid to one tablespoon of butter and one tablespoon of flour. For a thicker sauce, use one cup of liquid and increase butter and flour to two tablespoons each. For an even thicker sauce, use one cup of liquid and increase butter and flour to three tablespoons each.   *A*

SAUCE MADEIRA

2½ cups

2 cups Brown Sauce (see page 275)
½ cup dry Madeira

Heat the Brown Sauce in a small pan. Add the Madeira. Heat again, but do not allow the sauce to boil.   *A*

SAUCE MORNAY

2 cups

¼ to ½ cup grated Parmesan and Gruyère
  cheese, in equal amounts
2 cups Béchamel Sauce (see page 275)

Stir the grated cheese into the hot Béchamel Sauce. If the sauce is to be used for coating, reduce the quantity of cheese.   *A*

BLENDER MAYONNAISE AND HOLLANDAISE

1¼ cups

The blender will give you Mayonnaise and Hollandaise when you need it in a hurry, but do not expect the same volume that the conventional method produces.

Mayonnaise:

1 egg
¼ teaspoon salt
½ teaspoon dry mustard

2 tablespoons vinegar
1 cup salad oil

Place the egg, salt, mustard, vinegar, and one-quarter cup of oil in the blender at low speed. Remove the blender cover and add the remaining oil in a steady stream.

Hollandaise:

4 egg yolks
2 tablespoons lemon juice
¼ teaspoon salt

Pinch of cayenne pepper
8 tablespoons boiling butter

Place all the ingredients, except the butter, in the blender and give a few turns at low speed. Immediately remove the blender cover and add the heated butter in a steady stream.

MAYONNAISE

Approximately 1 to 1½ cups

Mayonnaise is a classic sauce for cold seafood—lobster, shrimp, and crab—and a binding sauce for cold meats and vegetables. The old wives tell us that it cannot be made in the presence of a witch or a pregnant woman. For lack of either in my kitchen during its preparation, I cannot vouch for the truth of their theory, but I can warn you against making it before or during a thunderstorm.

2 egg yolks
¼ teaspoon prepared Dijon mustard
Salt and pepper to taste

1 to 1½ cups olive oil, approximately
1 tablespoon lemon juice or wine vinegar, approximately

Place a mixing bowl on a wet towel. Add the egg yolks, mustard, and a pinch of salt and pepper. Beat with a wooden spoon or whisk. Add about two tablespoons of the oil, a drop at a time. Whisk.

(Continued)

When the oil is absorbed, gradually add the remainder while stirring. Make sure all the oil is absorbed before adding more. If the mixture is too thick, add a little lemon juice or vinegar. Correct the seasoning by adding more salt, pepper, and lemon juice or vinegar.

SAUCE MALTAISE

Approximately 1 cup

Sauce Maltaise is a variation of Hollandaise, orange-flavored Hollandaise. It is good with vegetables, including asparagus and artichokes.

3 egg yolks	4 teaspoons orange juice
1 teaspoon lemon juice	8 tablespoons hot, melted butter
Salt to taste	1 tablespoon grated orange rind
⅛ teaspoon white pepper	

Place the egg yolks, lemon juice, salt, pepper, and one teaspoon of orange juice in the blender. At low speed, gradually add the butter in a steady stream. Blend about fifteen seconds, or until the sauce is smooth and well-balanced.

Remove to a warm sauceboat and fold in the remaining orange juice and rind.

SAUCE MOUSSELINE

1 cup

Sauce Mousseline, a light version of Hollandaise, is served with fish or vegetables. It must be barely warm before folding in the whipped cream; otherwise the cream will separate.

3 egg yolks	8 tablespoons butter
Pinch of salt	Juice of ½ lemon
Pinch of pepper	⅔ cup heavy cream, whipped

In a small mixing bowl, whisk the egg yolks, salt, pepper, and a small piece of butter until thick. Add the lemon juice.

Place the bowl over a pan of warm water and whisk until very light. Add the remaining butter in small pieces. Fold in the whipped cream. Season to taste.

SAUCE VERTE I

2 cups

This is my favorite green sauce. It is delightfully fresh and is sufficiently delicate to serve with any cold fish.

1 bunch watercress
2 cups parsley, tightly packed
2 small bunches fresh tarragon

2 cups mayonnaise (see page 277)
2 tablespoons lemon juice
White pepper (optional)

Trim off the stalks of the watercress; use only the fresh leaves. Break off the heads of the parsley and strip the coarse stalks from the tarragon. Wash the greens thoroughly and drain well until they are free of moisture.

Combine the mayonnaise and greens in the blender and mix at high speed. Add the lemon juice and, if desired, the white pepper.

SAUCE VERTE II

Approximately 1 cup

This is another one of the many versions of green sauce. I find it goes very well with cold corned beef and makes an appetizing change from the more conventional green sauces that are made of mayonnaise and herbs, for the most part.

¼ cup finely chopped parsley
¼ cup finely chopped spinach
¼ cup finely chopped watercress
1½ tablespoons drained capers (if salty
    Italian capers are used, rinse and
    dry them)
½ clove garlic

1 tablespoon chopped sour
    cucumber pickle
1 slice white bread crumbled with
    crusts removed
Salt and black pepper
¼ cup olive oil
¼ cup wine vinegar

Crush together, preferably in a wooden bowl or in a food processor, the parsley, spinach, watercress, capers, garlic, pickle, bread, salt, and pepper.

Gradually stir in the oil and vinegar and correct the seasonings.   *A*

SAUCE NEWBURG

Approximately 2½ cups

I find this simplified method for Sauce Newburg ideal for using up cooked shrimp. Once, when there was a sizable amount of halibut left over, I reheated it in the sauce and, by serving it with well-seasoned brown rice, had enough for a luncheon.

4 tablespoons butter	2¼ cups heavy cream
1 tablespoon flour	Salt and pepper
¼ teaspoon paprika	3 egg yolks
1 tablespoon tomato paste	¼ cup dry sherry

Melt the butter in a saucepan over medium heat and add the flour, stirring. Add the paprika and tomato paste, and stir until blended.

Add two cups of the cream, stirring rapidly with the whisk. Cook, stirring, until well-blended. Add salt and pepper to taste.

Beat the yolks lightly and blend in the remaining cream. Add the yolk mixture to the sauce, stirring rapidly. Remove the saucepan from the heat immediately and continue stirring.

The sauce should now be thick enough to coat a spoon. Do not boil or the sauce will curdle. Add the sherry and stir. Heat thoroughly, but do not boil.   *A*

LOBSTER SAUCE

Approximately 3 to 4 cups

1 small carrot	1½ cups fish stock or clam juice
1 small onion	½ cup dry vermouth
1 rib celery	3 tablespoons flour
6 tablespoons butter	1 teaspoon tomato paste
1 pound uncooked whole lobster	½ cup heavy cream
1 bay leaf	Salt and pepper to taste
2 sprigs parsley	Lemon juice

Chop the carrot, onion, and celery very finely. Sauté in two tablespoons of butter for five or six minutes, being careful not to allow the vegetables to brown.

Split the lobster lengthwise, crack the claws, and place it, meat-side down, on the bed of vegetables in a large pan. Add the bay leaf and parsley sprigs. Pour in the fish stock and vermouth. Cook, with the lid on, for twenty minutes. Cool.

Remove all the meat from the body and claws of the lobster; cut into small pieces. Strain and reserve the liquid in the pan and discard the solids.

Melt four tablespoons of butter in a heavy pan. Stir in three tablespoons of flour and cook gently for three minutes, being careful not to brown. Off the heat, add one and one-quarter cups of strained cooking liquid. Cook for three minutes, stirring. Add tomato paste, heavy cream, and lobster meat. Season with salt, pepper, and lemon juice. *A*

SAUCE SCANDIA

Approximately ½ cup

Sauce Scandia is used for marinating cooked shrimp for either a cocktail tidbit or a first course. It can also be used as sauce for cubed, cooked white fish.

1 tablespoon mustard	Dash white pepper
1 teaspoon sugar	4 tablespoons salad oil or olive oil
1½ tablespoons wine vinegar	1 tablespoon fresh dill, chopped
½ teaspoon salt	1 teaspoon lemon juice

In a bowl blend the first five ingredients, then gradually add the olive oil. Stir in the dill and lemon juice, and correct the seasoning. *A*

SAUCE NANTUA

Approximately 1 cup

Sauce Nantua is good with poached fish fillets, or a whole poached sea bass or striped bass.

2 tablespoons unsalted butter	½ cup fish stock or clam juice
1½ tablespoons flour	2 teaspoons tomato paste
1 slice of onion	½ cup heavy cream
1 small slice of carrot	½ cup chopped cooked shrimp or lobster
1 bay leaf	Salt and pepper

Melt butter in saucepan; add flour, onion, carrot, and bay leaf. Cook for two to three minutes. Remove pan from heat and stir in fish stock or clam juice until smooth. Add tomato paste and heavy cream.

Return to the heat and cook the sauce four to five minutes more, stirring. Strain the sauce through a fine sieve, add shrimp or lobster, and season with salt and pepper. *A*

CARRIAGE HOUSE SAUCE

Approximately 1½ cups

1 cup sour cream
3 tablespoons lemon juice
1 tablespoon prepared mustard
2 tablespoons tomato purée

2 tablespoons vegetable oil
½ teaspoon celery salt
White pepper to taste
½ cup heavy cream

In a small bowl mix thoroughly all the ingredients, with the exception of the heavy cream. Whip the cream until thick.

Fold in the sour cream mixture. Adjust the seasoning with celery salt and pepper, if necessary. Refrigerate, covered.

A

CAPER SAUCE

Approximately 4 cups

⅓ cup butter
½ medium onion, chopped
⅓ cup flour
3 cups hot milk

1 teaspoon salt
3 or 4 twists of white pepper mill
2 to 3 parsley stalks or sprigs
⅛ teaspoon nutmeg

Make a *roux* by melting the butter in a heavy one-quart pan. Add the chopped onion and cook until golden. Add the flour and cook three to four minutes longer, stirring to prevent burning.

Heat the milk to just below the boiling point in a heavy pot. Remove from the heat and immediately pour it on the *roux*. Whisk or stir until smooth. Add the salt, pepper, parsley, and nutmeg, and cook at a gentle simmer for fifteen to twenty minutes. Strain through a fine sieve. If the sauce will not be used right away, stir now and again until it cools to prevent a skin forming.

For every cup of sauce add:

1 tablespoon chopped capers
Chopped parsley

½ cup heavy cream
Lemon juice to taste

Add the capers, parsley, cream, and lemon juice to taste. Mix well and correct the seasoning. Serve hot.

A

GOOSEBERRY SAUCE

Approximately 2 cups

Gooseberry Sauce is excellent served with grilled fish.

1 pound fresh gooseberries
4 to 6 tablespoons of sugar, or to taste

Top and tail the gooseberries. Cover them with cold water and bring slowly to a boil. Drain immediately. By now the gooseberries should give gently between the fingers.

Place one-quarter cup water in a skillet with the sugar and bring to a fast boil after the sugar has dissolved. Add the gooseberries and shake gently, turning them over in the syrup.

Pour the sauce around the fish or serve separately in a sauceboat.   *A*

MARINADE FOR LONDON BROIL

Approximately ½ cup

1 teaspoon salt
½ teaspoon black pepper
¼ teaspoon basil
¾ teaspoon rosemary

1 clove garlic, crushed
½ onion, chopped
1 tablespoon wine vinegar
2 tablespoons salad oil

Combine all the ingredients in a screw-top jar and shake. There is enough for marinating one flank steak.   *A*

SAUCE BEARNAISE

Approximately ¾ cup

Sauce Béarnaise is excellent with grilled meats.

1 shallot, chopped
6 peppercorns
1 tablespoon chopped tarragon
1 bay leaf
1 tablespoon chopped parsley

1 tablespoon chervil
4 tablespoons wine vinegar
2 egg yolks
8 tablespoons unsalted butter
Salt and pepper

(Continued)

In a saucepan, combine the shallot, peppercorns, tarragon, bay leaf, parsley, and chervil with the vinegar. Reduce, over low heat, until one tablespoon remains.

In another saucepan, beat the egg yolks with one tablespoon of butter. Strain the vinegar mixture into the egg yolks. Place the saucepan in hot water.

Melt the remaining butter until it foams. Pour it over the egg mixture in a steady stream. Stir over low heat until the sauce is thick. Correct the seasoning with salt and pepper.

SAUCE POIVRADE

Approximately 1½ cups

Sauce Poivrade is served with grilled steak.

1 cup Brown Sauce (see page 275)
1 tablespoon tarragon vinegar
1 tablespoon chopped capers

1 tablespoon tomato purée
1 tablespoon finely chopped parsley

Place all the ingredients, except the chopped parsley, in a small saucepan and bring to a boil. Stir in the chopped parsley before serving.   *A*

BASTING SAUCE

This is excellent for broiled lamb chops.

½ cup prepared mustard
2 tablespoons soy sauce
1 clove garlic

1 teaspoon rosemary
½ teaspoon ginger
2 tablespoons oil

Combine all the ingredients in a bowl and store in a screw-top jar in the refrigerator.   *A*

SAUCE CUMBERLAND

Approximately ¾ to 1 cup

Sauce Cumberland goes well with ham—hot or cold—smoked tongue, and most of the cold meats. Homemade, it is infinitely better than the store-bought variety.

1 orange
1 lemon
¼ cup water
¼ cup port wine
4 tablespoons red currant jelly

½ tablespoon prepared mustard
1 tablespoon vinegar
Salt
Cayenne pepper

Peel the orange and lemon very thinly without taking off any of the white pith. Squeeze the fruit and set aside the juice.

Cut the peels into very thin shreds, julienned. Cook them in one-quarter cup of water for five minutes and drain.

Place the lemon and orange shreds back in the pan. Add the port wine, red currant jelly, mustard, lemon and orange juices, vinegar, salt, and a pinch of cayenne. Stir until the solids are dissolved.

Simmer for five minutes and cool before serving. The sauce keeps well, refrigerated.   *A*

SAUCE CHASSEUR

Approximately 2 cups

Leftover roasted chicken is very good if reheated in this sauce and served with rice.

1 tablespoon butter
1 small onion, diced
2 mushrooms, sliced thinly

½ cup dry white wine
1 teaspoon tomato purée
2 cups Brown Sauce (see page 275)

Melt the butter in a small skillet or saucepan. Add the onion and cook for three or four minutes, but do not burn it. Add the mushrooms and cook for three or four minutes more.

Pour in the white wine and boil for five minutes or so. Stir in the tomato purée and Brown Sauce. Reheat.   *A*

SAUCE BIGARADE

Approximately 1½ cups

Serve with duck and game.

1 orange
½ cup dry red wine

1 tablespoon red currant jelly
1 cup Brown Sauce (see page 275)

Peel the orange, taking care not to include any of the white pith. Squeeze the orange and set the juice aside. Slice the orange peel and cut it into very thin julienned strips. Drop the peels into boiling water for three to four minutes to blanch, then strain.

Place the peels and all the other ingredients into a small pan and bring to a boil.   *A*

BARBECUE SAUCE FOR CHICKEN

Approximately ¾ cup

1 heaping tablespoon peanut butter
4 tablespoons fresh lemon juice
4 tablespoons finely chopped onion

¼ cup olive oil or salad oil
½ teaspoon salt
¼ teaspoon freshly ground pepper

Mix the peanut butter with lemon juice until smooth. Stir in the chopped onion and gradually add the oil. Mix until smooth. Season with salt and pepper.   *A*

SAUCE TARTARE

Approximately 1½ cups

2 hard-boiled eggs
2 raw egg yolks
1 tablespoon Dijon mustard
¼ teaspoon salt
1 cup oil

3 tablespoons minced sour pickle
3 to 4 tablespoons minced capers
3 to 4 tablespoons minced parsley, chives,
     or tarragon
Lemon juice

Sieve the yolks of the hard-boiled eggs, and chop the whites coarsely.

In a bowl, mix the sieved and raw yolks with mustard and salt. Using an electric beater at slow speed, add the oil drop by drop to begin with. When it is being absorbed, the mixture will become creamy.

Pour the remainder of the oil in slowly while continuing to beat. Stir in the pickle, capers, herbs, and lemon juice. Adjust the lemon juice to taste. Add the chopped egg whites and mix.

PESTO

Approximately 1½ cups

Pesto served with pasta or a vegetable, such as finely julienned zucchini, is a wonderful stand-by. I usually make it in high summer when basil is plentiful. It keeps well frozen. The recipe can be doubled, tripled, or more without difficulty.

1 cup fresh basil leaves, tightly packed
¼ cup pignoli nuts
1 clove garlic, crushed with
   1 teaspoon of salt

¼ cup Parmesan cheese
2 tablespoons butter
2 tablespoons olive oil

In a blender or food processor blend together the basil, pignoli nuts, and garlic. Add the Parmesan cheese and butter, and blend until smooth. Beat in the olive oil.   *AB*

CURRY SAUCE

Approximately 3 cups

This sauce is for vegetables, lamb, beef, and seafood.

2 tablespoons oil
2 tablespoons chopped onion
2 tablespoons curry powder
1 tablespoon flour

1 small clove garlic, crushed
2 dried apricots, chopped fine
2½ cups chicken stock
⅓ cup raisins

Heat the oil in a heavy saucepan. Add the onion and cook, stirring for several minutes, but do not burn.

Stir in the curry powder and flour and cook for two minutes. Add the garlic and apricots. Remove from the heat and pour in the stock. Return to gentle heat and whisk until thick. Stir in the raisins.   *AB*

TOMATO SAUCE

Approximately 3 cups

1 tablespoon butter
1 tablespoon olive oil
2 cups finely chopped onion
1 clove garlic, finely minced
½ teaspoon chopped thyme
1 bay leaf

1 teaspoon dried basil
4 ripe tomatoes, peeled, cored, and
  chopped
Salt and pepper
2 tablespoons tomato paste
½ teaspoon sugar

Heat the butter and oil in a saucepan, and add the onion and garlic. Cook until the onion is wilted. Add the remaining ingredients. Simmer until the sauce is thickened.

GREEN TOMATO CHUTNEY

6 pounds green tomatoes
4½ pounds hard, green apples
3 large onions
1½ pounds brown sugar

1½ ounces mustard seed
1½ teaspoons cayenne pepper
3 tablespoons salt
4½ pints white malt vinegar

Drop the tomatoes into boiling water. Count to ten and lift them out. When cool enough to handle, remove the skins and quarter them. Peel, core, and dice the apples. Peel and slice the onions.

Place all the ingredients in a large non-aluminum pan and bring slowly to a boil. Lower the heat and simmer gently, covered, for about two hours. Cool. Store in sterilized glass jars.

TERIYAKI SAUCE

Approximately 2½ cups

1 bottle soy sauce,
  (ten ounces)
1 bottle Teriyaki sauce,
  (ten ounces)

1 large clove garlic, mashed with
  1 teaspoon coarse salt
1 finger-length fresh green ginger,
  chopped

Bring all the ingredients to a boil in a heavy pan. Reduce the heat and simmer for five to six minutes. Strain and store in bottles. It keeps indefinitely. *AB*

MUSTARD SAUCE

4 servings

This sauce is excellent with artichokes and cauliflower.

3 tablespoons boiling water
2 tablespoons hot Dijon mustard
½ cup olive oil

Salt and pepper to taste
Lemon juice to taste
1 tablespoon finely chopped parsley

In a bowl add the boiling water to the mustard and mix well. Drop by drop, stir in the olive oil.

Season to taste with salt, pepper, and lemon juice. Be sparing with the salt. Mix in the parsley.
A

HORSERADISH SAUCE

Approximately 1½ cups

1 cup grated fresh horseradish root
¾ cup sour cream

Salt and pepper to taste
Lemon juice to taste

Peel and grate a piece of fresh horseradish and mix with the sour cream. Season to taste with salt, pepper, and a few drops of lemon juice.
A

HORSERADISH AND APPLESAUCE

Horseradish and applesauce are the perfect accompaniment for boiled beef.

Mix together equal parts fresh Horseradish Sauce (see recipe above) and unsweetened apple purée.
A

VINAIGRETTE SAUCE

Approximately ¾ cup

2 tablespoons red wine vinegar
1 teaspoon prepared Dijon mustard
1 teaspoon lemon juice
½ teaspoon sugar

½ teaspoon salt
Freshly ground black pepper
10 tablespoons olive oil, or half olive and
    half vegetable oil

Shake the vinegar, mustard, lemon juice, sugar, salt, and pepper together in a screw-top bottle to dissolve the solids. Add the oil and shake again.   *A*

QUICK ASPIC JELLY

Approximately 1½ cups

1 egg white
1 egg shell, crushed
1 small onion, chopped

1½ cups cold chicken, veal, or fish stock
1 tablespoon unflavored gelatin
2 tablespoons dry Madeira

Mix the egg white, egg shell, and chopped onion in a bowl with your hands. Combine them with the stock in a saucepan and mix. Bring very slowly almost to the boiling point over low heat. Reduce the heat and simmer gently ten minutes. *Do not let the mixture boil.*

Strain into another container through three or four thicknesses of cheesecloth, wrung out in warm water.

Soften the gelatin by sprinkling it over one-half cup of the strained stock. Dissolve over low heat and add to the clarified stock. Allow to cool. Stir in the Madeira.

CRANBERRY SAUCE

Approximately 4 cups

2 oranges
½ cup red currant jelly
½ cup port
1½ to 2 cups sugar

2 sticks cinnamon and ¼ teaspoon whole
    allspice tied in cheesecloth
2 cups fresh cranberries, washed and
    picked over

Cut the peel of one orange into fine strips. Simmer the peels in water for two to three minutes; drain.

Combine the juice of both oranges, the jelly, wine, sugar, and spice bag. Bring to a boil, then simmer five minutes.

Remove the spices; add the cranberries and orange peel. Bring to a full, rolling boil until the berries pop.   *A*

BREAD SAUCE

Approximately 2 cups

8 slices of white bread, crusts removed
1½ cups half-and-half
1 small onion stuck with 3 or 4 cloves
Pinch of freshly grated nutmeg

Salt
Freshly ground white pepper
Pinch of cayenne pepper
4 tablespoons heavy cream (optional)

Grate the bread to make crumbs. Place the half-and-half and onion in a small pan and heat gently almost to the boiling point. Do this very slowly over very low heat to draw out the flavor of the onion and cloves.

Remove the onion and stir in the bread crumbs. Continue stirring until all the half-and-half has been absorbed. Season with nutmeg, salt, and both peppers. If you wish to use heavy cream, stir it in at this point. Serve warm with a little cayenne sprinkled on top.   *A*

BRANDY SAUCE

Approximately ¾ cup

Use this sauce on steamed puddings.

1 egg, separated
¾ cup confectioners' sugar
Salt

½ cup heavy cream
3 tablespoons brandy

Beat the egg white until stiff. Add the confectioners' sugar and beat until the sugar disappears. Add the salt and egg yolk. Whip the heavy cream. Fold it into the sauce mixture. Add the brandy and chill.   *A*

HARD SAUCE

Approximately 2½ cups

2 cups confectioners' sugar
8 tablespoons unsalted butter, softened

3 tablespoons brandy
¼ cup heavy cream

Add the sugar gradually to the softened butter, using an electric beater. Mix until well-blended.

Add the brandy and mix again. Beat in the heavy cream. Chill thoroughly before serving.

AB

SAUCE SABAYON

Approximately 2½ cups

½ cup sugar
4 egg yolks

2 whole eggs
2 cups dry white wine

Place the sugar and all the eggs in the top half of a double boiler over hot—not boiling—water, and beat until thick and lemon-colored. Add the wine and beat until the mixture is thick and heavy—a ribbon will form when the beater is lifted out.

Set the pan over a bowl of ice and continue to beat until the sauce is cold. Refrigerate until needed.

A

SAUCE DIJONNAISE

Approximately 1 cup

1 package (12 ounces) frozen raspberries, drained
½ cup black currant preserves

Rub both together through a fine sieve.

AB

RASPBERRY JAM SAUCE

Approximately ½ cup

½ cup raspberry jam
¼ cup water
Juice of 1 lemon

Dissolve the raspberry jam in the water and lemon juice over low heat.   *A*

ORANGE SAUCE

Approximately 2½ cups

5 egg yolks
½ cup granulated sugar
2 tablespoons grated orange rind

½ cup Cointreau
1 cup heavy cream

Select a bowl that will fit over a saucepan that has three to four inches of hot water in it. Bring to a boil.

Add the yolks, sugar, and orange rind. With an electric hand beater, beat until the yolks are thick and yellow.

Place the bowl over another bowl of chopped ice. Stir in half the liqueur and continue beating until the mixture is cold. Beat the cream until it holds definite peaks. Fold it into the egg yolk mixture with the rest of the liqueur.   *A*

APRICOT SAUCE

Approximately 1½ cups

1½ cups apricot jam
½ cup water

Sugar
2 tablespoons Kirsch or other liqueur

Mix the jam with water. Cook gently for eight to ten minutes, stirring to prevent burning. Rub through a fine sieve. Add sugar to taste and the liqueur.   *A*

BUTTERSCOTCH SAUCE

Approximately 3 cups

⅔ cup white corn syrup
1¼ cups light brown sugar, tightly packed
4 tablespoons butter

¼ teaspoon salt
⅔ cup heavy cream

Cook all the ingredients, except the cream, to the consistency of heavy syrup. Cool. Stir in the cream.

A

CREME ANGLAISE

Approximately 2½ cups

4 large egg yolks
2 cups hot milk

¼ cup sugar
2 tablespoons Grand Marnier (optional)

Beat the egg yolks; add the hot milk and sugar. Cook over hot water in the top half of a double boiler until the back of a wooden spoon is generously coated. On no account allow the custard to boil or it will curdle. Remove from the heat. Stir until cool. Stir in the liqueur. Refrigerate until needed.

A

CHOCOLATE SAUCE

Approximately 1½ cups

6 ounces (6 squares) unsweetened
   chocolate
1 cup water

½ cup sugar
1 teaspoon almond extract

Over low heat melt the chocolate in a little of the water. Add the sugar, the remaining water, and the almond extract. Dissolve the ingredients completely and simmer gently for ten minutes.

A

PRALINE POWDER

Approximately 1½ cups

¾ cup sugar
¼ cup water

¼ teaspoon cream of tartar
½ cup blanched almonds

Place all the ingredients in a heavy pan. Heat, and stir until the sugar dissolves. Continue to heat, without stirring, until the color is dark amber.

Pour onto a lightly greased cookie sheet and cool. Break into rough pieces and pulverize them in a blender. *AB*

Breads, Cakes, and Cookies

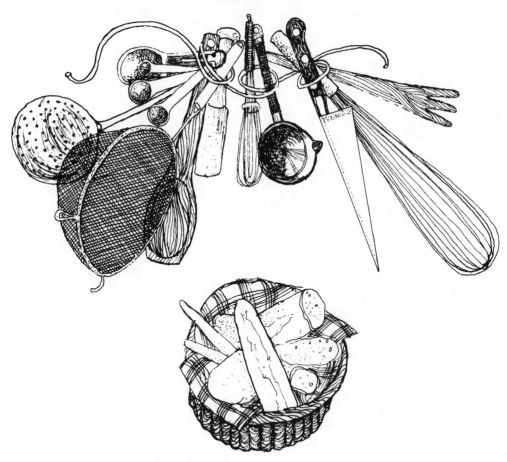

Breads, Cakes, and Cookies

There is little that comes out of the commercial baker's oven that could possibly be the staff of life. Some of the Italian and French breads and occasionally a protein or whole-wheat loaf are worth the journey to the store. I have discovered quite recently two recipes for whole-wheat bread that have solved my dilemma. They are included in Bernard Clayton, Jr.'s splendid *The Breads of France.* With my recipes for soda bread and biscuits, I have more than enough of the staff of life to maintain a healthy balance.

Cookies and cakes, on the other hand, are legion and there are few I dislike, but I have chosen the most useful and, in my opinion, the most popular. I find comfort in the knowledge that somewhere in my kitchen there is something sweet, no matter how small, to satisfy that craving at the end of a meal when I am not having dessert.

I have also included two recipes for pie shells. The All-Purpose Pastry is exactly what it says. It is used in both sweet and savory recipes (quiches, for example), whereas Pâte Sucrée may be used for sweet pies. It is rich, firm, easy to handle, and bakes like a cookie dough.

ALL-PURPOSE PASTRY

1 nine-inch pie shell

2 cups flour
½ teaspoon salt
1 stick (½ cup) sweet butter

3 tablespoons vegetable shortening
2½ to 3 tablespoons cold water

Blend all the ingredients, except the water, with a pastry cutter or knife. Gradually add the water, as little as possible, but sufficient to bind the pastry.

On a pastry board or cloth, smear with the heel of the hand, starting from the outside, and pressing hard. Form the pastry into a ball, wrap, and chill it for about two hours before rolling out.

Heat oven to 400°F.

Roll the pastry one-eighth of an inch thick. Line a nine-inch pie dish with the dough. Trim the pastry and prick it with a fork. Bake for fifteen to twenty minutes.

Glaze:

1 egg beaten with 1 tablespoon water

Brush the pie shell with the beaten egg. Reduce the temperature to 350°F. and bake ten minutes more.

PATE SUCREE

2 nine-inch pie shells

2 cups all-purpose flour
2½ sticks (1¼ cups) sweet butter, softened
   and cut into pieces
½ cup superfine sugar

¼ teaspoon salt
1 egg, beaten lightly with a fork
1 egg yolk

Place the flour in the middle of the working table. Make a well in the center and add all the other ingredients. Gather the dough, with a pastry scraper or your fingers, into a compact mound.

Place the dough close to you on the table, and with the heel of your hand, smear a portion about the size of a golf ball about ten inches forward. Keep your fingers pointed upward. Repeat, smearing pieces of the dough forward, until it has all been processed.

Gather the dough into a ball and repeat the operation once more. The two smearings help to homogenize the ingredients, making a well-blended dough.

Roll out the dough to one-eighth to one-quarter-inch thickness and fit it into the appropriate pastry pan.

BAKING POWDER BISCUITS

Approximately 24 biscuits

2 cups all-purpose flour
4 level teaspoons baking powder
Pinch of salt

12 tablespoons unsalted butter
Milk to moisten
1 egg yolk mixed with 1 tablespoon water

Heat oven to 450°F.

Sift the flour, baking powder, and salt into a bowl.

Divide the butter into small pieces and cut it into the flour with a pastry blender or your fingertips. It should resemble coarse cornmeal. Moisten with about four tablespoons of milk to blend.

Gather the dough into a ball and roll it out on a floured board to roughly three-quarters inch thick. Cut out the biscuits with a plain cookie cutter no larger than three-quarters inch in diameter.

Brush with the egg yolk and bake on a greased sheet for fifteen minutes.

BROWN SODA BREAD

1 loaf

2 cups all-purpose flour
3 teaspoons sugar
2 teaspoons baking soda

2 teaspoons salt
4½ cups whole-wheat flour
2½ cups buttermilk

Heat oven to 425°F.

In a bowl, sift together the all-purpose flour, sugar, baking soda, and salt. Thoroughly stir in the whole-wheat flour and make a well in the center of the mixture.

Stir in the buttermilk to make a soft, elastic dough that is neither too dry nor too moist. Add a little more buttermilk, if necessary, to reach this consistency. Work the dough as little as possible to combine the ingredients, and knead it lightly and quickly into a ball in the mixing bowl.

(Continued)

Transfer the dough to a floured, lightly greased baking sheet and pat it into a circle about one and one-half inches thick. With a floured knife, cut a cross about one-quarter-inch deep on the top and brush the surface with milk.

Place the bread in a hot oven for twenty-five minutes; reduce the heat to moderate (350°F.), and bake it fifteen minutes longer, or until it sounds hollow when tapped with the knuckles.

If the crust seems too hard, wrap the bread in a damp tea towel. Let the loaf cool on a wire rack. Soda bread becomes stale quickly, but the loaf should not be cut until about four hours after baking.

B

PAIN COMPLET

3 braided loaves

Starter:

2 cups warm water (105° to 115°F.)
½ cup nonfat dry milk

1 teaspoon dry yeast
3 cups whole-wheat flour

At least twelve hours beforehand, pour the water, milk, yeast, and flour in a large bowl and stir to blend all of the ingredients.

Cover with plastic wrap and leave at room temperature (70° to 75°F.) for twelve hours or overnight. Longer fermentation develops a more pronounced wheaty flavor.

Dough:

All of the starter
½ cup warm water (105° to 115°F.)
2 teaspoons dry yeast
¼ cup nonfat dry milk

1 tablespoon salt
¼ cup honey
1 cup all-purpose flour
2 cups whole-wheat flour, approximately

Remove and save the plastic wrap. Stir down the starter. Pour in the water, yeast, milk, and salt. Stir to dissolve and add the honey.

When blended, add one cup of all-purpose flour and beat with twenty-five strong strokes before stirring in the whole-wheat flour, one-half cup at a time. Do not rush. Let each addition of whole wheat absorb its full quota of moisture before continuing. If all of the flour is dumped into the mixture at once, it may suddenly become too dense and firm.

When it is a solid mass but soft, scrape down the sides of the bowl and turn out onto a flour-dusted work surface.

Kneading may be sticky in the beginning, so toss down liberal sprinkles of flour on the work surface and work it into the dough. A dough scraper is handy to keep the film of dough scraped off the work surface. Knead for six minutes with a strong one-two-three motion of push-turn-fold until the ball of dough is smooth and elastic.

Wash and grease a bowl and drop the dough into it. Cover tightly with plastic wrap and leave at room temperature (70° to 75°F.) until the dough doubles in volume, about an hour and fifteen minutes.

Turn the dough onto a floured work surface and knead it briefly to press out the gas bubbles. Prepare the braids or *nattes* by dividing the dough into three large pieces, and dividing each of these into three smaller pieces. Roll the pieces into balls and allow to rest for about three minutes.

Form the strands to be braided by pressing down and rolling each ball with the palm. As a strand lengthens, place both palms on it and gently roll it back and forth while exerting a slight outward pull with both hands—not too much or the dough might tear. If a strand pulls back, move to others and return when it has relaxed.

Individual strands will be about twelve to fourteen inches long. Place three strands parallel. Braid from the center. Pinch the ends of the strands together tightly and complete the braid on the other end. Place the completed braid on a greased baking sheet. Repeat for the other two loaves.

Cover the braids with wax paper and leave them at room temperature (70° to 75°F.) until they are nearly double in volume. If the ends should spring open, carefully pinch them together again.

Glaze:

1 egg, beaten
1 tablespoon milk

Heat oven to 380°F. twenty minutes before baking time.

Uncover the braids and brush them with the beaten egg-milk glaze. Place them on a baking sheet on the middle shelf of the oven.

At the end of thirty minutes, turn the baking sheet around so loaves will be exposed equally to temperature variations. Bake fifteen minutes longer.

The braids are done when the bottom crusts are deep brown and the loaves sound hard and hollow when tapped with a forefinger.

The braids are fragile when they come from the oven, so slip a spatula under each braid when you work it loose from the baking sheet and carry it to test or cool. It may stick if the glaze has run onto the baking sheet.

Place the braids on a metal rack to cool. This is delicious toasted.   *B*

GALETTE PERSANE

3 round flatbreads

Starter:

1 package dry yeast
1 cup cool water (70° to 75°F.)
1½ cups whole-wheat flour, stone-ground preferred

Sprinkle yeast in water in a small bowl and stir until it is dissolved. Pour in whole-wheat flour and blend to make a thick batter.

Cover the bowl with plastic wrap and leave at room temperature (70° to 75°F.) for twenty-four hours. During this time the batter will rise and fall as it ferments.

Sponge:

All of the starter
1 cup cool water (70° to 75°F.)
1½ cups whole-wheat flour, stone-ground preferred

Into a large bowl, pour all of the starter. Add water and whole-wheat flour to make a thick batter. Cover the bowl with plastic wrap. This should be left to mature a minimum of twelve hours. The longer the period, up to twenty-four hours, the more robust the flavor will be.

Dough:

All of the sponge
2 teaspoons salt
½ cup cool water (70° to 75°F.)

1 tablespoon olive oil
⅓ cup wheat germ
2½ cups unbleached flour, approximately

Remove the plastic wrap and stir down the sponge, which will be light and puffy. Add the salt, water, olive oil, and wheat germ. Blend with the sponge. Add unbleached flour, one-half cup at a time, stirring it in with a large wooden spoon or rubber scraper. When the batter gets too heavy to stir with the utensil, sprinkle it with flour and work it with the hands.

When the dough is a solid body, lift it from the bowl. Drop the dough on the work surface which has been sprinkled lightly with flour. Knead with a strong push-turn-fold motion for about seven minutes. Add sprinkles of flour if the dough is sticky.

Now and then lift the dough above the table and bring it down hard with a crash. It is good for the gluten. This will be a solid dough and, unlike all-white dough, not very elastic.

Return the dough to the large bowl (washed and greased) and cover with plastic wrap. Leave it at room temperature (70° to 75°F.) until dough has doubled in volume, about an hour and fifteen minutes.

Three pounds of dough will make three round loaves six inches in diameter.

Punch down the dough and knead to press out the bubbles. Divide the dough and shape into balls. Allow them to rest for a few moments.

Press one ball flat with the palm of the hand—about six inches in diameter and three-quarters inch thick. Place on a greased baking sheet. Repeat for the other pieces.

Cover the *galettes* with wax paper or a cloth and leave at room temperature (70° to 75°F.) until double in volume, about forty minutes.

Heat oven to 425°F. twenty minutes before baking. With a sharp razor, slash four *deep* cuts (one-half inch) across the top of the loaf. Make four more deep cuts in the other direction.

Place on a baking sheet on the middle shelf of the oven and bake for forty minutes. When loaves are light golden brown, tap the bottom crust with the forefinger and if it sounds hard and hollow, the bread is baked.

Place the loaves on a metal rack to cool. To serve, break the *galette* along the deep cuts.

SIMNEL CAKE

Simnel Cake is an Easter tradition, but is good at any time of year. It keeps well. I store it and deliberately forget it. Then there is that wonderful surprise on a chilly autumn day when I need something to nibble on with my four o'clock tea.

8 ounces all-purpose flour plus
  2 tablespoons
Pinch of salt
½ teaspoon each: nutmeg, cinnamon,
  allspice
6 ounces unsalted butter
6 ounces dark brown sugar
3 eggs, lightly beaten
1 pound currants
12 ounces golden raisins

4 ounces mixed candied fruits
4 ounces chopped almonds
1 tablespoon black treacle (dark molasses
  will do)
¼ cup milk
2 pounds almond paste
½ cup jam
1 egg yolk mixed with a little oil
Granulated sugar for dusting

Heat oven to 300°F.

Line the bottom and sides of an eight-inch cake pan with buttered wax paper.

Sift together the eight ounces of flour, salt, and spices.

(Continued)

Cream the butter and sugar until very light. I do this in the mixer. Add lightly beaten eggs, a little at a time, sprinkling with the sifted flour and beating well after each addition. Mix the fruits and almonds with the two tablespoons of flour.

Melt the treacle or molasses in the milk. Cool. Stir the floured fruits into the batter and add the milk and treacle, enough to make a fairly stiff batter.

Spoon half the mixture into the prepared cake pan. Smooth the surface with the back of a level spoon. Roll out one pound of the almond paste into a circle eight inches in diameter. Place it on top of the batter and spoon the rest of the batter on top of it.

Bake in the middle of the oven for about three and one-half hours, or until a knife inserted comes out dry. (Be careful not to go as deep as the almond paste, because the paste would give you a false reading.)

Cool the cake on a rack. Heat the jam. When the cake is cool, brush with the jam and cover with the other pound of almond paste rolled out to fit. Mark the top in triangles. I use the back of a knife to do this. Form eleven small balls from any remaining almond paste and arrange them around the edge of the cake. (The eleven balls represent the eleven apostles, leaving out Judas, the twelfth.)

Brush lightly with the egg and oil glaze. Brown the cake under the broiler, taking care it does not burn. Dust with granulated sugar. The cake keeps for a very long time in an airtight tin or container.

ANNA LEMON'S PLUM CAKE

Anna Lemon was my grandmother on the maternal side. She was, apparently, a remarkable Victorian. She died before I was old enough to know her. Her hospitality was known far and wide. She would give instructions to set the dining table for four extra people, just in case her tea-time guests should decide to stay for dinner.

This plum cake has been in the family for four generations. When I was young and roaming the globe, one arrived every Christmas no matter where I was. It keeps indefinitely, that is, if you don't like it, which is unlikely.

¾ pound flour	5 large eggs
1 teaspoon baking powder	1 teaspoon almond extract
1 pound currants	4 ounces ground almonds
1 pound raisins	½ cup cognac
¾ pound butter	Almond Icing (see next page)
¾ pound granulated sugar	Granulated sugar for dusting

Heat oven to 325°F.

Line an eight-and-one-half-inch springform cake pan with nonstick parchment.

Sift together the flour and baking powder. Mix the dried fruits with a little of the flour to coat them thoroughly.

Beat the butter until it is soft. Add the sugar gradually and beat until the butter is light in color and texture. This is best done in a mixer, but in my grandmother's day the beating was done in a large porcelain bowl with a long-handled spoon.

Add the eggs, one at a time, and the almond extract, beating thoroughly after each addition. Stir in the fruits and ground almonds.

Spoon the batter into the prepared cake pan and bake on the middle shelf of the oven for three to three and one-half hours. If the top of cake is taking on too much color, cover it with a piece of brown paper. Test with a toothpick. If it comes out clean, the cake is done.

While the cake is still hot, dribble cognac over it. The cognac will soak in.

Almond Icing:

½ pound ground almonds
½ pound granulated sugar
½ pound confectioners' sugar
2 large egg yolks

4 tablespoons hot water
1 teaspoon almond extract
¼ cup apricot jam
2 tablespoons water

Mix together in a small pan the almonds, the sugars, egg yolks, hot water, and almond extract. Stir over low heat until melted and combined to make a smooth paste.

In another small pan, heat the apricot jam and water, and cook until slightly reduced. Brush the top and sides of the cake with the jam.

Roll out the almond paste and fit it over the cake like a cap, pressing firmly to make it stick. Decorate with cutouts of almond paste and dust with granulated sugar.

ORANGE CAKE

1 cup butter , at room temperature
1 cup sugar
3 eggs, separated
2 cups flour
1 teaspoon baking powder
1 teaspoon baking soda
1 cup sour cream

Grated rind of 1 orange
½ cup chopped walnuts or pecans
¼ cup orange juice
⅓ cup Grand Marnier or Cointreau
Toasted whole almonds for decoration
Confectioners' sugar

(Continued)

Heat oven to 350°F.

Butter and flour one tube (angel food) cake pan.

Cream together the butter and sugar until light and fluffy. Beat in the egg yolks one at a time. Sift together the flour, baking powder, and baking soda. Add them to the butter mixture, alternating with the sour cream, and stirring until smooth. Stir in the orange rind and chopped nuts.

Beat the egg whites until stiff but not dry, and fold them into the batter. Pour the batter into a prepared pan.

Bake for forty-five to fifty minutes, or until done.

Combine the orange juice and liqueur and spoon them over the cake while it is still hot. Cool before removing from the pan. Decorate the top with almonds and dust lightly with confectioners' sugar.   *B*

OLD-FASHIONED FRUITCAKE

About 6 to 8 cakes

1 pound raisins

1 pound currants

1 pound candied lemon peel

1 pound candied orange peel

1 pound candied citron

1 pound candied cherries

1 pound candied pineapple

1 pound shelled walnuts

1 pound shelled pecans

5 cups flour

1 pound butter

1 pound dark brown sugar

15 eggs

¾ cup brandy

Heat oven to 300°F.

Line six to eight nine-by-five-by-two-and-one-half-inch bread pans with aluminum foil.

Cut up the fruits and chop the nuts. Stir in one cup of flour.

Cream the butter and sugar. Add the eggs, one at a time, and beat after each addition. (It will look curdled.)

Stir in the remaining four cups of flour. Add the batter to the cut-up fruit. The dough will be moist and stiff.

Pack the batter in foil-lined bread pans and bake at 300°F. for about four and one-half hours.

Turn the cakes out onto racks and peel off the foil. When cool, douse them well with brandy and wrap tightly in foil. Store for three to four weeks to ripen. To serve, slice thin with a sharp knife.

CHOCOLATE LAYER CAKE

3 eight-inch layers

It was the birthday of Steve Halsey, a good friend of mine, and I was giving a small dinner party for him. A cake was called for and, as he is still very young, a small one that would accommodate the required number of candles. I selected a well- and-truly tried recipe for a chocolate layer cake, one that I knew would not take up too much of my time.

As if by signal, as soon as I attempted to put it all together, the telephone rang nonstop and the door had to be opened several times. To shorten the tale, I left out the beaten egg whites, discovering my mistake after the pans had been filled.

I simply could not begin all over again and let it be, hoping by the time we got to the champagne and toasts, no one would be a bit the wiser. I need not have worried, for it turned out to be the chocolate cake I had been looking for all my life, moist and dark and certainly enough chocolate for the most rabid addict—which only goes to show!

¾ cup Dutch cocoa
1¾ cups sugar
1 whole egg and 3 yolks (freeze remaining whites for future use)
½ cup milk
8 tablespoons butter
2 cups flour, sifted

½ teaspoon salt
1 teaspoon baking soda
1 teaspoon baking powder
1 cup sour cream
1 teaspoon vanilla
¼ teaspoon almond extract

Heat oven to 350°F.

Line three eight-inch baking pans with nonstick baker's paper.

Combine the cocoa with three-quarters cup sugar, one egg yolk, and the milk. Cook over very low heat until the mixture is thick. Cool.

Cream the butter and the remaining cup of sugar until fluffy. Beat in one whole egg and two yolks.

Sift the flour, salt, baking soda, and baking powder together.

Fold in the sifted flour, sour cream, and batter, alternating one after another. Beat in the cocoa mixture, vanilla, and almond extract.

Pour the batter into the baking pans. Bake thirty to thirty-five minutes. Do not overcook. Turn out onto racks. Chocolate Icing (see next page).

CHOCOLATE ICING

Approximately 1½ cups

This icing may be made ahead and frozen until needed.

6 ounces semisweet chocolate
2 ounces unsweetened chocolate
2 tablespoons strong, prepared,
 instant coffee

1 teaspoon vanilla extract or rum
1 tablespoon corn syrup
½ cup heavy cream, approximately

Over low heat melt the chocolates with the coffee and vanilla or rum flavoring. Add the corn syrup. Mix well. Stir in the cream. Cool. *AB*

CHOCOLATE TORTE

1 cup almonds
4 squares semisweet chocolate
½ cup soft butter
⅔ cup sugar

Pinch of salt
3 eggs
1 tablespoon dark rum
¼ cup fine white bread crumbs

Heat oven to 375°F.
Butter the bottom of an eight-inch cake pan and place a round of wax paper over the butter.
Grind the nuts finely. Melt the chocolate. Cream the butter until soft; beat in the sugar and salt gradually until the butter is fluffy.
Beating by hand, add the eggs one at a time, being careful not to overbeat. Stir in the melted chocolate, rum, bread crumbs, and nuts.
Pour the batter into the pan and bake for thirty minutes. Cool twenty-five minutes and turn out onto a cake rack. Let the cake set for two hours before applying the icing.

Icing:

2 squares unsweetened chocolate
2 squares semisweet chocolate
¼ pound soft butter

2 teaspoons honey
Sliced, blanched almonds for decoration

Melt the chocolates together. Stir in the butter and honey. Cool slightly and pour over the cake. Decorate the top with a border of sliced, blanched almonds.

SHORTBREAD

5 cups flour
Pinch of salt
1 pound butter

1½ cups sugar
1 teaspoon vanilla extract

Heat oven to 350°F.

Butter a fifteen-and-three-quarter-by-ten-and-one-half-inch jelly-roll pan.

Sift together the flour and salt. Cut the butter into small pieces and rub into the flour with your fingertips. Add the sugar and vanilla extract, and continue blending until it becomes a heavy paste.

Spread mixture in the prepared pan and pat down evenly. It will be about one inch thick. Prick with the tines of a fork.

Bake for twenty-five to thirty minutes. The cake must not brown. Cut into triangles while warm. Store in an airtight container.   *B*

COUNTRY HOST GINGERBREAD

Rona Deme, an English friend of mine and owner of the Country Host in New York City, makes and sells in her store the very best of English country fare. Her gingerbread is one of my favorites, moist and dark as night.

Cheese and gingerbread make good companions. In England, the perfect cheese would be Wensledale, which may be found here in stores that specialize in cheeses.

½ cup unsalted butter
1 cup sugar
1 egg
½ cup molasses
2 cups flour
1 teaspoon baking soda

½ teaspoon salt
1 teaspoon cinnamon
½ teaspoon cloves
½ teaspoon ginger
1 cup boiling water

Heat oven to 350°F.

Butter six four-inch loaf pans.

Cream the butter and sugar until light. Beat in the egg and molasses.

Sift together the flour, baking soda, salt, and spices. Mix with the batter. Quickly stir in one cup of boiling water and spoon the batter into the loaf pans, half filling them.

Bake for forty minutes; rest the loaves for five minutes, then turn them out onto wire racks to cool.

GINGERBREAD

40 large pieces

Gingerbread and apple purée, gingerbread and good Cheddar cheese, are both very English, satisfying and healthful.

12 ounces butter
1½ cups sugar
4½ teaspoons baking soda
3 cups molasses
7½ cups flour
6 teaspoons cinnamon

6 teaspoons ginger
2 teaspoons ground cloves
6 teaspoons baking powder
Pinch of salt
4½ cups boiling water
6 eggs, beaten

Heat oven to 325°F.

Butter and flour two jelly-roll pans, or pans the same size but deeper.

Cream the butter and sugar. Beat three teaspoons of baking soda and the molasses together, and add them to the butter.

Sift together the flour, spices, baking powder, and salt. Add one and one-half teaspoons of baking soda to boiling water. Add the water and sifted dry ingredients alternately to the butter mixture.

Fold in the beaten eggs. Place the batter in the prepared pans.

Bake for twenty to thirty minutes. Cool on wire racks.

ALMOND PETITS FOURS

1 cup whole blanched almonds, ground
1 cup granulated sugar
3 tablespoons flour
2 egg whites

1 cup Praline Powder (see page 295)
Confectioners' sugar
1 cup whole unblanched almonds

Heat oven to 350°F.

Mix together the ground almonds, sugar, and flour, and work them through a coarse sieve. Moisten the almond mixture with three-quarters of the lightly beaten egg whites. Pound the mixture to bind it together. Work in the Praline Powder.

Divide the mixture into small walnut-sized balls. Roll them first in the remaining beaten egg white, then in the confectioners' sugar. Place a whole almond on each petit four. Set the petits fours on parchment paper.

Bake for fifteen to twenty minutes, or until lightly browned. Cool, then remove from the parchment.

B

ALMOND BUTTER COOKIES

3 dozen cookies

⅔ cup butter
½ cup granulated sugar
½ cup light brown sugar
1 egg
1 teaspoon vanilla

1 tablespoon grated orange rind
2 cups flour
1 teaspoon salt
½ teaspoon baking powder
¾ cup toasted, diced, or slivered almonds

Heat oven to 400°F.

Beat the butter until creamy. Gradually beat in the granulated sugar and the brown sugar until the mixture is light and fluffy. Beat in the egg, the vanilla, and the rind.

Sift together the flour, salt, and baking powder. Stir the flour mixture into the batter. Mix in the nuts.

Form one-inch balls of the dough. Place the balls on a lightly greased baking sheet. Flatten each ball with the bottom of a tumbler dipped in confectioners' sugar, if necessary, to prevent sticking.

Bake six to eight minutes, or until the edges are lightly browned. Cool on a rack.   *B*

OREGON FILBERT CRUNCHIES

16 cookies

¼ cup light corn syrup
¼ cup butter
⅓ cup light brown sugar

⅓ cup finely chopped filberts
½ cup flour
⅛ teaspoon salt

Heat the oven to 375°F.

Place the corn syrup, butter, and sugar in a saucepan and heat, stirring until the butter melts. Remove from the heat and stir in the nuts, flour, and salt.

Drop the dough by teaspoonfuls, about three inches apart, onto lightly greased baking sheets. Bake for eight minutes, or until the cookies are lightly browned around the edges.

Let the cookies stand five minutes, before removing them to a rack to cool.   *B*

WALNUT WAFERS

Approximately 48 pieces

1 cup soft butter
½ cup brown sugar
½ cup granulated sugar
2 eggs
2 teaspoons vanilla

1 teaspoon grated lemon rind
2¾ cups flour
1½ teaspoons salt
½ teaspoon baking soda
1½ cups very finely ground walnuts

Cream the butter thoroughly. Gradually beat in the brown sugar and the granulated sugar until very light and creamy.

Beat in the eggs, one at a time, very well. Beat in the vanilla and lemon rind.

Sift the flour, salt, and soda together and stir into the batter. Stir in the nuts.

Shape the mixture on wax paper into two rolls about two inches in diameter. The mixture will be soft. Refrigerate. As the mixture begins to harden, form the rolls into even cylinders. Once the rolls are firm, wrap them in aluminum foil and freeze overnight.

Heat oven to 400°F.

Remove the wrapping, cut each roll into slices one-eighth inch thick, and place them on a lightly greased baking sheet. Bake about eight minutes, or until the cookies start to brown around the edges. Cool on a rack. *B*

BROWN AND SPICE SQUARES

2 cups dark brown sugar, firmly packed
1 teaspoon ground allspice
1 teaspoon cinnamon
½ teaspoon nutmeg
Pinch of salt
½ cup cocoa
2 cups flour

1 teaspoon baking powder
3 eggs
2 tablespoons bourbon
1 tablespoon vanilla
¼ cup dark molasses
1½ cups finely chopped walnuts or pecans

Heat oven to 350°F.

Butter a ten-by-fifteen-inch rimmed baking sheet.

Stir together the sugar, allspice, cinnamon, nutmeg, salt, cocoa, flour, and baking powder until well-blended. Add the eggs, bourbon, vanilla, and molasses, and beat until thoroughly mixed. Stir in the nuts.

Spread the batter on the prepared baking sheet. Bake for thirty minutes. Cut in squares while still warm.

GINGERSNAPS

10 dozen cookies

¾ cup butter
2 cups sugar
4 cups flour
1½ teaspoons baking soda
3 teaspoons ginger

½ teaspoon cinnamon
¼ teaspoon cloves
2 eggs
½ cup molasses
2 teaspoons vinegar

Heat oven to 350°F.

Cream together the butter and sugar until light and pale in color. Sift the flour, baking soda, and spices together.

Add the eggs one at a time to the sugar and butter mixture; then add the molasses and the vinegar. Stir in the dry ingredients a third at a time. Mix well.

Drop the batter on a greased cookie sheet a tablespoon at a time about two inches apart, and bake for approximately fifteen minutes.   B

SWEETMEATS

A small piece of this confection satisfies the craving for something sweet after dinner and replaces the dessert. Frozen, it lasts indefinitely. Attractively wrapped, it makes a very acceptable Christmas gift.

1½ cups butter
2½ cups brown sugar, tightly packed
2½ cups flour

Heat oven to 375°F.

Cream the butter and sugar until light and fluffy. Mix in the flour gradually while beating.

Spread the mixture evenly on a fifteen-and-three-quarter-by-ten-and-one-half-inch baking sheet, smoothing with the fingertips. Bake for fifteen minutes. Remove from oven. Cool, but do not turn off the oven.

Topping:

1 cup brown sugar
4 eggs, lightly beaten
2 tablespoons flour

2 cups chopped walnuts
1 cup shredded coconut
Granulated sugar

Mix all the ingredients, except the granulated sugar, and pour over the baked base.

Bake for twenty minutes. Sprinkle with granulated sugar while hot. Cut in squares and store in an airtight container.   B

SOUR CREAM COOKIES

½ pound sweet butter
1 cup light brown sugar
2 eggs
1 teaspoon vanilla or almond extract

2 cups flour
½ tablespoon baking soda
½ cup sour cream
1 cup finely chopped pecans

Heat oven to 375°F.

Grease two baking sheets.

Cream the butter and sugar until light and fluffy. Add the eggs one at a time and the vanilla or almond extract, and beat thoroughly after each addition.

Sift the flour and baking soda together. Mix them into the sugar and eggs, alternating with the sour cream. Stir in the chopped pecans.

Drop the batter onto greased baking sheets in teaspoonfuls. Bake twenty to twenty-five minutes.

Stuffings

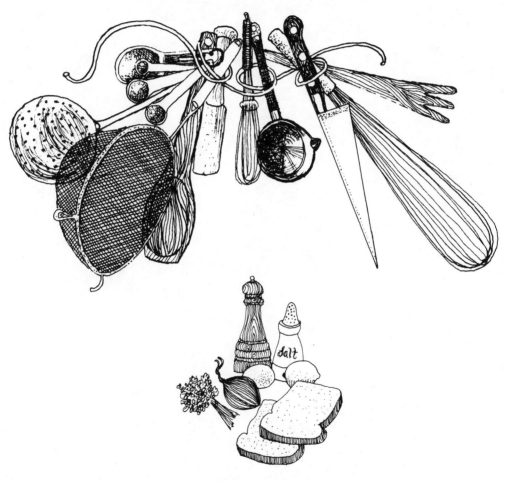

Stuffings

As if we do not have enough ways to serve the all-popular chicken, here are four marvelous stuffings for those of you who like a good old-fashioned roasted bird, well-seasoned, and basted with unsalted butter. I prefer the three- to three-and-one-half-pound chicken, cooked in a 400°F. oven for one hour—a little longer for those who shrink from the slight trace of red at the joints.

The one stuffing given here for turkey is simple and satisfying. Select small turkeys—preferably hens not weighing more than ten pounds, twelve at the most.

HERB STUFFING FOR CHICKEN

Enough for 1 chicken

1 medium onion, chopped
4 tablespoons butter
4 tablespoons ground ham or bacon
1 tablespoon chopped parsley

1 teaspoon thyme
½ cup bread crumbs
1 egg plus 1 egg yolk
Salt and pepper to taste

Sauté the onion slowly in the butter until soft and golden, but not browned. In a bowl add the onion and the juices from the pan, and all remaining ingredients. Season the mixture to taste with salt and pepper.

OYSTER STUFFING FOR CHICKEN

Enough for 1 chicken

1 to 1½ dozen oysters, shucked and
   cut into fours
10 tablespoons white bread crumbs,
   made from stale bread
5 tablespoons chopped suet
1 heaping tablespoon chopped parsley
Grated rind of ½ lemon

1 heaping teaspoon thyme
⅛ teaspoon mace
⅛ teaspoon nutmeg
Pinch of cayenne pepper
1 large egg, beaten
Salt and pepper to taste

In a bowl mix all the ingredients well, and season mixture to taste with salt and pepper.

HAZELNUT STUFFING FOR CHICKEN

Enough for 1 chicken

1 large onion, chopped
4 tablespoons butter
½ cup fresh white bread crumbs
¼ cup hazelnuts, lightly grilled
   and chopped
4 knobs preserved ginger, chopped

Juice of 1 lemon
Grated rind of ½ lemon
1 large egg, beaten
Salt and freshly ground black pepper
   to taste
2 tablespoons chopped parsley

Sauté the onion in the butter until soft. Place a lid on the pan so the onion does not brown.

Transfer the onion mixture to a bowl and add the remaining ingredients in the order they are given, mixing thoroughly each time.

PARSLEY AND LEMON STUFFING FOR CHICKEN OR TURKEY

Enough for 1 turkey

1 loaf of bread, grated to crumbs
Rind of 2 lemons, grated
Juice of 1 lemon
Salt and freshly ground black pepper
1 teaspoon lemon-thyme

1 teaspoon dried marjoram
4 ounces chopped parsley
8 ounces butter, creamed
3 eggs, beaten

Spread the bread crumbs on baking sheets and dry them in the oven. Do not allow them to color. Weigh out eight ounces.

Mix the crumbs with the lemon rind and juice. Mix in the remaining herbs and chopped parsley. Blend the mixture with butter and stir in the beaten eggs.

STUFFING FOR TURKEY

Enough for 1 turkey

1 turkey liver
8 ounces melted butter
1 pound lean pork, ground
1 pound lean veal, ground
2 ounces hazelnuts, ground

2 eggs, beaten
½ cup fresh white bread crumbs
1 teaspoon chopped parsley
1 teaspoon crushed thyme
Salt and pepper

Sauté the turkey liver in a little butter, and chop it coarsely. Mix all the ingredients in a bowl.

Stuff the bird, making sure the filling is not packed solid. Leave room for expansion.

Menus

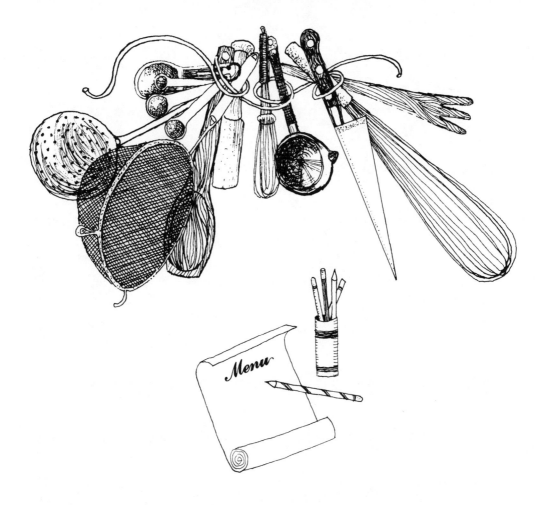

MENUS FOR SPECIAL OCCASIONS

THANKSGIVING

Thanksgiving is literally a time for giving thanks and has little to do with feasting. Today family and friends gather to celebrate and give thanks, much in the same way the early settlers gave thanks for survival.

The Pilgrims' menu was obviously restricted to what they grew and the fruits of sea and land. With the exception of brown bread and butter, celery, and sweetmeats, I have made up this menu from native ingredients. It is a menu that can, for the greater part, be prepared in advance, leaving the host free to be with the guests. Two traditional Thanksgiving dishes are prepared differently in these recipes.

Boiled Turkey makes a welcome change from the eternal roasted bird, and Pumpkin Soup, although well-known in Europe, is seldom served in America. Make the servings small.

Oysters, Lemon Wedges
Thin Brown Bread and Butter
Pumpkin Soup (page 64)
Boiled Turkey and Celery Sauce (page 97)
Cranberry Ice (page 267)
Sweetmeats (page 315)

CHRISTMAS

Christmas would not be complete without Plum Pudding as it was made in my family for many generations. When I was a small boy, plum puddings, Christmas cakes, and plum cakes were made in August or September. The puddings were hung from hooks on the kitchen ceiling, shriveled and wrinkled and hard as iron. The children of the house were allowed to assist. This was one of the few times they could enter the kitchen.

The cakes were prepared at about the same time and often had silver charms and coins—occasionally even a golden guinea, a coin that no longer exists—baked into them. The cakes were soused with brandy or rum and securely wrapped until it was time to ice and decorate them.

This Christmas menu is a simple one with little or no last-minute work. Make the servings small. Serve a glass of dry sherry with the consommé, a good Bordeaux with the pheasant, and vintage port after the fruit.

Double Consommé (page 62)
Braised Pheasant (page 103)
Artichokes
Plum Pudding (page 245), With Hard Sauce (page 292)
Fresh Fruit

BUFFET

This is one of my favorite buffet menus, one that caters to most tastes and is prepared in advance with the exception of filling the chocolate roll, which should be done an hour or so before it is served. If you have difficulty finding bass to poach, use another fish and serve it in exactly the same way.

Green Bean Salad (page 215)
Glazed Corned Beef (page 118)
Poached Striped Bass (page 72), With Sauce Verte I (page 279)
Venetian Chocolate Roll (page 261)
Compote of Fruits (page 248)

BREAKFAST

Breaking one's fast, even if it is late in the morning, is to my mind still breakfast, and I have never found it necessary to use the coined word "brunch." But, the later breakfast is served, the greater the variety of dishes one can offer and the closer one comes to the hearty breakfast eaten by my ancestors: steaks, game, eggs, fish, and ale—good hearty fare to sustain one through a hard day's work, or play.

Creamed, Smoked Haddock (page 74)
Kidneys and Bacon (page 161)
Cold Ham
Baking Powder Biscuits (page 301)
Pain Complet, Toasted (page 302), and Marmalade

SUMMER BUFFET

A summer buffet, in my opinion, is one that can be prepared well in advance and assembled a short time before the guests are ushered to the table. Fish, chicken, vegetables, and fruit maintain a good balance and present inviting contrasts in color and in texture. When I use this particular menu, I start by poaching the chicken or hen two days ahead of time, the fish on the day before, and, in the morning of the day itself, I wash and hull the fruit. The food is perfect for the hot days of August.

Cold Poached Striped Bass, (page 72), With Sauce Verte I (page 279)
Pollo Tonnato (page 93)
Tomato Salad (page 217)
Strawberries Rue du Bac (page 264)

WINTER BUFFET

In the winter months, I like to offer hot and hearty food. For a buffet, I choose dishes that are prepared ahead of time and easy to serve and eat. My personal instinct is to shy away from buffet foods that need more than a fork to handle. My winter buffet requires a fork and spoon only—soup is served in cups.

Casserole of Lamb freezes well, should there be any left over, and Paella, in a pinch, can be reheated.

Greek Egg and Lemon Soup, Hot, (page 59)
Paella (page 170)
Casserole of Lamb (page 130)
Green Salad, Pignoli Nuts (page 212)
Bread-and-Butter Pudding (page 242)

SUPPER

Supper after the theater should appear simple, no matter how much time has been spent on its preparation. Chicken Pie takes time, but it is time well spent. Serving it hot requires only reheating for the necessary time. The mushrooms can be baked in the same oven and, the Coffee Granita is ready to serve from the freezer and does away with the need to serve hot coffee later.

Baked Mushrooms (page 45)
Chicken Pie (page 94)
Coffee Granita (page 255)

SUMMER MENUS

Iced Cucumber Soup (page 60)
Virginia Baked Chicken (page 85)
Tomato Salad (page 217)
Compote of Red Plums (page 247)

Mushroom Consommé (page 63)
Jambon Persillé (page 141)
Peaches and Sauce Dijonnaise (page 263)

Spinach Soufflé (page 225)
Salad Tennessee (page 217)
Raspberry Sorbet (page 266)

Shrimp, Avocado, and Carriage House
Sauce (page 47)
Fidget Pie (page 138)
Salad
Summer Pudding (page 246)

Iced Borscht (page 60)
Poached Salmon Steaks (page 73)
Cucumber Salad (page 213)
Tortoni (page 269)

SUMMER MENUS

Oeufs Indiens (page 201)
Butterflied Leg of Lamb (page 124)
Potato and Beet Salad (page 216)
Raspberry Fool (page 264)

Spinach Salad *Queen Mary* (page 213)
Carriage House Terrine (page 34)
Baked Toast (page 34)
Compote of Apricots (page 248)

Cold Cream of Celery Soup—Sans
Crème (page 55)
Cold Poached Striped Bass (page 72),
Sauce Verte I (page 279)
Mushroom Salad (page 214)
Strawberries Cardinal (page 265)

Vegetable Beignets (page 31)
Pollo Tonnato (page 93)
Plum Grasmere (page 251)

Melons and Ginger (page 46)
Chicken Breasts en Papillote (page 89),
With Mint Butter (page 274)
Soufflé Monte Cristo (page 235)

AUTUMN MENUS

Potage St. Germain (page 57)
Casserole of Beef (page 112)
Salad
Deep-Dish Apple Pie (page 251)
Cheddar Cheese

Pilaf (page 46)
Noix d'Agneau Braisé (page 127)
Beet and Endive Salad (page 216)
Pecan Meringue Torte (page 259)

Eggs Florentine (page 204)
Codfish Steaks (page 75)
Steamed Potatoes (page 195)
Queen of Puddings (page 243)

Consommé (page 63)
Chou Farci (page 171)
Green Rice (page 168)
Apple Rings (page 249)

Kohlrabi Vinaigrette (page 41)
Smoked Haddock Soufflé (page 223)
Ginger Pudding (page 245)

AUTUMN MENUS

Oeufs Verts en Cocottes (page 203)
Casserole of Lamb (page 130)
Chou-fleur Panache (page 188)
St. John's Iced Lime Soufflé (page 232)

Potage Poires de Terre (page 58)
Pot Roast (page 113)
Boiled Potatoes
Apple Purée, Gingerbread (page 312)

Pumpkin Soup (page 64)
Boiled Turkey With Celery Sauce
(page 97)
Brussels Sprouts and Water Chestnuts
(page 182)
Chocolate Soufflé (page 230)

Indian River Soup (page 59)
Curried Vegetables (page 172)
Brown Rice
Fresh Fruit

Double Consommé (page 62)
Chicken Pie (page 94)
Salad
Venetian Chocolate Roll (page 261)

WINTER MENUS

Baked Mushrooms (page 45)

Oxtail and White Grapes (page 162)

Pullman Pudding (page 244)

Scotch Broth I (pages 65 and 66)

Braised Tongue

Salad

Apple Charlotte (page 252)

Oeufs aux Crevettes (page 203)

Carbonnades Flamandes (page 112)

Steamed Potatoes (page 195)

Cranberry Ice (page 267)

Artichokes With Mustard Sauce (page 43)

Nancy's Casserole of Chicken (page 90)

Brown Rice

Ginger Pudding (page 245) with
Whipped Cream

Cream of Carrot Soup—Sans Crème
(page 54)

Baked Red Snapper (page 73)

Salade de Haricots Verts (page 215)

Crème Brûlée Mocha (page 256)

WINTER MENUS

Celeriac Rémoulade (page 41)

Braised Pheasant (page 103), With
Bread Sauce (page 291)

Braised Endive (page 180)

Apple Meringue (page 258)

Individual Pizzas (page 32)

Chicken "243" (page 91)

Parsnip Purée (page 191)

Apple Rings (page 249)

Vindaloo Soup (page 55)

Pork Chops and Yellow Plums (page 139)

Potato Purée (page 193)

Queen of Puddings (page 243)

Smoked Eel (page 47), Horseradish Sauce
(page 289)

Civet de Lapin de Bordeaux (page 104)

Salad

Sweetmeats (page 315)

Cold Tomato Consommé (page 64)

New England Corned Beef (page 117)

Apricot Soufflé (page 228)

SPRING MENUS

Apple, Grapefruit, and Bell Pepper Salad
(page 218)

Leg of Lamb With Apricot and Rice
Stuffing (page 125)

Deep-Dish Rhubarb Pie (page 250)

Avocado and Tomato Ice (page 40)

Cottage Pie (page 109)

Carrots Vichy (page 182)

Crème Brûlée aux Fruits (page 256)

Greek Egg and Lemon Soup (page 59)

Roast Chicken (page 84)

Watercress and Green Peas (page 184)

Iced Coffee Soufflé (page 236)

Asparagus (page 42) Vinaigrette
(page 290)

Carre d'Agneau (page 129)

Pommes de Terre Boulangere (page 194)

Ile Flotant (page 257)

Cheese Soufflé (page 224)

Truite en Papillote (page 72)

Cucumber Salad (page 213)

Fruit Flan (page 254)

SPRING MENUS

Oeufs en Gelée (page 205)

Roast Duck (page 99), With
Orange Sauce (page 293)

Watercress Salad (page 212)

Sorbet au Champagne (page 265)

Sorrel Soup (page 56)

Saumon en Papillote (page 71)

Steamed Potatoes (page 195)

Cinnamon Ice Cream (page 268)

Mushroom Soufflé (page 226)

Cold Meat Loaf de Luxe (page 108)

Bean Salad (page 215)

Strawberries Rue du Bac (page 264)

Dieter's Vegetable Soup (page 53)

Moules Marinière (page 79)

Green Salad, Pignoli Nuts (page 212)

Melons and Ginger (page 46)

Tomatoes Antiboise (page 40)

Salmi of Duck (page 101)

Strawberry Sorbet (page 266)

Weights, Measures, and Metric Conversions

Weights, Measures, and Metric Conversions

WEIGHTS AND MEASURES:

A pinch = amount that can be picked up between finger and thumb
1 teaspoon = ⅓ tablespoon
1 tablespoon = 3 teaspoons
2 tablespoons = ⅛ cup or 1 fluid ounce
4 tablespoons = ¼ cup or 2 ounces
5⅓ tablespoons = ⅓ cup or 2⅔ ounces
8 tablespoons = ½ cup or 4 ounces
16 tablespoons = 1 cup or 8 ounces
¼ cup = 4 tablespoons
⅜ cup = 5 tablespoons or ¼ cup plus 2 tablespoons
⅝ cup = 10 tablespoons or ½ cup plus 2 tablespoons
⅞ cup = ¾ cup plus 2 tablespoons
1 cup = ½ pint or 8 fluid ounces
2 cups = 1 pint or 16 fluid ounces
2 pints = 1 quart, liquid, or 4 cups
4 quarts = 1 gallon, liquid
8 dry quarts = 1 peck
4 pecks = 1 bushel
1 pound = 16 ounces

METRIC CONVERSION TABLE:

Dry Ingredients

Ounces to Grams:

Ounces	Grams	Ounces	Grams
1	28.35	9	255.15
2	56.70	10	283.50
3	85.05	11	311.85
4	113.40	12	340.20
5	141.75	13	368.55
6	170.10	14	396.90
7	198.45	15	425.25
8	226.80	16	453.60

Grams to Ounces:

Grams	Ounces	Grams	Ounces
1	0.03	9	0.32
2	0.07	10	0.35
3	0.11	11	0.39
4	0.14	12	0.42
5	0.18	13	0.46
6	0.21	14	0.49
7	0.25	15	0.53
8	0.28	16	0.57

Pounds to Kilograms:

Pounds	Kilograms
1	0.45
2	0.91
3	1.36
4	1.81
5	2.27

Kilograms to Pounds:

Kilograms	Pounds
1	2.205
2	4.41
3	6.61
4	8.82
5	11.02

Liquid Ingredients

Liquid Ounces to Milliliters:

Liquid Ounces	Milliliters	Liquid Ounces	Milliliters
1	29.57	6	177.44
2	59.15	7	207.02
3	88.72	8	236.59
4	118.30	9	266.16
5	147.87	10	295.73

Milliliters to Liquid Ounces:

Milliliters	Liquid Ounces	Milliliters	Liquid Ounces
1	0.03	6	0.20
2	0.07	7	0.24
3	0.10	8	0.27
4	0.14	9	0.30
5	0.17	10	0.33

Quarts to Liters: / Liters to Quarts:

Quarts	Liters	Liters	Quarts
1	0.95	1	1.06
2	1.89	2	2.11
3	2.84	3	3.17
4	3.79	4	4.23
5	4.73	5	5.28

Gallons to Liters: / Liters to Gallons:

Gallons	Liters	Liters	Gallons
1	3.78	1	0.26
2	7.57	2	0.53
3	11.36	3	0.79
4	15.14	4	1.06
5	18.93	5	1.32

Hints and Tips

VEGETABLES:

To store watercress, rinse it under cold water. Shake off the excess water. Place it in a metal bowl, stalks down, with a little water in the bottom. Cover with plastic wrap tied around the bowl.

To store salad greens and parsley, wash and dry them. Seal in a plastic bag.

To store root vegetables, cut off any green shoots and seal vegetables in plastic bags to prevent moisture loss.

Melons may be refrigerated provided they are securely sealed in plastic bags.

Refresh wilted celery by steeping it in a bowl containing one quart of water and one tablespoon of sugar.

Peeled potatoes will not darken if left in a bowl of water mixed with milk. Use four cups of water to one of milk.

To clean mushrooms—two pounds or more—fill a large bowl with tepid water, throw in a handful of flour, mix thoroughly, put in the mushrooms, swish for a minute or two and drain.

Use a collander over a pan of water to simulate a steamer.

Cook green vegetables uncovered.

If by accident a soup is too salty, cook a potato in it until soft. It will absorb much of the salt.

A piece of dry toasted bread on top of cooking cabbage absorbs odors.

FRUITS:

Peeled apples, pears, peaches, and other fruits will not darken if left in acidulated water—one quart of water to which two teaspoons of lemon juice or vinegar, or one teaspoon of ascorbic acid has been added.

Fruits, such as oranges, apples, and pears, have a longer life in the refrigerator if sealed in plastic wrapping—moisture loss is cut down.

EGGS:

Separate eggs while they are cold.

Beat egg whites at room temperature.

The shell of a brown egg is less fragile than that of a white egg and a brown egg is easier to separate. Otherwise, there is no difference.

Pierce the broad end of eggs with a needle or a gadget made for that purpose, before boiling them. The trapped gas will escape and the shell will not crack.

Roll hard-boiled eggs on a hard surface to crack the shell and drop them into cold water before removing the shell.

Freeze egg whites in individual plastic ice-cube containers. When solid, wrap with plastic wrap.

If you have an extra egg yolk or two, cover with water in a small dish and freeze. When thawed, it comes in handy for glazing pastry.

When beating egg whites in a copper bowl add a pinch of salt, which will have the same chemical action on egg whites as cream of tartar in a porcelain bowl—both will toughen the skin on the egg white air bubble. This ensures a lighter soufflé.

To resurrect egg-bound sauces, such as Hollandaise, add a tablespoon of boiling water.

If mayonnaise separates, begin all over again with one egg yolk, adding the curdled mixture gradually and continue adding the required amount of oil.

BAKED GOODS:

Chill a prepared dish for a hot soufflé before filling it. To bake a soufflé, place it on a baking sheet for easier handling.

Use a piece of coarse canvas as a surface for rolling pastry.

Brush pastry shells with an egg-based glaze halfway through baking to seal them so that when filled they will not have soggy bottoms.

Freeze crusts of bread and unused slices until enough for crumbs. Bake bread in the oven at 250°F. for approximately one and one-half hours. Crush the baked bread with a bottle or rolling pan. Season as needed.

DAIRY PRODUCTS:

Clarify butter half a pound at a time. It keeps well refrigerated. To clarify, heat gently in a heavy pan. Remove scum and strain the clear fat into a clean container for future use. The milk solids that are left after clarifying may be used in soups.

A thin film of oil or butter in the pan used for boiling milk makes for easier cleaning.

Chill cream and whisk thoroughly before beating, or place cream in the freezer for three or four minutes. Also, chill bowl, and the egg beater or mixing blades.

MEATS:

Before freezing poultry brush all over with vegetable oil, chill, and seal with plastic wrap.

Sprinkle meats with salt or other seasonings halfway through broiling or roasting, not in the beginning.

Grill bacon in the oven on a rack over a jelly-roll pan at 350°F. for approximately twenty minutes.

MISCELLANEOUS:

Coarse salt and a lemon clean copper.

To decant vintage port wine, strain through a nylon stocking rinsed in cold water.

SAUCES:

A full can of tomato paste is rarely used at one time. Freeze what is left in small glass jars.

If you must cover sauces, place a piece of paper toweling over the pan, then the lid. The paper will catch condensation that would otherwise drop on the sauce and thin it.

Refrigerate an opened bottle of vinegar to prevent fermentation.

A word of advice: No matter what directions are given for seasoning a dish, taste it several times and correct it to suit your palate.

Index